Muslim Girls and the Other France

Muslim Girls
and the
Other France

Race, Identity Politics, & Social Exclusion

Trica Danielle Keaton

Foreword by Manthia Diawara

Indiana University Press
Bloomington & Indianapolis

This book is a publication of
Indiana University Press
601 North Morton Street
Bloomington, IN 47404-3797 USA

http://iupress.indiana.edu
Telephone orders   800-842-6796
Fax orders   812-855-7931
Orders by e-mail   iuporder@indiana.edu

The paper used in this publication meets the minimum
requirements of American National Standard for
Information Sciences—Permanence of Paper for
Printed Library Materials, ANSI Z39.48-1984.

Manufactured in the United States of America

Library of Congress Cataloging-in-Publication Data

Keaton, Trica Danielle.
    Muslim girls and the other France : race, identity politics, and
social exclusion / Trica Danielle Keaton ; Foreword by Manthia
Diawara.
        p. cm.
    Includes bibliographical references and index.
    ISBN 978-0-253-34719-0 (cloth : alk. paper) — ISBN 978-0-253-21834-6
(pbk. : alk. paper)
    1. Muslim girls—France—Social conditions. 2. North
Africans—Cultural assimilation—France. 3. Veils—France—
Social aspects. 4. Social conflict—France—Religious aspects.
5. Marginality, Social—France. I. Title.
    HQ1170.K4 2006
    305.235'2'0882970944—dc22
                                                    2005023414

    2 3 4 5 11 10 09 08

For Dorothy, my sisters and brothers, and Roy

Contents

Foreword by Manthia Diawara   ix
Acknowledgments   xiii

Introduction   *1*

1 Unmixing French "National Identity"   *32*

2 Structured Exclusion: *Public Housing in the French Outer City*   *58*

3 Transmitting a "Common Culture": *Symbolic Violence Realized*   *90*

4 Counterforces: *Educational Inequality and Relative Resistance*   *127*

5 Beyond Identity: *Muslim Girls and the Politics of Their Existence*   *157*

Epilogue: *And So It Goes . . .*   *193*

Notes   *197*
Bibliography   *205*
Index   *215*

Foreword

Dear France,

You have sowed "Liberté, Égalité, et Fraternité" in your remotest colonies, and now, as they say in America, "The chickens have come home to roost." French Arabs and Africans have come to you to ask for more individual rights. They belong to you and you belong to them, because you have carried them in your womb. They need you most to realize their dream of democracy, equal rights with your other children, and individual dignity. And you, France, you need them as you meet the new global challenges of migration, transnational markets, and multiple identity positions. From now on the world will judge you according to whether they embrace or reject your doctrine of universalism. France, your position as torch-bearer of democracy in the world will depend on their welfare.

Dr. Trica D. Keaton's new book provides the most in-depth analysis of the predicament of French Arabs and Africans living in the suburbs of Paris—your capital and symbolic city. As an African American, Professor Keaton has experienced racism first-hand in America. But it is as a social scientist—who has studied with the best of your intellectuals—that she looks at your new citizens and candidates for "Liberté, Égalité, et Fraternité." Trica Keaton spent more than six years doing fieldwork and archival research on children of African and Arab descent who were born in Paris and its suburbs. She followed them at school—where they were taught the values of assimilation, national unity, and the universal equality of individuals. And she went with them to their neighborhoods and homes, where they were discriminated against by your police and public institutions. She found many contradictions between what you promised them through education, on the one hand, and what they experienced daily, on the other hand.

France, you may not like what you are going to find in Dr. Keaton's book. But remember what Jean-Paul Sartre once said in his introduction to L. S. Senghor's book *Anthologie de la nouvelle poesie nègre et malgache de langue française.* Sartre argued that French people would not like being perceived and judged by those whom they had colonized. Since they had always looked at the colonized and judged them, they would not enjoy hearing from them that colonialism was oppressive and evil. But, for Sartre, it was necessary for Frenchmen to listen to what the Black African, the Arab, and other wretched of the earth had to say. Conditions in those days were such that decolonization movements had heated up—there was Indochina, and Algeria soon after. In Paris, the Negritude poets had returned the gaze, and French people were their object of perception in a rapidly changing world. Sartre correctly thought that it was important for the French people to try to understand what the Other was saying. Sartre went as far as to call Senghor's anthology the most committed in France at the time.

Trica Keaton's book is not about the colonizer and colonized, nor even about immigration, although it could be read that way. It is about your children whose ancestors may have issued from colonialism, or even slavery. Counting the French Caribbeans, today, there are more than eight million people of Arab and African descent living in France. They suffer humiliation at the hands of the authorities, and their civil and citizenship rights are continually violated by people who treat them as foreigners simply on the basis of the color of their skin. This book is mainly about their experiences in the "Metropole."

In one sense, one can read the book through the lens of such great African American writers and activists as Richard Wright, James Baldwin, and Malcolm X. In their radical demand for citizenship, equal rights, and belonging in America, they told the "White Man [to] Listen"; and they threatened the "Fire Next Time." Malcolm X was one of the first to relate the struggle of African Americans in the U.S. to that of other people of color in Europe. Looking at the riots in Birmingham, England, in the 1960s, he cautioned the British that if they were not careful, they would end up with a situation similar to that of the U.S. Professor Keaton's book also contains an implicit warning to you, France, not to reenact American racism in your country. Your Black and Arab children are pleading with you to grant them their full citizenship, to respect their individuality, and to stop American-like ghettoes from surrounding them, separating them from your other children.

But it is as a social scientist that Dr. Keaton reserves her most pressing question for you, France. She calls it "the French dilemma," borrowing the expression from the Swedish sociologist Gunnar Myrdal, who spoke of "the American dilemma." Trica D. Keaton's extensive research has revealed to her that there are "fundamental contradictions between [a] highly abstracted notion of universalism and the lived reality of ethnic distinction and racialized discrimination against people of non-European origins and of color." In other words, your children of Arab and African descent are both assimilated culturally and excluded socially. To borrow an expression from W. E. B. Du Bois—the father of race sociology in America—they experience a double consciousness as the manifestation of living simultaneously within and behind the veil. Therein lies the paradox for you, France: position the veil in one way for a particular result, or another for a totally different outcome. Adjust the definition of "universalism" in light of new modernities and alternative globalizations, or maintain the old concept of French universalism, so dear to the National Front and other conservatives and racists. Either way you will have a different France: democratic and dynamic, or old, conservative, and xenophobic.

The first choice is obviously what all of us, who love you, France, wish for. However, to be flexible with the definition of universalism does not mean to fall back on relativism or to retreat from reason, or even to lock ourselves into some form of fixed identity politics. It means that a strategy has to be found to include your "Other" children in the nation, without reducing them to an outdated identity of Frenchness, or ethnic absolutism. It means mobilizing everyone toward a common goal of "Liberté, Égalité, et Fraternité" without taking away their soul. Finally it means realizing that people from different origins embrace their French identity in a different manner, without using that difference to divide them. A multicultural France is what we're calling for—a country that is still in the making, and yet is the beacon of democracy and reason. Your universalism is one that keeps rediscovering its essence in its new members, instead of being represented as fixed and timeless. We have to dare to think of a France that is not yet completed, and whose future depends also on the children of African and Arab descent.

Next to this dream of a multicultural France, an absolutist and ethnocentric model of universalism currently prevails in most institutions and public spheres. It picks on trivial symbols, such as Arab girls' wearing the veil to go to school, to exclude them from your family. It denies French citizenship to Black children born in the suburbs of Paris because their parents came here illegally. It mobilizes the images of radical Imams, lawbreakers, and the unemployed to demonize whole communities that it declares unfit to be included in your family. In short, this tendency relies on stereotypes and other outward forms of representation as weapons in a war against the

"Other." It tries to maintain your children of African and Arab descent in a position that Pierre Bourdieu calls "beings perceived" as foreigners, and not as French.

France, if you stay on the course of ethnic absolutism, you will be forced to reject not only some of your children, but also the idealism that made you famed around the world: "Liberté, Égalité, et Fraternité." The universalism you should want to defend is freedom and democracy for the oppressed, not some unitary way of being French in this global world. The universalism you should extend to the world is the French hospitality and inclusion of the oppressed in your family instead of sending them back at the mercy of dictators, religious fanatics, and intolerant cultural environments. France, you need a new and, as usual, courageous universalism that can cope with the modern global challenges, instead of retreating from them.

Finally, France, you do not need to take sides in the identity discourses and political struggle between the National Front and the veiled Muslim girls. They're both symptoms of a changing world in which their roles are diminishing. They may hide behind your flag or envelop themselves in it, but they are not the torch-bearers. You are, France. Dr. Keaton's book shows that it is not the veil that is the problem, but the schools and the environment in which the children grow up. Her excellent research reveals, to anybody who is willing to read it, how you, France, can solve your dilemma. I hope that you'll have the courage to read it.

Sincerely,
Manthia Diawara
New York, Accra, Paris
January 17, 2005

Acknowledgments

Expressing my thanks and acknowledging the wealth of people who contributed their insights and voice to this effort is no small task. First and foremost, I must thank all the girls—who became young women over the course of my fieldwork—who shared their personal lives with me, as well as the countless others who informed this analysis. I am especially indebted to numerous scholars whose critical comments on early and subsequent incarnations of this book had an immeasurable impact on the final product. And while none are responsible for its content or conclusions, this work would have been impossible in their absence. Thank you, Mom (Dorothy Jean Holman), George Bond, VèVè Clark, Lambros Comitas, Jeanette Demeestère, Anne Haas Dyson, Lily Wong Fillmore, Janet Hart, Bennetta Jules-Rosette, Michel Maffesoli, Pedro Noguera, Danielle Roth-Johnson, Stephen Small, Tyler Stovall, and Loïc Wacquant. As well, I must thank Remi Lenoir and Francine Muel-Dreyfus, whose support and penetrating questions greatly facilitated the completion of this project while I was in France as a Chateaubriand Fellow. They provided me with an intellectual home in the Centre de sociologie de l'éducation et de la culture of the École des hautes études en sciences sociales (EHESS). Moreover, thanks to them and Loïc Wacquant, I had the great fortune of meeting Pierre Bourdieu, Manthia Diawara, and Franck Poupeau. Professor Bourdieu's seminar at EHESS, which he generously invited me to join, has left a lasting impression on both me and this work, and I greatly appreciate his kind encouragement and incisive advice. He is missed. I have insufficient words to thank Manthia Diawara, who has been both a pillar and source of sustenance from the first day that we met in Pierre Bourdieu's seminar. Similarly, the generosity and kindness shown to me by Franck Poupeau, who was Bourdieu's graduate student and assistant, are incalculable.

I reserve a special, heartfelt thanks to a host of others who directly contributed to this work or advanced its publication, including Gregory Anderson, Marie-Clémentine Bendo, Françoise Boliya, Velma Bury, Claude Clegg, Christopher Daniels, Pierre Jacques Derainne, Omar Dia, Prentis Goodman, Mathew Guterl, Melinda Herron, Sory Koité, Jan Lebow, Sara Miangu Mas, John McCluskey, Charlie Nelms, Thomas Pollard, Karen Robinson, Jacqueline Rodin,

Boris Seguin, John Stanfield, and other colleagues in the Department of African American and African Diaspora Studies at Indiana University, Bloomington, and most recently Laïla Amine. I owe a very large debt of gratitude to Roy Jensen, whose reading and re-reading of the manuscript was more than I should have ever asked from one whom I call friend—*mange takk*. Finally, I must also thank the W. E. B. Du Bois Institute for African and African American Research at Harvard University, for its support of me as a non-resident Fellow; many at Teachers College-Columbia University; the Office of Academic Support and Diversity at Indiana University, Bloomington; the staff at *Canal, le magazine de Pantin,* especially Pierre Gernez; and the editors at Indiana University Press, in particular Rebecca Tolen. I also gratefully acknowledge *Anthropology and Education Quarterly* for allowing me to use materials published in that journal that were drawn from portions of this book.

**Muslim Girls and the Other France**

Introduction

I was born French, but for me, the way I see it, it's only in France that I'm French because our parents are foreign. But [in France] you have to be French. You have to be French to do anything here, like at school, or how you're educated. But in my head, I'm a foreigner.
—**Mariama (of Malian origin)**[1]

Me, I find myself totally integrated in France, so I feel at home everywhere. Given that I was born in France, that I speak French, that my culture is French, that I learned French history, France is my country . . . My identity is French of Algerian origin, of Muslim religion.
—**Fatima (of Algerian origin)**

[W]e are French and Muslim and proud of it.
—**Protester against the law banning headscarves in schools**[2]

Individuals or groups are objectively defined not only by what they are, but by what they are reputed to be, a "being perceived" which, even if it closely depends on their being, is never totally reducible to this.
—**Pierre Bourdieu,** *The Logic of Practice*

When people think of France, they do not typically attribute the racialized[3] forms and formations of violence, so commonplace in the United States, to the French urban landscape. However, the targets and effects of identity politics, educational inequality, blighted public housing projects that risk becoming little more than feeders for prisons, and generalized feelings of insecurity are very much a different "normal" in multiethnic France and Europe. Though urban violence (both real and anticipated) derives from a variety of sources, image-savvy politicians and media "experts" have identified, shaped, and honed "suitable enemies,"[4] enemies whom the public is taught to fear. In France, they are youths of immigration and of color from the outer cities—those high-rise public housing complexes on the periphery of urban centers. The sum and summation of all such enemies are Muslims, and most visibly headscarf-wearing Muslim girls. However, the underlying factors contributing to the public's alarm have less to do with reported increases in urban violence over the years and more with one glaring realization. Because France has failed to discern its grown and evolving populations of non-Europeans—an estimated four to five million of whom are Muslim[5]—its carefully crafted nation-state is now a more diverse state of ethnic nationals whose French-born or -reared children have come home to roost . . . permanently. That is, the consequences of history are making themselves felt in France. More importantly, these youths are shaping a "new" France and are one face of the Europe of tomorrow. Therein lies the actual source of the public's fears, which are now amplified by the attacks of September 11, 2001, in the U.S. and of March 11, 2004, in Spain, suicide bombings in Morocco and the Middle East, the expanding war on terror, and memories of wars and attacks previously visited upon French shores, such as the bombings of the mid-1980s and the summer of 1995. These memories are roused by threats of more attacks, spurred by the 2004 law banning "Islamic" headscarves and by the deportation of "radical" Imams allegedly for "spreading extremist Islamic thought,"[6] and by the kidnapping and subsequent release of French journalists in Iraq toward the end of 2004, also in response to the headscarf ban.

In the absence of a necessary conversation about the systemic causes of urban violence, a politicized rhetoric conjures an imaginary hydra of immigration, itself seen as the threat to France's coveted "national identity." Yet the real challenge to the national representation and culture is posed by stigmatized youths of non-European origins who assert that they are French and expect to be treated as such in their country: France. As young people from the outer cities, they are typecast as violent delinquents, feared as terrorists in the making, and objectified as criminals—the fodder of prisons and the targets of racialized profiling, secular laws, and curfews that apply solely to their neighborhoods. While they are made to be seen by the public as living manifestations of every social ill, what they are not *perceived* as is French. Born or raised in France, the only country that they know well, they did not become French through any conscious social movement or through political demands. Rather, they were made so through social structures and more directly through French national education, whose historical and expressed objective remains franco-conformity—an arrogant assimilationism toward the "national identity" in keeping with the interest of national unity (Noiriel 1988, 1992; Weil 1996, 1997; Bleich 1998).[7] Such youths are not, however, accorded the social recognition and currency that assimilation presumes.

Drawing from a multiyear study, this book examines this paradox in the lives of Muslim girls of African origins, and of youths of color in general, living in the French outer cities. The literature on the topic of Muslims in France continues to expand, though it typically focuses on North African or Maghrebin Muslims, and is often in French (Ben Jelloun 1984; Leveau 1986; Sayad 1991; Kepel 1991; Etienne 1989; Lacoste-Dujardin 1992; Hargreaves 1993, 1997; Cesari 1994; Raissiguier 1994; Khosrokhavar 1997; Wihtol de Wenden and Leveau 2001; Venel 1999; Gaspard 2004).[8] This attention to Maghrebin experiences is largely due to sociohistorical factors that drive a type of "Algerian exceptionalism." These factors include the fact that Algeria was a settler colony from the 1830s to 1962, as opposed to a protectorate; its bitter, bloody war of independence, which reached French soil; massive immigration and family recruitment from Algeria; and the fact that many Algerians hold dual Algerian and French nationality. Thus "Muslims" and "Muslim issues" become quasi-synonymous with the Magrebins and more specifically Arabs in discourse, writings, and public perception. The headscarf ban, for example, is portrayed as affecting only "Arabs," and not West Africans or Asians.[9] Nonetheless, anti-Arab violence and sentiment have been on the rise in France for more than two decades, as have intolerance and violence toward those identified as minority groups in general (Taguieff 1987; Tribalat 1995; Geisser 2003; CNCDH 2000–2002; 2004; Bleich 2003).

Although the majority of my focal participants[10] are of North African origin, they represent a range of ethno-national origins, colors, and color consciousness. In fact, in the U.S. context, some would be identified as "black,"[11] not Arab. This study seeks, then, to bridge that gap somewhat, by focusing on teenage girls of North and West African origins whose experiences merge through the politics of national identity and social exclusion in France. While these youths have highly diverse national origins, their ways of being and knowing are fashioned toward "ethnic sameness and differentiation: a changing sameness," as Paul Gilroy (1993, xi) describes it. Here, the African Diaspora is understood not merely as a brutal dispersal, but more as a site of separation and interconnection of Africans and African descent groups throughout the world, converging in places like the inner and outer cities. It is from this context that their self-understandings emerge. The accent in this analysis is placed, then, on that which unites them rather than what distinguishes them, in order to render more transparent the mechanisms fostering "unity within heterogeneity," as Stuart Hall (1990, 235) correctly phrases it.

As outer-city youths, they have been constituted as a social problem, and as youths of color, a denied racialized question in a French society that posits itself as operating out of a type of humanist universalism, a society that purports to be color-blind and race-free. Moreover, they are living expressions of a decidedly French dilemma in being simultaneously socially excluded and culturally assimilated while being defined as a threat to the "national identity." The creation of legislation targeting and banning the so-called Islamic headscarf—identified with a supposed rise in fundamentalism and intolerance in the outer cities—effectively illustrates this point, especially since educational policies have been in place to address this very issue since 1995. And yet few actual cases of Muslim girls wearing a headscarf in the public schools have been documented, though the law is likely to increase that number, as girls resist it. The headscarf has been made to symbolize something antipodal to French values and culture, which then triggers those statist practices (i.e., laws and policies) aimed at franco-conformity. Resistance triggers other actions, namely the expulsion from the schools and the country of youths whose life chances are already compromised by a dysfunctional educational system. But, more to the point, these youths expose fundamental contradictions between that highly abstracted notion of universalism and the lived reality of ethnic distinction and racialized discrimination against people of non-European origins and of color.

Indeed, these youths and their assertions that they are French or "French of 'x' origin" (e.g., of Senegalese or Tunisian origin) become, then, the litmus test for ideologies of inclusion and models of assimilation, because their self-understandings pose an acute challenge to popular perceptions, discourses of belonging, and a "national identity." Muslim girls have been fashioned as the quintessential other vis-à-vis French culture and the national representation in the courts of public and private opinion. Their complexities are often reduced to tropes of gendered oppression associated with controversial acts such as honor killing, imposed veiling and seclusion, forced marriage, polygamy, repudiation, and excision, forms of violence that have also become the stuff of urban legends. Speciously attributed solely to Muslims, these acts frontally clash with the idea of human rights and tolerance taught in French schools, schools that ironically expel headscarf-wearing Muslim girls should they refuse to remove their head covering on the school's grounds. Moreover, these measures diminish the importance of other pressing social problems affecting the life chances of these youths—including poor living conditions and educational inequality. They also serve to reinforce a seemingly inelastic notion of a "national identity," itself buttressed by subjective interpretations of French secularism, *la laïcité* (Barbier 1995; Coq 1999; Poulat 2003).

To be defined as a problem, in the language of W. E. B. Du Bois, is not without its effects. For some youths a type of double, if not triple, consciousness emerges that leads them to measure themselves through the contemptuous eyes of others.[12] The "psychological wage of Frenchness," to slightly alter Du Bois's phrase, compels certain youths to distance themselves from negative representations and practices identified with their presumed cultures in favor of the national representation nurtured in their schools, which is equated with gender equality. High-profile cases in the media are instructive illustrations of this point, such as that of Hawa Gréou, a fifty-nine-year-old French resident from Mali who received a stiff prison sentence for having excised forty-eight girls in France, which I discuss in chapter 5. To the Malian community's surprise and dismay, she was denounced by a French-raised girl whom she had excised. Then there is the case of Fatoumata, a French high school student of Senegalese origin whose father held her in Senegal against her will pending a forced marriage, taken up in chapter 1. The more tragic cases include the murders of Nazmiyé, a fifteen-year-old girl of Turkish origin, and Sohane Benziane, an eighteen-year-old of Algerian origin, over questions of shame and honor, patriarchy, and machoism, issues I develop in this analysis in relation to the experiences of my focal participants.

The backdrop to this entire scenario is a sexually liberal, media-oriented Parisian society, to which these teens are exposed wherever they go. Going for a walk, riding the metro, or watching television can be a challenge for the more modest among them, since they may be faced with life-size billboards and advertisements wherein nudity and sensuality sell anything from lingerie to car insurance. More-over, unlike in their parents' countries of origin and in their homes, nudity is not taboo on French television. These in-your-face kinds of media make the expectation of modesty more complex for some Muslim girls who continually walk a swaying tightrope in being the transcultural teenagers that their social locations have fashioned. In this light, their narratives merit greater attention not because they represent the totality of Muslim girls' lived realities, but because their stories reveal valuable and alarming developments within na-tional identity politics structured by social exclusion and reinforced by gender constraints.

In sharing their stories, I cannot stress too much that the vio-lence experienced by some of my participants and documented in this study should not be generalized to all Muslims or Africans. Some are, nonetheless, subjected to unspeakable crimes and have been silenced by the forces responsible. It is my hope to give voice to such youths, particularly the ones whom I have come to know. It is also my intent to place a very real human face on a host of pressing problems affecting the life chances of youths from the French outer cities, ranging from dashed hopes and dreams to the broader, inter-nalized effects of residential and educational segregation in French society. Despite long-standing affirmative action initiatives, an aver-age of sixty thousand youths left the French schools between 1990 and 2000 without any meaningful certifications or diplomas. An es-timated 40 percent of the diploma-less are without work in a coun-try where unemployment rates hover around 10 percent (at times higher) nationally (DEP 2003; INSEE 1999, 2004).

On Race and Classifications

In this context, the self-understandings of Muslim youths sig-nify critical change in a French society clinging to its "national iden-tity" amidst unanticipated and often unwanted social mutations that these young people come to represent. Ill-prepared to embrace these youths as French, France finds itself facing several pressing so-cial questions, most notably, what will be the effects of stigmatized youths of color's claims on a social fiction termed a "national iden-tity" in a society that constitutes them as perpetual outsiders or im-migrants? And what happens when public institutions attempt to level cultural differences among youths of varying African origins *in* schools while those differences are amplified *outside* of schools? One clear implication is that these youths lay bare the flawed nature of the classifications used in France, while making the social reality of race—contingent upon struggles over classifications and structures of meaning—salient in a French society hostile to this notion. It is also a society in which social race comes to justify and explain existing divisions and differences, much as "racialized barriers," to use Stephen Small's (1994) term, and color consciousness operate in the U.S. and England. Indeed, U.S. understandings and applications of "race" are rejected in France and measured against notions of universalism. Moreover, U.S. notions of hypodescent (the "one drop rule," according to which any traceable African ancestry makes one black) do not obtain in a France that eschews [avoid] categories defined and described in terms of "race" and ethnicity. Nonetheless, these "suitable enemies," anchored in the French context, play a pivotal role in the racialization of the "national identity." Because of this, this racialization permeates social structures and more specifically those elements of urban social life with which youths of color and immigration are identified, such as dead-end vocational tracks, prisons, and the outer cities themselves.

Already, "race" discourse is prevalent in French society, so much so that one commonly hears people describe themselves and others as *noir* (black), *beur* (Arab), or *blanc* (white), and use "ethnic roots" (e.g., *Gaulois*) to mark distinction and difference. Some even identify as "black" rather than *noir*, and this usage connects them to a U.S. type of consciousness permeating France and parts of Europe. The title alone of Gaston Kelman's (2003) controversial book mocking identity politics in France speaks volumes: *Je suis noir et je n'aime pas le manioc* (I'm black, and I don't like yams). The putative markers of "race"—skin color, hair, features, language varieties, and by extension family name, religion, and ways of being—have long-standing social meanings in France, underpinned and enlivened by ideologies and policies acting on them. Scientific racism, which legitimized chattel slavery and colonization, is the most obvious example. And, clearly, views such as those espoused by Arthur de Gobineau in *The Inequality of the Human Races* (1853) structured both racialist thought and policies in and beyond France, despite Haitian anthropologist Anténor Firmin's fierce rebuttal, *The Equality of the Human Race* (1885), which went largely ignored.

In many ways, there exists a "French dilemma," similar to what Gunnar Myrdal (1944/1975) identified as an "American dilemma," having to do with the patent contradictions in France between the cherished national values of "Liberty, Equality, Fraternity, and Secularism" (*Liberté, Egalité, Fraternité,* and *Laïcité*) and the consistent prac-

Worldly rather than spiritual

tice of targeted racialized discrimination. In the French context, such discrimination, as a social problem, is frequently subsumed in issues of social inequality and immigration, or conflated with xenophobia. In other words, people of color are supposedly discriminated against because they are "immigrants" or feared foreigners, not necessarily because they are African or Asian or "black" (De Rudder, Poiret, and Vourc'h 2000). But the fact that a thing is not racially named does not mean it is not racialized. The twist in the French context, compared to the United States, is that it is much more difficult to prove racialized discrimination within the population identified officially as "French," because their ethnic origins are not documented (Simon 2000; Tribalat 1995; Simon and Stavo-Debauge 2002). Various anti-racist organizations[13] have acknowledged that it is necessary to "un-mix" the official category of "French" in order to document and more effectively combat racialized discrimination, despite state and public resistance to this prospect.[14] It is critical to emphasize, all the same, that documenting ethnic origins (implying "race") is considered discriminatory according to the French constitution, and cutting against those universalist principles inhering in the construct of a citizen-individual attached to a nation-state. Moreover, such classifications are viewed through perceptions shaped during the Vichy regime and still conjure up dreaded memories and images of ethnic labeling in France during the Nazi era.

And yet, anti-racist groups, both statist and independent of the state,[15] continue to show that racialized discrimination manifests itself in the most basic social structures, including employment, housing, education, social services, the criminal justice system, and relations with the police. While I examine these issues vis-à-vis the lived experiences of my participants, such realities are, in effect, what constitute social race as a persistent entity, despite the discrediting of biological "race" and the decoding of the human genome. In his study of international race politics, sociologist Michael Banton reminds us of the danger of reproducing through connotation the very thing one seeks to dismantle: "the international anti-racist movement has never known quite what to do about the ways in which the language of race can reinforce the identification of biological and social difference" (2002, 3). And yet, as sociologist Loïc Wacquant rightly states when comparing these young people to similar "suitable enemies" in the United States, "foreigners and quasi-foreigners would be the 'blacks' of Europe" (1999b, 216).

Appearances, however, are deceiving, and reality is quite another matter. To ascribe a black/white paradigm to the French context or frame human relations in such neat terms is to err. Although extremely powerful, such reasoning applies only problematically to these youths, whose origins lie on the *continent* of Africa, where historical migration, invasion, partition, and mixing—indeed, geopolitics—disrupt attempts to identify them in neat black/white terms, despite popular discourse. To uncritically view Arabs as "white" (as do the U.S. census and popular understandings) and sub-Saharan Africans as "black," or to desire (s)kinship with people on the basis of their physical appearance or "looks" (as people commonly do who are conditioned by black/white paradigms) is equally to err. It further leaves little room for people to self-understand outside narrow categories reified into representations of culture. The point is that the supposed markers of "race" can be erroneous indicators of ethnic and national origins, and do not signify culture. After all, people who self-understand as African or Arab have a variety of complexions and features. More to the point, being perceived as African or Arab in French society has never carried the same advantages as being perceived as French, which signifies European ancestry and, increasingly, "whiteness." The formation and claiming of a self-representation articulated as French or "French of 'x' origin" by youth of color and immigration become, then, a signpost in France. It announces what may be a transformation in the official classification system, should these youths continue to be distinguished, and distinguish themselves, from the *français-français* ("French-French," the supposedly unequivocal or "old stock" French).

"National Identity" and Nationality: Symbolic Struggles over Representation

In France, the politics of identity exist within a state of tension between an ideology of national unity and a reality of ethnic diversity. At the nexus of this tension lie stigmatized youths of color assimilated toward the "national identity." Culture, those historically accumulated and socially formed, embodied, and transmitted ways of being and knowing, is a very real stake in this context, in which the authority to *name* or *constitute* who is French (and who is not) in an exclusionary fashion contributes to perceiving the "national identity" as being reserved for a select(ed) group. Understood in this manner, "national identity" becomes a social fact and a highly coveted form of symbolic capital having the quality of nobility. That is, it is morphed into an entity within French society that legitimizes belonging upon its acknowledgment, or disqualification when breached:

> In the symbolic struggle for the production of common sense or, more pre-
> cisely, for the monopoly over legitmate naming, agents put into action the
> symbolic capital that they have acquired in previous struggles and which
> may be juridically guaranteed. Thus titles of nobility [like nationality] rep-
> resent true titles of symbolic property which give one a right to share in
> the profits of recognition (Bourdieu 1990a, 134).

Constituting a nation-state demands that it be recognized as such
by society, and the nation-state is consecrated through *de jure* titles
designating a "nationality." It demands, too, a corresponding national representation attached to entities such as an official language
and culture, vague notions of common descent, "ambiguous identities" (to borrow from scholar Étienne Balibar) and mechanisms for
incorporating diversity (Noiriel 1992; Balibar and Wallerstein 1991;
Thiesse 1999). Challenges to the national representation have important social and political implications for the national educational
system in France, whose expressed goal is to reproduce and transmit
a unitary, irreducible "common culture" to which all young people
are expected to conform in the interest of the nation.

French "national identity" and nationality are products of the
revolution and the forging of the nation-state. Through colonialism
to the period of economic euphoria known as the *trente glorieuses*
(thirty glorious [years], 1945–1974) to the present, these entities
have remained central to political debates and struggles over complex issues and problems, such as immigration, social exclusion, and
racism. The social movements of the 1970s and 1980s were spearheaded by youths of immigrant origin who rallied to bring attention
to these concerns, while militating to have citizenship rights accorded to long-term immigrant residents in France (Wihtol de Wenden 1999; Wihtol de Wenden and Leveau 2001). Though they failed
in their efforts, this debate periodically reemerges in local elections.[16] More critically, these multiethnic movements highlighted
the contradictory principles embedded in the concepts of French
"national identity," nationality, and citizenship, which manifestly
hinged on having and asserting rights attached to a representation
from which youth of immigration and of color were excluded. In
other words, a principal aim of such movements was to validate a
new type of French citizen, a product not of one culture but of multiple cultures who insisted on *le droit à la différence* (the right to difference) without being assigned different rights. Moreover, since
belief in a French "national identity" and national culture have become a concern of politics and public opinion, the symbolic strategies of these youths were an attempt to disrupt a singular notion of

Frenchness by intentionally seizing a self-representation that deviated from this popular idea. It should also not be overlooked that, as Tahar Ben Jelloun rightly asserts, "Among certain Maghrebins, notably the Algerians, becoming French is considered . . . a type of treason" (1984, 142), an assertion also articulated by West Africans that shapes and informs how these youths self-understand (Poiret 1996; Quiminal ct al. 1997; Diawara 2003).

The symbolic power that inheres in the authority to determine what constitutes a "national identity" necessarily expresses itself at both macro and micro levels of French society, and is enforced by the state through its National Codes. As important as the belief in this representation is, what has become more critical is the need to be documented and to have French nationality: symbolic capital at work. In 1986, for example, legislation was enacted that placed greater emphasis on defining French nationality and a "national identity," which historically hinged on the socialization of potential nationals through institutions such as the schools. In France, as political scientist Patrick Weil argues, "One's bond to the nation no longer results from a personal allegiance to the King, but rather from having been educated in French society, and from one's past residence." He further states that "Republican law bases nationality on socialization more than on ethnic background or on a voluntary or contractual act, [and] on the acquisition of social codes more than on origin and place of birth" (1997, 19–20). So important was the belief in the socialization process that it was determined that birth on French soil, rather than only blood descent (as was the case in such countries as Germany), would determine nationality in France. In his analysis, Weil clearly outlines the important history of immigration and naturalization legislation in the country, from the Constitution of 1791 through the Fifth Republic, in order to demonstrate how these laws set the tone for contemporary reforms to naturalization legislation.

Notable among these reforms were the 1993 Méhaignerie and the infamous Pasqua laws. Together, they rendered it more difficult for children of foreign-born immigrants from undesired countries to acquire French nationality, and they created an inhospitable climate for their parents by making it more difficult to enter the country, unite families, and attain residency. These measures also sanctioned random ID checks of those perceived as "immigrants," treating people as criminals because of their appearance, because they were seen as "immigrants," even if they were not. One particularly contested aspect of these laws was their requirement that the children of immigrants, who are predominantly of African and Asian origins, establish their nationality by formally expressing a desire to be French, making a declaration of intent between the ages of sixteen and twenty-one. Although the 1993 law was overturned in 1998, it nonetheless wreaked havoc in the lives of youths who were forced to live in a nebulous, liminal space in the only country that many knew and called home until reaching their majority.[17] Further, requests for nationality could be denied if a person had a criminal record, which is not unlikely among those outer-city youths who are also engaged in alternative economies, and some have been deported to their parents' home countries. Then there are the sad cases of youths who believe they already are nationals simply because they have no memories of a life outside of France. In this book, I highlight cases that illustrate the lived consequences of this legislation, whose current incarnation is unsurprisingly viewed with suspicion and contempt by people from stigmatized groups seeking naturalization. Picking up on this point, Weil argues that one critical reason for requiring young people to demonstrate their desire for French nationality was to avoid the recurring problem of their not knowing whether they were actually nationals of the country. Yet in actuality, as Weil argues, by requiring youths of this generation to make such a declaration, France was asking more of them than it did of former immigrants of European origins, thereby "breaking with the egalitarian and universal practice upon which [the country] is founded" (quoted in Venel 1999, 103). Much of the confusion derives from the multiple changes in the naturalization laws and the lack of informed personnel to explain these changes to a public that is equally ill-informed.

These destabilizing laws, coupled with existing educational policy that proscribes the wearing of "conspicuous" religious symbols in the schools—and potentially in other public arenas, such as hospitals—are shaping how youths of immigrant origin self-understand in contemporary France. In this context marked by high unemployment, feelings of frustration, and generalized disenchantment, the politicization of a "French national identity" renders it a scarce commodity to which employment, even in those jobs once shunned by the *français-français,* is attached. As Tahar Ben Jelloun affirms, "people are afraid of no longer corresponding to the image they have of themselves" (1984, 24), afraid—perhaps—of seeing turned against them the violence that a colonial past and current cruel social patterns have unleashed. While calling oneself *rebeu* (Arab) or *kebla* or *renoi* (Black or Noir), terms common in popular youth culture, can be interpreted as a form of resistance against disparaging representations, calling oneself French (and believing it) appropriates the rights attached to both citizenship (e.g., the right to vote) and nationality (e.g., the right to be and work in France, in security) in both material and symbolic ways. Ironically, despite the multiple barriers that they confront, these young people (like others of their generation) exhibit practices and opinions traditionally associated with a French "national identity." After all, they are products of one common institution that begins at the formative age of two or three in France: national education. On the one hand, the French school teaches them that they are French through its ideology of a "common culture" in a system whose gatekeepers are hostile to multiculturalism and change.[18] On the other hand, young people are reared in segregated neighborhoods and schools that clearly belie those very teachings.

The assertions by France's "suitable enemies" that they are French, and that the country they live in is *their* country, are a clear expression of symbolic power, to borrow a concept from Pierre Bourdieu (1990b), that is, practices aimed at preserving or transforming social reality by shaping its representations in ways that can perpetuate the status quo. Their assertions become symbolic violence (i.e., more disguised, subtle forms of violence exercised with complicity) when they derive from "the categories of perception that the world imposes" (but whose imposition is not perceived) (Bourdieu 1990b, 141). Although "national identities" are reified social fictions indicative of a legitimized domination à la Weber, their symbolic force resides in the cultural distinctions believed to be held by a powerful and privileged few. When constructed as a precious and limited commodity allowing exclusive access, these representations become all the more valuable, desirable, and contested. Because they are largely unquestioned in the contexts where they are imposed (the schools and society) these classifications, expressed as "identities," appear universal, or simply seem natural to the general public, including these youths. Again, therein lies the violence. It becomes, therefore, not only interesting but critical to connect identity politics with social institutions in order to demonstrate more broadly how those very politics—structured by those institutions—contribute to maintaining a status quo, despite resistance to them.

Beyond "Identity" to Identity Politics

What terms can be used to denote and analyze how people self-understand without violating a fundamental tenet of social science:

never use one social fact to analyze another (Durkheim 1993)? The use of the term "identity" exemplifies this thorny problem in being derived from commonsense discourses that make the existence of an "identity," national or otherwise, possible. In this analysis, I grapple with just this problem in framing my work in terms of identity politics, which implies using concepts, themes, and interests that are conditioned by institutional contexts and lay understandings. Yet, in an attempt to name such phenomena, one set of connotations is ultimately replaced by another, and the signifiers and concepts obfuscate as much as they clarify. This appears to be the case with the term "identity," as opposed to other signifiers such as "self-identification." As social scientists Rogers Brubaker and Frederick Cooper argue,

> The problem is that "nation," "race," and "identity" are used analytically a good deal of the time more or less as they are used in practice, in an implicitly or explicitly reifying manner, in a manner that implies or asserts that "nations," "races," and "identities" "exist" and that people "have" a "nationality," a "race," an "identity." (2000, 6)

These social scientists zero in on the ambiguity attached to the language of "identity," which is expected to serve as both a "category of social and political practice" and a "category of social and political analysis" (2000, 2). In other words, this single term is expected to accommodate so many purposes that it ultimately becomes diluted, thus meaningless.

While one can find truth in these arguments, one must also question a fundamental issue at the heart of this debate. That is, in so ardently attempting to name the rose, are we overlooking the real work of analyzing the phenomena that account for the rose's existence, and, more important, its acceptance as social reality? What is at issue is the necessity for epistemological clarity and the necessity to "deconstruct the notion of identity" in order to carry out the very real work of refuting "myths of insularity," cultural singularity, and the authenticity of a particular group (Benoist 1977, 16). This point was central in discussions of these themes in Claude Lévi-Strauss's seminar on identity at the Collège de France in Paris in 1974–1975 (Lévi-Strauss 1977). In attempting to analyze how the "other" is constituted (with the realization that one is always someone else's other), one must account for both the subjective and objective dimensions of the dynamic that results in the formation of the sociopolitical self. In the debate rightly foregrounded by Brubaker and Cooper, however, is the focus on the terminology obscuring other important issues? Such issues would include understanding how the dialectic of identification operates within struggles over cultural legitimacy between peoples and groups through the act of assigning oneself and one's "other" to socially distinct categories. The examination of others' social worlds necessarily compels the scholar to practice a level of epistemological vigilance that most lay people, such as those in the media, can and do ignore. However, the scholar must perforce attempt to break from preconceived ideas, and especially from the reification of culture expressed as an "identity." This is not easy.

Fundamentally, I examine the sociopolitical construction of self: that is, what Craig Calhoun terms "the politics of identity" (1994). This process of person formation is complex, as it involves ideological descriptors (e.g., French, immigrant, or Muslim, and even girl) that are recast in terms of a prescribed culture that is presumed to connote a common heritage and shared modes of thought, values, dispositions, and even, perhaps, physical appearances. As Calhoun compellingly argues, the politics of identity "involve[s] refusing, diminishing, or displacing identities others wish to recognize in individuals . . . politics either starting from or aiming at claimed identities of protagonists" (19, 21). However, this process is not the result merely of individual will; it is an "implicit recognition of a range of authoritative others [based on] the unquestioned acceptance of the apparent order of social categories," as Calhoun argues further (11). Thus, affirming oneself as French carries with it a tacit understanding that there is power attached to this classification, a power that, in a stratified France, is transformed into rights and economic opportunities. By the same token, to be a demonized Muslim of non-European origins and aver that one is French is to transcend the narrow representation of the "authoritative other" while consciously or unconsciously appropriating the categories of dominance and distinction that command recognition within French society. The equation of "Muslim of non-European origins" with "French" also defies the simplicity of these categories, and therein lies the complication. An important aspect of "identity" struggles, for those people seeking to preserve a given representation, is the capacity to maintain authority by publicly stigmatizing an undesirable population, as the prevailing U.S. and European trope of the immigrant as invader, job stealer, and leech on the public funds effectively shows. The efficiency of such a maneuver expresses itself in the ease with which such amalgams come to manipulate public opinion such that the stigmatized become the sole authors of their stigmatization.

The concept of identity politics, as I employ it, accurately applies in this context simply because it draws attention to the authority, and thereby complicity and interests, aimed at formalizing and normalizing a social fact called an "identity." And yet the waters of identity politics are never quite as clear as one would wish, as the polemical voice of bell hooks reminds us:

> a totalizing critique of "subjectivity, essence, identity" can seem very threatening to marginalized groups, for whom it has been an active gesture of political resistance to name one's identity as part of a struggle to challenge domination. (1994, 78)

Challenging domination through naming "one's identity" is the essence of a dialectic of identification, a dance involving the naming and renaming of self in response to an "other." hooks's observation applies tellingly to the French context and those young people who are averring that they are French by challenging (knowingly and unknowingly) the fundamental terms of inclusion in their economically and socially troubled homeland. Protesters against the current law banning religious symbols in schools drive home this point. Headscarf-wearing protesters draped in the French flag, marching down the streets and singing the Marseillaise (the French national anthem once claimed by the extreme right), defiantly manifest the contested image inscribed on their signs: *Françaises, Musulmanes* (Frenchwomen, Muslim women). If it were not an issue, there would be no need to proclaim it. On one level, such assertions are forms of resistance to rejection and exclusion that speak to these women's desire, if not demand, to be recognized and accorded the same dignity as any other French person. On another, their claims and assertions further reify as much as they describe a social prescription of a "national identity" whose symbolic force resides in its regenerated and unanalyzed use.

Thinking Globally and Seeing Locally: Why Care about France?

In many apparent and not so apparent ways, these young people resemble many teenagers that one could readily encounter in one's communities, classes, or homes, or simply on the streets. This "come-along generation," as I once heard the acclaimed Haitian novelist and scholar Edwidge Dandicat describe the children of immigrants during a conference in Paris, did not choose their exile. Although

Dandicat was referring to young people who accompanied their parents to foreign, sometimes hostile lands, I found that this statement harbors some truth for urban youth of color in France. That is, they did not *choose* France per se, but France is often the only country that they know well, the one that they call home. A certain recognizable familiarity resonates in their experiences and connects their lived realities to those of similarly marginalized young people in the African Diaspora who face intergenerational, socioeconomic exclusion that is furthered by their schooling. To enter into their world and bear witness to their struggles (and successes) is a way of understanding the interconnections between local and global contexts, indeed between the periphery and the metropolis. What better exemplifies this point than educational systems wherein the children of immigrants and other unpopular groups find themselves at odds with people and policies that oppose their ways of being, which are not truly understood nor particularly valued? Because often precious little is known about the complex backgrounds of such young people or what is expected of them socially and culturally (and the forces guiding those expectations), it becomes all the more critical for the general public to learn more about their actual experiences, from their perspectives.

Another important point to keep in mind is that the educational system can work remarkably well in France, as it can elsewhere. However, the people for whom it works most poorly are the ones with the least power to counter its devastating and long-term effects. And, as elsewhere, there are controversial policies in France that further complicate how young people are received and schooled in French society. Among them are residential and educational segregation, affirmative action, high-stakes testing, academic tracking, and selection biases in school choice, measures derived from broader political forces operating at the state level. Moreover, the very real effect of many of these policies is that the school becomes the surest means of reproducing social inequality. While social reproduction theories most associated with Pierre Bourdieu have been heavily criticized for being overly mechanistic, denying resistance, and asserting a preexisting, unbreakable social order, inequalities are reproduced all the same through educational structures. The result is that the most vulnerable members of society are further subordinated by these forces, that is, the young who inherit their parents' socioeconomic precariousness and disadvantage. And yet they do resist those forces, as Bourdieu argues in responding to those criticisms:

I do not see how relations of domination, whether material or symbolic, could possibly operate without implying, activating resistance. *The dominated, in any social universe, can always exert a certain force,* inasmuch as belonging to a field means by definition that one is capable of producing effects in it. (Bourdieu and Wacquant 1992, 80)

Rather than being mechanistic, the process is dramatically dynamic, since people *of* and *in* social structures of power, privilege, and prejudice seek to both preserve and transform their positions within those structures. My point here is that social relations—indeed acts of resistance and agency themselves—cannot be abstracted or disconnected from the historical, ideological, and institutional context in which they are embedded and which they also shape.

Further, as I will show, the young people in my study exercise resistance and agency in multiple ways, which include defying patriarchal expectations or battling to remain in coveted non-vocational studies and ability tracks, at any cost, against the verdicts of their communities and schools that attempt to neutralize such acts of defiance. These efforts can, however, wind up producing the opposite effect. That is, rather than emancipating them, these actions can also further entrench these young people in their conditions of poverty and marginalization, the very things they are intended to combat. Secular national education is the centerpiece in these complexities, whose ideological force serves to assimilate youths in ways that are not unlike the mission of the common schools formerly advocated in the United States (Tyack 1974). The very real difference, however, is that the French model remains largely intact, and the idea of a "common culture," transmitted through the schools, is not the loaded issue that it is in places such as the United States. In fact, issues of cultural literacy and multiculturalism are only beginning to emerge as curricular questions with the growing presence of young people of non-European origins in French schools. Coupled with these factors are antagonisms between various racialized groups (i.e., Afro-French, Euro-French, and migrants of differing national origins) who share common neighborhoods that are marked by long-term economic misery. During this period in which the volatile discourse of nationalism perpetuates notions of French purity, popular myths concerning a French "national identity" become especially appealing to working-class *français-français* who have been conditioned to see their non-European neighbors as simply beneath them (Garcia, Poupeau, and Proteau 1998). Consequently, so-called immigrants become identified in political and popular discourses as the cause of personal economic lack, if not of all the general woes of the country

(Miles 1982; Small 1994; Wieviorka 1995; Taguieff and Tribalat 1998). These woes become defined in terms of racialist ideologies, themselves recast as nationalistic interests, and used against those perceived as usurping scarce resources, such as housing, jobs, social services, and even the "national identity." The perspectives of France's "suitable enemies" converge, then, at the intersection of local and global contexts with other racialized young people defined as social problems. Further, their cases force us to rethink some pertinent social questions in this new millennium, in which we walk on shifting sands of belonging and are forced to ask ourselves less who we are and more how we are perceived.

Reflections on Paris and the Craft of Fieldwork in a Parisian Outer City

Urban cities are complex by definition. Paris is complex in its own way. In the summer of 1995, I began fieldwork in the City of Light, which was reeling from the worst urban violence of that decade, attacks for which France's Muslim population, then more than three million, was collectively held responsible for the actions of a few. Having already experienced the panic and fury wrought by the bombings in 1986, I found a certain irony in returning to Paris at a time when the city was rocked once again, this time by a series of bombs planted in commuter trains.[19] While a young man of Algerian origin, Khaled Kelkal, was blamed and subsequently martyred once the media aired images of him being shot and killed by the police during a botched arrest attempt, those tragedies tainted all Muslims in their wake (as have more recent ones). My participants, their families, and their friends were collectively tried in the courts of public opinion for crimes in which they were not involved and over which they had no control. Their visible appearance, or as they say, their *tête*, made them "suitable enemies" for a public seeking revenge for these acts of violence, a French public that appeared not to comprehend why, yet again, they had been targeted by those identified as "Islamic fundamentalists." And while many Muslim groups and individuals denounced these bombings as inhumane and cowardly, some even expressing an enormous sense of shame over such violence, this shame was second only to the fear and hatred that these acts would unleash in a country where Muslims were already on such tenuous ground. France and its Muslim communities are joined at the hip by a long, often violent relationship, conditioned by colonialism and war, but public rage at the time of those attacks (assisted by irresponsible media imagery) rendered it difficult to abstract individual innocence in a climate where guilt was easily assigned to Muslims in general:

> After these bombings, we were all suspects . . . If you come through an airport or a train station, all eyes are on you. People are picked up according to their complexion or because they have frizzy hair. (quoted in the *International Herald Tribune*, September 8, 1995)

World events, as they stand, have exposed these old wounds, resurrected submerged bigotries and hate, and aroused mistrust on all sides. And suspicion continues to be the order of the day, especially of anyone making inquiries about the experiences of Muslims and Muslim youths in France. Every category to which researchers are assigned comes into play in contexts such as these. My appearance and nationality made me suspect, as much as did my asking questions or having views that deviated from the public's outrage over the suffering brought about by attacks that touched so many. Indeed, it is often overlooked that Muslims were also victims of these attacks.

When I entered this field of lived tragedies, other relevant events were also unfolding, including the violent expulsion of African families (including babies) from the country (reminiscent of Interior Minister Charles Pasqua's deportation of more than a hundred Malian immigrants, shackled hand and foot, in 1987).[20] Educational policy proscribing "proselytizing" symbols of religious affiliation was also instituted in 1995, which portended current legislation designed to do the same thing. And as if that were not enough, matters intensified when France was hit by extensive public transportation strikes that paralyzed the city for a record number of months. I found myself walking, hitching, and pondering inventive ways to get to my research sites, as frequent metro strikes and slowdowns became part of the experience of living in Paris. Shortly thereafter, in scenes reminiscent of May 68, came the massive protests by university students against educational inequalities. Demonstrations were not often peaceful, and confrontations with the police sometimes erupted into physical violence engulfing anyone in its path. These themes would reemerge during large-scale demonstrations and strikes involving all sectors of national education beginning in 1998, which continue and will continue as long as the systemic causes of inequality go unaddressed. In short, it was the worst and the best of times to be in Paris, and the best and the worst of times to explore the lives of Muslim girls in the outer cities.

Over the years, I would come to know this "other France" quite well, thanks to the forces of serendipity that helped me gain access. Researchers often describe gaining entry to their site as one of the main difficulties they face in fieldwork. For me, gaining access was the result of having quickly glanced at a dissertation lying on the desk of one of my former professors (Bennetta Jules Rosette) during a visit. Almost nonchalantly this professor added, "Marie-Ange is a teacher in Paris." Well, that was like a sweet melody to my ears, as I was a bit anxious about finding reliable contacts affiliated with the public school system who might know or have Muslim students. I gladly accepted Marie-Ange's address and subsequently wrote her a letter detailing my project, along with a brief outline of my professional and personal background. Shortly thereafter, I received a small white envelope in the mail with the notation *par avion* written upon it, indicating that it was from France, and more precisely from Marie-Ange. I immediately exhaled a huge sigh of relief, as one seemingly formidable problem dissipated with her invitation to contact her once I had arrived in Paris.

When Marie-Ange and I finally met, we almost immediately discovered a type of sisterhood, though we hailed from very different parts of the world—she from the Antilles and I from a small town in northern Ohio. Though the places we called home felt lightyears apart, we were, nonetheless, walking expressions of the African Diaspora. Marie-Ange often mused that with my hair in braids I could "pass" for any number of people of African origins living in Paris, especially since I speak French. In fact, her reflections were also warnings, because my looks and that very fluency made me subject to the same treatment that non-European-looking people suffer in France. Manthia Diawara poignantly documents this treatment using "reverse anthropology," a twist on colonial models that constitutes Europeans and European cities as objects and fields of study to be investigated by Africans, as opposed to the other way around. Diawara's aim is to examine the "silences of the Parisians about the brutality against African immigrants [who] traveled to France to find work, [and] . . . find only shame and humiliation at the hands of the French police" (2003, 43). Diawara has had such experiences himself in both the U.S. and France. He argues further from personal and observed experiences: "Every encounter with a CRS policeman, an immigration officer, a racist cabdriver or café waiter, or patronizing French intellectual at a reception or a dinner sends me back to my poem 'The Stranger,'" a poem about the rejection and hostilities experienced by African immigrants in France (153).

This ugliness manifested itself to me in two typical ways—denial of housing and racialized profiling. At times, I and friends of African origin were selectively made to show our tickets on commuter trains, or were followed in supermarkets or department stores by Black men (who are increasingly employed as security guards and police officers in the belief that they can manage and control other African-derived people). And then there are those memorable occasions when we were stopped dead in our tracks with demands for our papers, when we were doing nothing more than, like anyone else, being on the streets of Paris, in the metros, or in a taxi (where Diawara was also accosted). Ironically, Paris, which so many expatriate and exiled Black Americans from the nineteenth century to the present have perceived as a haven from U.S. racism, has rarely been a safe and liberating sanctuary for the descendants of those enslaved and colonized by France (Gondola 2004). To be sure, U.S. race terror, its structural manifestations, and the threat of physical violence—lynchings, random beatings, and rape—fueled emigration to Paris during the pre–Civil Rights era. Moreover, migration narratives imbued with tales of an all-embracing Parisian society where neither Jim nor Jacques Crow resided were compelling, and played decisive roles in the formation of an image of a color-blind France that continues to pull U.S. Blacks to the City of Light (Robeson 1936; Drake 1982; Irele 1981/1991; Fabre 1993; Stovall 1996; Wright 2003). Although Black internationalists worked to dispel this notion from the turn of the century through the 1960s (for example, René Maran, Tiemoko Garan Kouyaté, Claude McKay, Alioune Diop, W. E. B. Du Bois, Mercer Cook, James Baldwin, and William Gardner Smith), Paris has been and remains significant to African Americans precisely because of that myth. More importantly, Paris has been an essential meeting ground, a space for Black cosmopolitanism, intellectualism, and border crossings seemingly available nowhere else, despite the reality of inimical treatment of people of African origin (Jules-Rosette 1998; Julien 2000; Edwards 2003). And while Black Americans were once shielded from this treatment by their nationality or by speaking English or French with an American accent, distinguishing themselves from the Afro-French (or Black French), these resources offer little protection today. Fake passports are easily obtained, and African Americans are not the only Blacks with American passports. Neither are we the only speakers of English in this diaspora city where transcultural cross-fertilizations make it difficult to know who is who, and from which part of the diaspora people hail.

Because I am both a Black woman and a researcher, my desire to document what I feel to be an important shift in identity and cultural politics in France also exposed me to much of the same discrimination and antagonism confronted by people of African origin in Paris. Yet, with that said, I cannot stress enough that I also had a relative freedom of mobility, thanks to identification cards showing my affiliation to some of the more prestigious universities in Paris. I also had the aegis of my nationality, although it was not always an asset in doing fieldwork of this nature, particularly when anti-U.S. sentiment was running high or when I faced anti-black discrimination and hostilities from people ranging from the neighborhood baker to personnel at the American Embassy, who never immediately took me to be American. Otherwise, I was a "being perceived" from any number of African countries or the Caribbean, or as someone trying to "pass" as a Black American, subject again to the same disregard and disdain. And while I have spent a number of years learning French and have taken pride in masking my U.S. accent, such diligence came with unanticipated costs. That is, in concealing that notorious linguistic marker, I also exposed myself to the uglier side of human relations in urban France. However, what was a hardship for me personally was, interestingly, an asset for me as a researcher. Living the experience of racism necessarily sensitized me to the hostilities and incivilities typically reserved for those with whom I'm assigned (s)kinship relations and with whom I desire greater kinship. But certainly my experiences pale in comparison to documented examples of outright violence experienced by people of African origin and other "suitable enemies" in France. Through their eyes and my own experiences, Paris is both appalling and sublime, like a number of diaspora cities. It is perhaps for those reasons that I am continually drawn toward the complexities of these places, despite the hostile reception I may receive, a reception predicated on the prevailing despised categories of the day, be they defined by class, "race," color, gender, nationality, or national origins.

In negotiating those difficulties and complexities of space and place, I approached this work from an interdisciplinary perspective. I see social reality as being structured by sociohistorical forces and constitutive of systems of relations (both symbolic and material) that have been shaped by human activity on social institutions. This perspective invites a type of relational thinking about research design and methods in both theory and practice. That is to say, it encourages the researcher to view the whole of her project reflexively, understanding that her tools, her self, and her set of propositions are interlinked in the crafting of her object of study. Within this context my appearance, color, hairstyle, presumed nationality and religion, gender, situated knowledge, and methods were all interconnected, a fact often revealed to me during fieldwork. To illustrate this point, as a non-Muslim, U.S.-born and -reared Black woman, a scholar, and a descendant of African captives enslaved in the United States (as opposed to other parts of the African Diaspora), I am the product of multiple systems of education, some more formal than others. Every aspect of my being became, therefore, a non-neutral, active element in each phase of my research, which continually surfaced as a factor in its negotiation. For example, I was frequently taken for a Muslim, because of my topic and perceptions of what a "Muslim" presumably looked like. In fact, it was pointed out to me that the headbands I wear, which cover the front of my hair, suggested as much, and when I dined out, waiters often warned me when a dish I had ordered contained pork. Alternatively, I was considered a living example of televised American culture (given my nationality), and sometimes (less incredible these days) either a CIA agent or an inspector from the school district (since I was taking notes and making observations in troubled classrooms and schools). Clearly, the role of the researcher is neither neutral nor ideologically free. And, as I have learned, researchers are also research tools operating under assumptions and limitations that inhere in the process of doing fieldwork, particularly in a foreign country. For me, it was sometimes difficult to observe interactions between different groups and individuals without immediately attributing them to the black/white schism that typically frames racialized relations in the U.S. Though certain American and French situations and events appeared identical on the surface—for example, public housing in France vis-à-vis the U.S.A.—clear distinctions emerged between them on a deeper reading, as I elucidate in this book. Although startling similarities exist, it is critical to move beyond surface appearances, and this was one of the many struggles I faced in doing fieldwork in the French outer cities.

Methods

This study is as much about my journey, my observations, and my participation in a familiar yet foreign country as it is about the Muslim girls and numerous others who shared their lives and stories. This has been a long, exciting, yet often very painful multiyear adventure involving fieldwork and other methods of data genera-

estudiar personas, grupos etnicos

tion (e.g., ethnographic observations, interviews, surveys, and journals) put to the test in exploring this "other France." I began this study in the fall of 1995 and continued into the following summer. I returned in December 1997, in the 1998–1999 and 2000–2001 academic years, and during the summers of 2001 and 2003. In February 2004, I returned to spend five months in the neighborhoods highlighted in this study, to record any further transformations and developments, especially in light of world events in which Muslims held, once again, center stage. This has allowed me to situate and re-situate my findings within that context.

My primary research sites were a middle school, a multitrack, general studies high school, and a vocational school, all located just outside Paris in Pantin, a borough of the economically depressed *département* of Seine-Saint-Denis. I attended the same classes my participants did and participated in their curricular and extra-curricular activities, ranging from class discussions to philanthropic pursuits. Through guided tours of the sprawling public housing complex, *la cité des Courtillières*, where the majority of my participants live, and through my volunteering in events in this neighborhood, my access and presence became "normalized." This process seemed to be aided by my origins and "looks," since most of the local population appeared to be of African descent.

self governing township

I was initially introduced to my participants by Marie-Ange, who was a teacher at the middle school. She invited me to classes whose student populations, as I learned from student self-introductions, were entirely of North and West African origin. She also introduced me to one of her former students, Aïcha, who was attending the general studies high school I discuss in chapter 4. After I had established trust and rapport with Marie-Ange and Aïcha, and with their assistance, my contacts snowballed at all sites. In Marie-Ange's middle school class, I focused on four girls (Habiba, Rima, Fatou, and Su'ad) whose willingness to participate, coupled with the consent of school officials and their parents, made them ideal for this study. I remained in contact with these girls through written correspondence after my return to the U.S. in 1996 and again in 1997, and when I came back to France during the academic year 1998–1999, they agreed to continue working with me, giving a measure of continuity to the study. In this analysis, I focus on fourteen youths, who form a cross section of the Muslim students whom I have met during the course of my fieldwork. However, since 2000, I have remained in close contact with only those five students, Aïcha, Habiba, Rima, Fatou, and Su'ad, whose growth and coming of age I have witnessed.

In addition to informal and formal interviews with them, I formally interviewed members of their families when possible, educators and staff at their high schools, members of community advocacy associations, and just about anyone else who was willing to talk with the *américaine*, as I came to be generally known. Though these methods yielded a wealth of data, I also wanted to find a way to document students' private moments, outside of our immediate interactions, in order to access their thoughts and activities that were eclipsed during observations and interviews. Providing the girls with personal journals addressed this concern and served multiple purposes beyond their intended use. For example, not only did I obtain written excerpts of their writing styles, I additionally had examples of their language varieties, including home, peer, and national languages, which certain young people unconsciously conflate. Through these journals, I became privy to more reflective critiques of difficult issues raised during interviews or noted during observations. In order to probe more deeply into their practices and views, I additionally attached a series of questions to the inside cover of each journal, along with excerpts from books, blind copies from previous interviews, and newspaper articles that spoke to concerns of a more personal nature. In many cases, these stimuli allowed students to discuss sensitive topics about which they felt shame or that they were reluctant to broach during a recorded interview, such as polygamy, excision, seclusion, lying, or veiling requirements. Moreover, these texts served to lower their affective filter once they realized that I was already aware of these issues and that someone else had revealed practices that could threaten the positive self-image that they initially sought to convey.

Equally instructive were data from students' cumulative files at their schools, which contained valuable socioeconomic and family information, grades, birth certificates, and medical histories. For example, certain students had turbulent home environments that the schools documented together with disciplinary problems. One striking example is a participant I call Anita, who was removed from an abusive family environment with the help of the school's social services representative. Another example is Amina, whose father periodically threw away her books and class notes during the school year because he believed that she had received enough schooling.

Using data constructed through these methods, I was able to corroborate responses and compare them with answers to a multiple-question survey that I developed and distributed to nearly one hundred students.[21] This tool proved highly useful in eliciting succinct information from participants about their background, self-understandings, and interests. More importantly, I was able to verify participants' nationality in school records and gain insights into how their self-representations compared with the formal demographics of their schools and neighborhoods, whose populations, in educational discourse, were both characterized as predominantly North and West African and Muslim. It should be noted all the same that school records and census data indicate that the majority population in these areas is officially French.

Limitations of the Study

Like many other researchers, I also took fieldnotes, although I have found that they can be as disruptive as they are useful in the school context. I noted conversations and information conveyed throughout my fieldwork, and I also drew diagrams of class configurations and how students regrouped during their free time. I especially recorded important events or incidents that I intended to pursue later, either in interviews or in informal conversations. However, I found that there are significant drawbacks in keeping fieldnotes. That is, it is difficult to record and observe events without interrupting or missing other important happenings unfolding at one's site. Moreover, taking fieldnotes is conspicuous and can, therefore, be misinterpreted by those being observed, as when an instructor believed that I was evaluating her teaching because I was copying part of her lesson from the blackboard. After class, she cornered me in the hallway and said, "Listen, I just want to tell you that if you're looking for a specialist in pedagogy, I'm no specialist." I later had to harness all of my persuasive powers to convince her that my notes were for my own use and would not be shared with school inspectors. A similar incident occurred with one of her students, who was part of a class characterized as *débiles* (dimwits or morons), an insulting label that I heard certain outer-city teachers use to describe difficult students and through which some students had learned to see themselves. While taking my usual notes one day in a class where I had not been introduced, I noticed a girl glancing at me suspiciously from the front of the classroom. Agitated, she interrupted the teacher in the middle of her lesson and stated, "Excuse me, I don't mean to cut you off, and you have every right not to answer, but I think we have a right to know who this woman is. I see her taking notes, and well, is she a journalist or from the CIA or what? I think we have a right to know." And this student was entirely right. She had every right to know who I was and why I was taking notes in her classroom. The important point raised by these examples is that the taking of fieldnotes can be disruptive and misinterpreted in the field. All the same, doing fieldwork without them is akin to attempting to conduct a formal interview without a recorder. It can be done, but much can be lost in the process.

Throughout this journey, both my person and my personal convictions were continually tried and tested by events over which I had no control, but which affected my fieldwork nonetheless. For example, during the 1998–1999 academic year, I ran headlong into the student-teacher walkouts and demonstrations that resulted in the closing of public schools on several occasions—sometimes without notice—including my sites. And then there were the bombings of Sudan and Afghanistan, and later of Iraq during Ramadan, ordered by President Clinton. Following the bombing in Iraq, I reluctantly returned to my site, not knowing quite what to expect from Muslim students. In some cases, those who had greeted me with smiles before this event turned cold and distant in its wake. At one school, a student blocked my entrance as I approached her classroom. Standing in front of me and clearly angry, she looked me squarely in the eyes and asked, "Do you support your president's Monicagate?" Yes, "Monicagate": it had been strongly suggested in the media that these actions were an attempt by the president to "wag the dog" in order to divert attention from his then-alleged infidelities. Sadly for me, after those bombings, my image shifted for some students from that of their media-generated, popular understanding of an American to an American as the oppressor. This was particularly troubling for me, since I know first-hand what oppression feels like from being raised in poverty and segregation in the U.S. It took a great deal of work to reconnect with some students and demonstrate to them that I sincerely wanted to learn more about them. I illustrated that sincerity by participating in community activities organized in their neighborhood and at their schools.

The most rewarding moments were those times when I was invited to help with food and clothes drives for the needy, as many of the students were also involved in humanitarian relief efforts both in France and in North and West African countries. I also once stayed up until the wee hours of the morning with a dear Canadian friend at his office while his computers and computer skills generated a website for these students, something that allowed them to share their activities and philanthropic efforts with a broader international community. That which is global can indeed become local, as these experiences proved to me. Nonetheless, international news and events reverberated against this study, including the massacres in Algeria and the horrifying "ethnic" cleansing of Muslims in Kosovo, which risk exploding again as I write. These tragedies were broadcast daily in the media and were taken very much to heart by many of my participants, who did not see their Muslim selves as disconnected from those events. I should add that not everyone was comfortable with my presence at these sites, which are located in an area where neighborhoods and low-performing schools have been transformed into dumping grounds for economically disadvantaged immigrant families and their children. Moreover, residents and teachers expressed concern and even fear about how I would convey what I saw and experienced.

Another important challenge was created by the requirement of parental consent, in keeping with the protection of human subjects. While it is critical that researchers protect their participants at all costs, having to obtain written consent from the parents of Muslim girls hindered student participation in this project. Some parents refused to let their daughters participate at all, suspicious of a foreigner asking personal questions. Given the historical context leading to the presence of Muslims in France and the often tenuous relations produced from those tensions, it was not surprising that some parents would not allow their daughters to be in a study that focused on Muslims. Though many students wanted to lend their experiences to my project, many parents refused to give their consent, which reduced the size and richness of the pool of participants, especially in schools where the majority population was of African origin.

The crux of the problem in this context has much to do with how one conceptualizes these young people, which depends on the sociocultural lens through which one understands life experience and age. While most of my participants were between fifteen and nineteen years old, their status as "girls" or "young women" varies according to context. That is, though they are of marriageable age in many of their parents' cultures and countries of origin, a sixteen-year-old may be more girl than young woman at home, I learned, and yet more young woman than girl outside of it, in school or elsewhere. The importance and value of parental consent should not be minimized, and obtaining or not obtaining it raises ethical concerns and holds great potential for mistrust and harm. However, one must allow a researcher some latitude in determining the criteria that determine how one assigns individuals to such categories as "minor" and "adult." Researchers should not be forced to adhere to a narrowly defined template; the internal logic of the research context must be considered in making such determinations. In this study, I obtained parental and student consent, in keeping with Human Subjects requirements; nonetheless, the question of the emotional maturity of participants remains an intrinsic and ethical factor to be considered in doing research of this nature.

Another limitation was posed by inadequate census data and other gaps in statistical information concerning national origins and ethnicity in France, as previously discussed. Data were similarly lacking on religion; such information is considered personal and potentially prejudicial in France, and is therefore not available to the public. While these limitations and challenges affected the facility with which this project unfolded, the difficulties encountered were also occasions for me to critically grasp how I was the architect of this study. In other words, these obstacles were also opportunities for learning, which illustrate the beauty of being in the field where everything is subject to change, including the researcher herself.

Organization of this Journey

This book is organized into into five chapters, which open with brief abstracts outlining their content. Chapter 1, "Unmixing French 'National Identity,'" introduces my focal participants, while situating their lived experiences within the broader dynamic of the politics of French national identity. Their narratives describe a number of forces affecting their life-worlds, forces that compel them to activate a range of strategies in order to negotiate and to circumvent competing expectations. One issue highlighted in this chapter is forced marriage, against which national status becomes an effective means of self-defense. Chapter 2, "Structured Exclusion: Public Housing in the French Outer City," is an invitation into the neighborhood that these young people call home. This chapter documents in detail the oft-ignored experience of living in public housing in the famed City of Light. As an illustration, I focus on a housing project known as *la cité des Courtillières*. While it is not the worst example in the French outer cities, city officials have allowed it to degrade over the years into conditions of substandard living. It is also a structuring element in these young people's self-representation, the site where "their French and African-born-in-France identities" merge (Quiminal et al. 1997, 7). In chapter 3, "Transmitting a 'Common Culture': Symbolic Violence Realized," we move closer to the role that national education plays in French identity politics through its "common culture" ideology. In examining this issue, I draw upon the theories of

Pierre Bourdieu, who has consistently shown in his extensive writings how the school, as an extension of the state, is the site for the imposition and elaboration of the dominant culture and its categories of perception. I illustrate this point in relation to two core subjects representative of the country's patrimony, French literature and history. In chapter 4, "Counterforces: Educational Inequality and Relative Resistance," I take up the way that national education paradoxically includes and excludes youths in the "other France." While French affirmative action seeks to mitigate educational disparities, other mechanisms are at work that select and sort students toward downward mobility. The school, nonetheless, remains an integral element in shaping youths' self-understandings, but certain Muslim girls resist this shaping. That is, when the "common culture" conflicts with or tests the limits of their fundamental beliefs, practices, and modesty, they are not without their own forces and strategies. In chapter 5, "Beyond Identity: Muslim Girls and the Politics of Their Existence," I discuss my own connection to this journey through my first encounter with a Muslim teenager, a former in-law, who embodied the gendered constraints and very real forms of violence that certain girls both live with and die by. While I document abuse, as my participants insisted that I do, I also challenge the perception that such acts are committed solely by Muslims or Africans, and the cultural deficiencies Muslims or Africans are presumed to have. As I stress throughout this study, these youths resist all forms of constraints placed upon them, but some forces are not easily overcome. French secularism and the law banning religious symbols are examples treated in this chapter. Finally, the epilogue, "And So It Goes . . ." summarizes my key arguments and pertinent findings. I must stress that this landscape is always changing, transforming itself as I write.

1 Unmixing French "National Identity"

> To say that we're French means a lot of
> different things; it's almost like saying that
> we're Christian, almost, because most of the
> time, French people are Christian. Maybe on
> the outside we're French and on the inside
> we're Arab. But really, our problem is that
> our parents are immigrants, and when we go
> to Algeria, we're still immigrants. So, we're
> somewhere in the middle. That's how I see it.
> —**A participant in my study**

> I'm Senegalese before anything else. French
> nationality is a passport that opens doors to
> a lot of places where I wouldn't have access
> with just a residency card. That's how I see
> it . . . But at the same time, when I go to
> Senegal, I reach a point when the only thing
> I want to do is go back home. I actually miss
> France to that point when I'm over there.
> It's stronger than just the papers. So, I'm
> Senef; it's what the Senegalese say, and it
> fits perfectly. SENEF: Neither French nor
> Senegalese, but between the two.
> —**Quoted in Quiminal et al., "Les jeunes
> filles d'origine africaine en France"**

This chapter serves to introduce and situate my focal participants in relation to French national identity politics. In providing greater insights into their self-understandings, backgrounds, preoccupations, views, and observed behaviors, my aim is to show that their incorporation into French society has not been seamless, but has involved confusion and pain. Further, growing up in an increasingly hostile reception context complicates their adaptation, and often their self-understandings are a reflection of that complication.

As youths from the outer cities whose parents are foreign-born, they share similar worlds of experiences and are assigned many of the same social labels, such as "oppressed" or "submissive Muslim girls," "immigrants," and "kids from the projects," that is, kids from that "other France." Rarely are they seen for what they say they are: French nationals, indeed French girls. The legitimacy of their assertions is determined less by what they claim to be, and more by what they do, as it is their actions and strategies that ultimately say who they are, beyond the categories of perception by which they are identified. When examined in relation to broader questions of multiculturalism and national unity, these youths expose the foundational weakness of the latter (national unity) while exemplifying the former (multiculturalism) through "unmixing" a homogenized notion of Frenchness that is seemingly devoid of ethnic diversity.

Fundamental to their incorporation is the system of national education, seen by these youths as the means of overcoming and avoiding treatment they consider punitive. An example that I foreground is the prospect and promise of forced marriage, a pervasive international issue experienced by non-Muslims and Muslim girls alike. I begin with vignettes of three divergent cases interwoven with common threads, threads firmly attached to France and French national education.

Aïcha

My first meeting with Aïcha took place in my apartment the day following the second bombing near the St. Michel metro. Though I lived just one metro stop away from that station, she insisted on joining me at my home rather than meeting closer to her neighborhood. As anti-Muslim feeling was quite high, I was naturally concerned about her coming to my area. But for Aïcha, as I would learn, coming to me was a chance to get out of her neighborhood and be in "Paris," a seemingly mythological place that she appeared not to know and rarely visited, despite living only one metro stop outside its borders. On that day, as on most occasions, this slim teen was wearing her signature form-fitting Levi's 501 blue jeans and a T-shirt under a brown suede jacket. Slung over her back was a black leather knapsack, containing another accessory almost essential to her look, her *clopes et briquet* (cigarettes and lighter). Dark curls cascaded from the ponytail atop her head, which gave Aïcha the appearance of maturity, indeed a certain sensuality, noted by men who did classic double-takes when she passed by. Like other teens, she emphasized and deemphasized that sensuality according to context: according, that is, to whether she was at home, in school, or out and about with me.

At school, Aïcha, like her sisters, was considered a bright student, though "aggressive" was the epithet often used by teachers to describe her and her closest friends. As one put it,

> You feel this internal tension from them that's translated into a certain aggression . . . I wonder if it comes from what they live, you know, this tension between home— [*pause*] well, their parents have a certain way of living in France, a certain mentality, and then they, the girls living in France, are confronted by a world completely different.

Aïcha appeared keenly aware of those differences, some of which she conveyed in her journal: "I was raised in a cool way because I can easily talk to my mother about things, like about marriage. Otherwise, my parents are very strict. For example, I can't go out after 6:00 P.M. to visit a friend or do things like that. No way!" Although she often mentioned that her parents were strict, she noted certain ironies, such as being allowed to travel to Italy for five days on a school trip, although she had a strict curfew in France. She also noted during one of our conversations that her mother had found out that she smoked, did not tell her father, and only told her that it was bad for her health. She expected an altogether stronger reaction, one akin to the dreadful, heated exchange between her mother and eldest sister when her mother discovered that her sister had a boyfriend. Amidst accusations of lost virginity and relentless admonitions, Aïcha's sister screamed in self-defense, "You'll see, *maman*, the sheets will be red," meaning that her virginity was intact. That declaration seemed to end the argument, but it ignited talk of marriage for Aïcha's sister.

My first visit to her home was not long after that fight, and as well as being interested in meeting her parents and having a home-cooked *couscous*, I was looking forward to seeing Aïcha in that context, among her family. Would she be as unrestrained around them as she was with me? The question was answered immediately when Aïcha answered the door at my arrival. Her attire was drastically different from the styles she typically wore at school or outside of her neighborhood. Her high-heeled black boots and tight jeans and shirts had been replaced by a large, baggy T-shirt, sweatpants, and flat shoes. Even her hair was pulled back in a braided ponytail, which suggested a little girl rather than the cigarette-smoking, lipstick-wearing young woman I often saw. I was also struck by her changed demeanor; around her parents she was less talkative, less gregarious, and demure, the opposite of how she was at school and on outings with me.

Before that visit, Aïcha had shared aspects of her parents' background. Her parents came from Morocco, and like the parents of most of my participants, they had had little formal schooling in their home country. Her father speaks French, but her mother's French is limited, and at home the family communicates in a combination of Arabic and French. This situation has led to a type of dissonant acculturation described by Alejandro Portes and Rubén Rumbaut (2001), in which youths' cultural adaptation surpasses that of their parents, resulting in a role reversal vis-à-vis certain family tasks. While Aïcha's father was the clear head of the household, Aïcha and her elder sister managed certain family affairs for which literacy was essential, such as communicating with the bank, the post office, and social service providers.

Aïcha elucidated the extent of her religious convictions in the context of how she interprets being Muslim: "Me, I don't practice. I'm Muslim only because my parents are Muslim. Otherwise, if I had the right to choose a religion, I would say that I believe in God. That's all." Her self-understanding was less clear and consistent than this declaration would suggest, however, reflecting tensions inherent in straddling overlapping cultural spheres and competing expectations. At times, she referred to herself as a French Muslim, or simply as French, in contrast to what she wrote in her journal:

> Despite being French on paper, I'll always be an Arab, and it's not a simple paper that could change my culture. I was born in France. I have French culture, but I live with Moroccans. Every year, for *2 months*, I go to Morocco. I speak Moroccan, I eat Moroccan food. In fact, I have 2 cultures, French and the other, Moroccan. I practically have to be French in order to succeed in life, otherwise, you're screwed . . . So, I'm Muslim of Moroccan origin.

It was perhaps during our first conversation that Aïcha cogently summed it up: "Listen, let me put it to you this way. When I am in Morocco, people call me French, and when I live in France, they call me a dirty Arab. So I prefer to identify myself as 'Aïcha.'"

Fatou

Fatou had mastered the fine art of secrecy. Between hiding her poor academic record from her parents and keeping her home environment a mystery to her teachers, this young woman walked a swaying tightrope that was fast becoming unhinged. Laconic and self-effacing, Fatou drew my interest more for her actions than her words, and for the way that she came to represent the failure of French national education, which lets students like her fall through its cracks.[1] At nearly eighteen years old, she was only in the first year of high school, in a competitive general studies track, and failing that year for the second time. More importantly, she had run out of options, since the state was under no obligation to educate her beyond the age of sixteen, the age at which compulsory schooling ends in France. And while she had considerable difficulties in written French, as I could see in her journal and assignments, the more fundamental problem identified by educators was culture, that is, cultural deficits and difference. Educators offered cultural models to explain the persistent academic difficulties and downward mobility experienced by teenagers like Fatou. "There's an image of the culture that we want to give to them at school," stated one of her teachers, "and it does not correspond at all to what they're given in their families. There is a huge gap between the family's culture and the culture at the high school; they're not at all the same thing!" Or, as a teacher of Senegalese origin said,

> the fact that Fatou has problems in French is not tied to her culture because we have some DuPonts and Durands in our schools who have the same problem . . . I mean people who are 100% French; they make the same grammatical mistakes or errors in syntax as Fatou. So it's not a cultural problem; it's a societal problem in my opinion . . . If there is a cultural problem, it's perhaps Fatou's parents' culture that's the problem, not Fatou. After all, she was born here.

Indeed, Fatou was born in France, a country praised for its formidable language academy, the Académie française, which sets the standards of French in the nation. To speak French means to speak it according to Académie standards, which remain resistant to notions of language varieties. That is, recognition of a sort of "Fre-bonics" in French society is out of the question; the only language variety considered valid is that approved by the Académie, which is referred to as French. However, Fatou understood a couple of important things that educators were only beginning to comprehend. Although the forces of national education would eventually place her in a vocational track offering only limited opportunities, and while she understood that her chances of obtaining the *baccalauréat* (the diploma that is the key to stable employment) diminished with each year she failed to progress in a general studies track, Fatou did not abandon her schooling. She battled instead to stay in school and resisted vocational studies in order to follow in the footsteps of one of her academically successful sisters, whom she admired and who was completing nursing school. Fatou struggled to remain in the coveted general studies track, ultimately to her detriment. To be in this prestigious track is to carry that same prestige, prestige that legitimizes and distinguishes those in it from those who are not because the prize is being a student of those studies, not merely attaining the degree attached to them.

Fatou wielded, however, a relative power because of that very schooling. As literate children of parents who spoke very limited French and had almost no formal schooling, Fatou and her elder siblings became the interpreters of the school's communications with their parents regarding their academic performance. That is, Fatou and her siblings used the power of their literacy to avoid stigmatized vocational studies. In their eyes, that path led only to the poorly paid jobs held by their parents and other unfortunate African immigrants in France: street-sweeping and house-cleaning. Some educators reasoned, however, that their resistance to vocational studies—which could be completed more quickly than the general studies curriculum—was more gender-driven. In other words, educators believed that they were trying to stave off marriage through prolonged studies, as one of her male teachers, of Maghrebin origin, perspicaciously suggested:

> They have understood that according to Francis Bacon's system, "knowledge is power." OK. They have assimilated this fact very well, "knowledge is power." It's the only way to get ahead in a society that is mutilated, and that mutilates. At home, there's no problem; it's enough that they already know how to read and write. Anyway, they're expected to get married, have kids, and continue that life . . . it's the girls who have the most at stake.

When asked about this concern, Fatou vehemently retorted, "My father would never force me to get married. He knows we have to go to school." Some of her teachers did not share her conviction, believing instead that, if she failed again, her family would force her to marry against her will. One teacher hinted at this prospect in an e-mail message (written in English) describing a meeting with Fatou in which she advised her to pursue a vocational track:

> I asked her if she would be disconsidered [viewed negatively] at home if she chose a different career track, such as one that would allow a student to work part-time while studying the rest of the year. I explained it was, for some students, a viable solution that would allow them to obtain interesting careers even though their studies would not be as formal as their parents would wish them to be. I suggested that being paid, even a little, could give her some status at home. I finally asked her if her family would decide to force her to marry if she failed. She said it was not the case, but that they were expecting a lot from her, although she could not work properly at home.

As the fourth of sixteen children, all born and raised in France, Fatou shared a four-bedroom apartment with thirteen other siblings, her father, and his two wives. As scholars Catherine Quiminal, Babacar Diouf, and others point out in their study of girls of West African origin in France, "If one adds to this diversified family structure the fact that uncles, aunts and even cousins can live under the same roof, one imagines that girls have a nebulous, if not chaotic, image of an African family" (1997, 7), since in France a two-parent household with only two or three children is the norm. One must keep in mind, however, that polygamy is permissible, and often highly esteemed, in other societies. However, as scholar Christian Poiret notes in his study of African families in France, "girls [were] frustrated by the situation of polygamy in their family. They were revolted by the submissiveness of their mothers . . . they would like to live like girls of their age in French society" (1996, 312). In most Western countries, polygamy is denounced and illegal, which has engendered a delicate situation for young people like Fatou who must negotiate home traditions with homeland laws that criminalize such customs. Because of polygamy's illegality in France and the shame some girls felt about it, young people in such households have learned to refer to their co-mother as "aunt" to outsiders. Fatou did so until I was invited to her home. Again, polygamy is not as uncommon as it is popularly believed to be in France, and for young people like Fatou, it is part of their norm, along with other practices that popular understanding considers exterior to French culture. For Fatou, these complexities inhere in her self-understanding, expressed in her journal this way: "I have French nationality, but I am of Senegalese origin . . . I love my religion, and I admire my parents a great deal for the way they raised me. My religion is very important, but it is very, very hard to practice."

Fatima

"Brilliant" was usually the first word I heard at the mention of Fatima's name. According to her teachers, she was a "Muslim girl perfectly integrated into France" from "a well-integrated family" that provided an "encouraging home environment," and she was "destined to pursue advanced studies" in the French Ivy League. High academic achievement appeared the norm in Fatima's family; she had two elder sisters completing law and medical studies at elite universities in Paris, while another was at the top of her class in the prestigious science track in the high school that she and Fatima attended. Indeed, some force was clearly driving these young women to all possible zeniths, credited by teachers to the national educational system and a supportive home environment. However, as I would learn from the women in Fatima's family, their success had more to do with their father, whose treatment of his wife and daughters belied the image of perfect integration so affirmed by people who seemed to know nothing about Fatima's home life.

"My father is strict with the girls," Fatima told me during our first interview, in response to my query about her relationship with her parents. She emphasized that her younger brother had no curfew, while she and her sisters were expected home before 6 P.M. or sunset, whichever came first. "Going out at night is forbidden," Fatima stressed. "It's not even worth asking. We already know the answer. Going out at night," she vociferated, *"impossible!"* Fatima was also forbidden to participate in after-school activities subsidized by the state, such as excursions to plays, trips abroad, and concerts, and even to socialize with friends. Sometimes Fatima feigned uninterest to explain her consistent absence to questioning teachers and classmates, or, more often, she simply drew from an arsenal of pat excuses passed down from the eldest in her family, who already knew the terrain, to the youngest. She was also not allowed to participate in sports, because the courses were co-ed. Many other girls, also barred from physical education, expressed concern that rigorous sports could rupture their hymens. Despite assurances to the contrary from their instructors, the prospect of doubt being cast upon their virginity and the shame their families would feel outweighed any consequences the school might impose for not participating. In any case, this matter was easily resolved by neighborhood doctors who provided medical authorizations removing girls from gym class, which teachers openly decried, as I discuss in chapter 4.

Fatima described her mother as completely different from her father: "more cool," protective, and supportive, at times subtly subversive of her father's authority. For example, she allowed me to interview Fatima alone in my home and permitted her to stay past her curfew. However, she escorted her daughter to and from my door, while other girls were allowed to come alone or in small groups. I gradually learned, in these interviews, that Fatima's father was quite abusive to her mother and her sisters, motivating the eldest, and eventually Fatima, to study law (as detailed in chapter 5). In light of her home life and her teachers' clear ignorance of it, I taught Fatima certain techniques so that she could formally interview the women in her family about any preoccupations or concerns they had as Muslims living in France. From this open question emerged two prominent themes: their father's behavior and their education, the latter being a means of defense against the former. For their mother, whose own schooling was cut short by marriage, education was a way for girls to "liberate themselves," and school was "a sanctuary away from men."

As well as valuing schooling, students often expressed love of their religion and discussed their observance of its practices, although, like Fatima, most had "never set foot in a mosque." The only hint of Fatima's cultural-religious affiliation was a discreet gold necklace, frequently worn by Muslim and non-Muslim girls, from which hung an "Eye of Fatima" (a symbol of protection) and a charm engraved with a verse from the Koran. "I am Muslim," wrote Fatima in her journal. "I don't practice, really, but I observe Ramadan; I don't eat pork; I don't drink alcohol, and I try to have good relations with others, even if it's not always easy." And while she is Muslim, she lucidly articulated what she also is in French society:

> Me, I find myself totally integrated in France, so I feel at home everywhere. Given that I was born in France, that I speak French, that my culture is French, that I learned French history—France is my country . . . My identity is: French of Algerian origin, of Muslim religion.

She concluded with "I consider my identity an advantage and an asset."

The Others

One of the many ironies for these girls, as Aïcha notes, is that outside of France, in their parents' countries, they are assigned the very label that they are denied in their country—*française*—a negative identification that can signify that these girls are damaged goods in the matrimonial market, that is, as potential mates in their parents' home countries. Some parents believe that growing up in a sexually liberal France taints rather than tames girls, who are seen as promiscuous, potentially non-virgins, thus unacceptable as wives (Sayad 1991; Lacoste-Dujardin 1992; Amougou 1998). Thus daughters can find themselves at odds with their parents, whose cultural expectations clash with those of the receiving society in which their daughters mature and with which they identify:

> For them, the issue of integration within French society arises, on the one hand, through their demands for acceptance and recognition by "their country"—France. On the other hand, there is the issue of attempting to maintain a dialogue with their parents and their family . . . that allows them to acknowledge and freely express both their French and African-born-in-France identities. Their feelings, their opinions and values are often far removed from those of their parents. (Quiminal et al. 1997, 6–7)

It becomes difficult, then, to portray these young people in their full complexity without including all of these viscerally felt, competing issues. What follows is a brief presentation of the other participants derived from multiple data sources, including their student records. It should be noted that most of these students have failed at least one grade in either middle or high school, which is not uncommon in their district, as I show in chapter 4. Three of the eleven presented are in vocational studies. The remainder are in general studies in literature, science, and social studies tracks. Although I highlight these particular teenagers throughout this analysis, I will include data on other Muslim girls whose narratives also reveal telling aspects of identity politics in a country that is only beginning to address, with trepidation, its issues of diversity in the schools and society. These young women represent but a few of the faces making up contemporary, multiethnic France, which, as Fatima says, is their country.

Rima was the middle child of three children. She and the youngest were born and raised in France. The family had lived in several different buildings in the Courtillières, the public housing complex mentioned earlier and discussed in chapter 2. Her parents were from a village in Algeria. Her father was born in 1948, her mother in 1960. The father was a manual laborer; the mother was a housewife whose French was limited. French and an Algerian variety of Arabic were spoken in the home, and the children appeared to understand and speak Arabic at varying levels. Rima never lived in Algeria and her last visit was when she was nine years old. "I've always lived in France," she told me; "it's the only country that I really know. Of course, going to Algeria during vacation is great, but I don't think I would like to live there. In Algeria, the people and the way they think don't suit me."

Mariama, her five siblings, and their parents lived in the same building as Fatou, one of the most neglected buildings in the Courtillières. Her father, born in 1936 in a village in Mali, no longer worked, and her mother, born in 1952 also in Mali, was a housewife. Soninké and French were spoken in the home. Mariama was considered a problem student, and had been expelled for fighting, insolence, and threatening a teacher. She wanted to help the young people in her neighborhood, though she felt that they all had limited futures. She had never been to Mali. "I was born French," she said, "but for me, the way I see it, it's only in France that I'm French because our parents are foreign . . . In France, you have to be French."

Sylvie was considered a highly intelligent and capable student. Though born Jewish, she had converted to Islam, as had her two elder brothers, with whom she lived in public housing near her school. Her Tunisian parents, who were divorced, did not live with the children, nor did any other family member. She had not seen her father in several years; her mother visited periodically. Sylvie had never visited Tunisia. "My conversion to Islam was a long process. People had talked to me a lot about Islam. In the first place, my friends are Muslim, so I knew about it already. My best friend is Muslim and her parents treat me like their daughter."

Amina

Amina was considered capable of pursuing university studies, according to her teachers. Her father and mother were both from Algeria. I was unable to learn her father's employment status; her mother was a housewife. She lived in public housing near the school, and was the eldest of four children. It was well documented that her father obstructed her schooling, insisting that she quit and find work; on several occasions he threw away her books and study materials. Her mother sided with him, according to Amina, who added that her mother was submissive. She identified both as French of Algerian origin and as French: "People have to consider us French because the French government has given us opportunities, like going to school with French people, working with French people, and living with French people. We have the same opportunities as they do . . . I'm French because, after all, France has given us the same opportunities."

Habiba

Habiba and her seven siblings were all born in France. They lived in a three-bedroom apartment in one of the multistory buildings that residents called "rabbit cages" in the Courtillières. Her father worked in the service sector and was born in 1936; her mother was a housewife, born in 1953. The children spoke French to each other, but usually used an Algerian variety of Arabic with their parents, especially their mother, who spoke very limited French. Habiba traveled to Algeria almost every summer. She told me, "I was born here, but not my parents, so I'm French, but I am of foreign origin."

Su'ad

Habiba's sister Su'ad had had a turbulent educational background, having failed and repeated one year of elementary school, one year of middle school, and her first year in a general high school. The following year she was placed in a vocational school, though part of a unique class within the school whose students had spent their first year in general studies. The class had some status within the school, because its students could return to general studies if their grades improved, unlike the other students at this school, who were locked into vocational studies. Although she was Habiba's elder sister, she was in the same class as Habiba in middle and high school, and this was the first time that she had been separated from her younger sister (whom people often mistook for the elder). "In

France, I feel more Algerian and Muslim because there are a lot of foreigners who are Muslim here. But with my friends, we all have foreign origins, and we feel that we have a little something more than the 'French-French' because we're French and Algerian. So we can be French, and if we want to thumb our nose at the French, we can be Algerian."

Anita

Anita was born in Côte d'Ivoire and brought to France by her uncle. She described her home situation with her family in France as domestic servitude. She attempted suicide, ran away on more than one occasion, and was removed from her uncle's home by social services, which placed her in a shelter for girls. Comparatively, she expressed fond memories of life in Côte d'Ivoire. But those memories also included the intense pain suffered from her excision, which she felt scarred her for life. "You never forget it." She had also ruled out returning to her family in Côte d'Ivoire for a host of reasons, including the fact that there were too many children (fourteen) already and tension between her co-mothers. She was afraid that a marriage would be arranged for her should she return in disgrace, which the forced removal from her uncle's home essentially guaranteed in her eyes: "For them now, I'm just a *pute* [slut], living on my own." She had French nationality and called herself both French of Ivoirian origin and Ivoirian. "My life is so complicated . . . I was happy to come to France because I really like France. You know, for an African it's a land of dreams . . . Everyone dreams of coming here, but they don't know what it is."

Khadija

Khadija, overall, was considered a bright student, someone destined for higher education. She and her family resided in the same building as Aïcha, Habiba, and Su'ad, like them in an apartment intended for a much smaller household (Khadija's had nine members). Her father's employment status was unknown; her mother had little formal schooling and was a housewife. Both parents were Berber, born and raised in a village in Morocco. A Moroccan variety of Arabic was spoken in the home, with French. Khadija received formal religious instruction and wore the "veil" outside of school. She considered herself a practicing Muslim, which she defined as one who prays, reads the Koran, fasts, eats *halel,* and attends the mosque: "Personally, I want to wear the veil because I feel more Muslim, and according to the Koran, women are required to wear it."

Leïla

Leïla was the middle child of three, all born in France. Her father was born in 1937 in Morocco; he died when she was in second grade, and she failed that year and repeated it. Her mother, who had Moroccan nationality, was born in 1947 and did not work. She was considered a very intelligent student capable of university studies. "I come from two cultures," she explained, "one from my country of birth, France, and the other from my country of origin, Morocco, which was passed down through my parents, especially my mother . . . When I go to school, I act like French girls; when I go to the cinema or the museum, I am French. At home, when I'm with my mother, I'm both French and Muslim."

Assia

Assia was the eldest of three children, and her family did not live in public housing. Her mother and father were born and raised in Egypt, were university-educated, and had French nationality. As a student, she excelled in language, particularly Arabic, which her Arabic teacher said she spoke fluently. She went to Egypt every year and said she wanted to live there. Though she indicated that she was French of Egyptian origin, she felt that French nationality was necessary in order to be treated fairly in France: "I don't feel like I'm French. I'm French by acquisition, I mean on paper, in my passport and all that, but I am Egyptian."

Naïma

Naïma was the eldest of four children. All were born and raised in France. Her Algerian mother was divorced from her Egyptian father. The mother had a high school education; the father was university-educated and was a chemist. Naïma, unlike the other girls in my study, had a boyfriend, a fact she desperately hid from her mother and father. He was of Tunisian origin. The day before I was to interview her mother, she called my home in a panic to make sure I would not divulge her secret. She insisted that I note that she was still a virgin: "I like French culture because people are free, but when I think of my future, I know I have to marry a Muslim and respect my religion."

Other young people of non-European origins whom I surveyed and interviewed overwhelmingly self-identified in similar ways, only rarely indicating that they were strictly nationals of their parents' home countries. It is important to keep in mind that, with few exceptions, they have been primarily schooled and raised in the "other France," having visited their parents' homelands only occasionally, if at all. Their multitextured experiences open a window onto colliding cultural and social worlds, worlds in the outer cities and in French society where their self-understandings are forged.

French and Somewhere in the Middle

While complexity, in the truest sense of the term, accurately characterizes the lived realities of these girls, what makes their cases both paradoxical and intriguing within contemporary identity politics is not merely their educational difficulties, nor the emotionally challenging aspects of their lives, nor the size and condition of their households. What makes their cases salient and compelling is how they self-understand *despite* those difficulties and differences, and the strategies that they use (knowingly and unknowingly) to position themselves (while being positioned) within overlapping cultural worlds. Although they can be socially perceived as neither French in France, nor accepted at times as African or Arab in their parents' home countries, what these labels ignore is that they are living products of a "mixture whose parts remain indissociable," as anthropologist Jean-Loup Amselle argues (1998, 161), despite those very labels. In the total light of those aspects of these girls' lifestyle that appear extreme or alien to those outside of their experiences, what becomes critical is indeed that "mixture"—rather than cultural and classificatory specificity—which they come to represent. Their cases are noteworthy because this mixture stands against the mythos of cultural insularity or French authenticity symbolized by a "national identity" (Lévi-Strauss 1977).

While some describe this mixture as "French of 'x' origin," this self-understanding is not as clear-cut as it appears on the surface, nor does it reveal what motivates its assertion. That is, in their choice of self-representation, these youths are expressing both a conscious and unconscious need to retain a certain specificity (which this label allows) that distances them from the *français-français* who are their "other." It also allows distance from those who excoriate young people such as these for their complicated personal lives and the visible lifestyle differences that come to typify that complication. On the one hand, being French can imply "oppressor" to the girls and their families, since they place it in opposition to African, Arab, or Muslim, the "oppressed." This opposition derives from racialized antagonisms stemming from colonization, war, and pernicious immigration policies. Similarly, participants often juxtaposed being Muslim (implying "tolerant") to being Christian (implying "intolerant"), depending on how they had been treated in a French society they perceived as Christian. The issue was especially significant to Muslim girls because of the headscarf ban in the schools. Nonetheless, the "oppressor" is often seductive, making the products of seduction all the more desirable. The title of nobility—"French"—in French society is one such product, indicative of distinction, privilege, and authority that transcends the mere possession of French nationality.

These young people are aligning themselves with the "national identity" and exhibit behavior that is consistent with having grown up in France. As historian Gérard Noiriel argues (1988), they have been assimilated in the classical sense, as demonstrated by the fact that they speak French, attend French schools, are growing up in French society, and have ways of being similar to those of youths "of old French stock." A striking example is their expressions of youth culture and their membership in the international and transcultural hip-hop generation now well anchored in an increasingly diverse Europe among youths whose dress, language, movement, and attitude surpass perceived differences and national origins. In some cases the assertion of being French derives from a sense of obligation, as some participants noted. Others who do not have French nationality, yet feel themselves to be French nevertheless, argue that being educated all their lives in France makes them French: "I consider myself French. I do the same things as everyone: I go to school; I take the bus, I go shopping, etc. In fact, I'm just like the French. I'm like them except that I'm Moroccan."

For socially marginalized young people, relative power emerges in the seemingly simple act of naming themselves, in identifying themselves to an institution, and in disrupting its norms through their visible differences. Scholar Camille Lacoste-Dujardin illustrates this in her own research on North African (Maghrebin) women in France. As she argues, Muslim girls "have chosen to distinguish themselves in a fascinating way, that is, with the cultural weapons of French society rather than the criteria of their parents' Maghrebin culture" (1992, 251). This can also be said of girls of West African origin raised in France. Attempting, then, to rewrite the terms of membership through a combination of these factors reveals the real stakes in struggles to define a "national identity," which is used as a cultural weapon in identity politics. As Amselle discerns:

The ability to name, to give a first name, surname, or nickname is of course essential; it reveals the rifts and the relations of forces at work within a given social field. Social stakes constantly manifest themselves in this ability to name and the possibility of refusing to be named. Culture as a collective identity, as a classification, is thus continuously the subject of a political struggle, of a struggle for recognition that takes the shape of an incessant reclassification, such that even its appearance in a society must be subjected to constant redefinition. (1998, 41–42)

To identify oneself as "French" is to create both a category containing that which defines Frenchness (i.e., ways of knowing, values, a language standard, appearances, customs, tastes, etc.) and a category determining those groups and people who are outside of that definition, in this case Muslim girls and outer-city youths of color. However, there is a paradox at work in this process of "identity" formation. That is, these youths are tacitly affirming categories arbitrarily derived and deduced from principles that assume a universal common culture in France. Rearticulating those categories, though powerful, ultimately reinforces this social fiction, which reveals the degree to which understandings of "self" and "other" are deeply shaped by what these assigned categories are presumed to connote and legitimize: reified culture, harboring notions of "race," and social division.

Struggles over categories and classifications implying racialized distinctions are highly relevant in French national identity politics. Though constituted by the French state, these categories are part of the national commonsense, as the French census saliently reflects. That is, individuals are broadly classified as "French by birth," "foreigner," or "immigrant"; immigrants may be further categorized as "French by acquisition," or naturalized. In other words, "naturalized" people remain classified as "immigrants"—stigmatized outsiders in France—despite the change in their legal status (INSEE 1999).[2] According to the last census (1999), there are over six hundred fifty thousand documented people of African origin in France classified as "French by acquisition" and thus "immigrants," which could technically include people born in overseas French territories (such as the French Antilles), since the defining factor is birth off French soil (de Rudder, Poiret, and Vourc'h 2000). Further, the ethnic and national origins of those identified as "French by birth" are not investigated, rendering it nearly impossible to document the descendants of "immigrants" and thereby social phenomena particular to specific groups, such as racialized discrimination (Tribalat 1995; Simon and Stavo-Debauge 2002). After all, the idea is to foster a common culture and thereby a common "identity." The U.S. census is equally problematic in the opposite direction, attempting to document all possible distinctions while conflating "race" and national origin. This approach has given rise to some interesting anomalies among my students, such as African-born South Asian immigrants to the U.S. who self-identified as African American to capture their new status—African and American.

Similarly, annual reports issued by the CNCDH (Commission nationale consultative des droits de l'homme, National Consultative Commission on Human Rights) are instructive. The CNCDH is an advisory committee charged with providing policy analysis to the prime minister in keeping with existing French laws and United Nations human rights resolutions against all forms of discrimination. Comprising representatives from the Ministries of the Interior, Justice, Social and Urban Affairs, and Employment in addition to academics, clerics, and members of various associations (e.g., SOS Racisme), the CNCDH has published, since 1989, an annual report on the "battle against racism and xenophobia," as the organization terms it, in France. Drawing from police reports and public opinion polls, the CNCDH finds that France has experienced a "massive" increase in "racial threats" and violence against people identified as "Arab-Muslims," "immigrants," "blacks," and "Jews." While the number of reported acts dropped between 1998 and 2000, and again during 2003, it tripled between 2001 and 2002, reaching the highest level in ten years (CNCDH 2003, 49, 51; 2004). According to the Commission's findings, acts of racist and xenophobic violence were committed by people from multiple sectors of society, although it identified the extreme right and ultranationalist groups as the main aggressors. These acts were largely reactions to national and international events and issues (e.g., juvenile delinquency, feelings of insecurity and exclusion, attacks, war, and terror), which tend to "amplify the number and the gravity of these acts" (CNCDH 2003, 14–16). The Commission highlighted increased violence toward Jewish people, which it saw as fueled by the ongoing Israeli-Palestinian war, euphemized as a "conflict." It also discussed violence against Arabs, described as "Islamophobia," over the years, particularly in its 2004 report, linking it to historically rooted racism and current world events. The Commission determined that the underlying causes of such violence derived not from racism and xenophobia, but from the "economic crisis" in France that has engendered high unemployment and a perceived "loss of the French identity." More crucially, the Commission acknowledged that in France "racism is quite present daily," something confirmed by 70 percent of those polled. It also recognized "French society's relative passivity" in addressing these issues (CNCDH 2004).

These findings are, however, problematic for a number of reasons, particularly when the CNCDH attempts to measure racism based on public opinion polls, while failing to analyze the ideological and institutional manifestations of racism and xenophobia. Breadth is given instead of depth, similar to being shown the exterior of a house without being informed of its interior design. The CNCDH admits that its data are limited by the fact that France, unlike the United States, does not have a tradition of documenting racialized violence and discrimination and analyzing them according to ethnicity. Yet the more telling aspect of these reports is the categories used to distinguish the aggressors from those being aggressed; and therein emerge identity politics.

The report issued in 2000, which was extensively discussed in the media, remains highly instructive. In it, the CNCDH found, for example, that an alarming 69 percent of the "French" called themselves "racists" and indicated that there were too many "foreigners" in France. And while Arabs were identified as the main target of racism and xenophobia, those polled also stated that "there are too many blacks," that "Jews have too much power in France," and that "foreigners are too different" (2000, 16–18). The CNCDH notes "a hardening of public perceptions against immigrants as well as an increase in xenophobic and racist attitudes in France compared with previous years" (18). These findings appeared to be confirmed by the fact that 98 percent of those polled indicated that racism was widespread in the country. And 78 percent identified the French school system as the institution most capable of unifying France's diverse populations, by transmitting a "common culture."

However, the more interesting question raised by these findings is not whether French people are racists, but who is being classified as "French." That is, the Commission failed to problematize the general category of "French people" used in its study, which is important given that many members of the groups about whom racist attitudes are held are also tax-paying French citizens. What is revealed, then, in this understanding is a more embedded form of racism that preconceives the national representation in singular terms which exclude certain sectors of French society. After all, to whom does this category refer? Equally problematic are the unanalyzed categories of "foreigners" and "immigrants," into which those perceived as not French (in this case people of African origin) are placed. While I do not mean to minimize the importance of examining the critical issue of racism in France, identifying who is racist remains unaddressed in official studies such as these. What's more, when the media report these findings uncritically, they spread misinformation that reinforces a representation whereby "French people" connotes simply European or "white," which remains unseen by those whose reality is taken as the norm.

And yet France too has its "model minorities," who, as in the U.S., are accorded a type of honorary "whiteness." A hint of the categories of perception that may lie ahead was published in the February 20, 2004, edition of the left-leaning newspaper *Libération.* In an effort to dismantle socialist party strongholds in regions heavily populated by people of North African origins, President Jacques Chirac's conservative party courted popular *beur,* or Arab, candidates who had been highly critical of the socialist party. In *Libération,* these candidates were euphemistically referred to as *les Français visibles,* that is, "visible French," a supposedly "race-neutral" term used to avoid more loaded descriptors such as "French of color." The point here is that these struggles over classifications illustrate the difficulty France is facing in attempting to name its citizens of non-European origins, who are typically called "people issued from immigration" or, again, "French by acquisition." These terms are used ironically by both outer-city youths and the extreme right, reflecting the same symbolic violence that produces similar ends: maintaining social divisions.

And yet there are contradictions too, a point well illustrated by the much-touted national celebrations following France's World Cup victory in 1997. A rainbow of people waved the French flag in honor of a multiethnic team. These festivities were seen as celebrating France's diversity, especially since a French Muslim of Algerian origin (Zinedine Zidane) had scored the crucial goal, becoming an iconic figure in France. France's football team came to symbolize a type of paradoxical inclusion that is not often recognized at the societal level. This image of a "racially" unified France was only solidified with front-page headlines proclaiming "La France: black, blanc, beur" (France: black, white, Arab) in reference to its triumphant star players: Christian Karembeu, Lilian Thuram, and Zidane. One wonders, however, what would have been the politics of diversity had this multicultural French national team lost the World Cup. Would "black, white, and Arab" still have symbolized *la France*? Then there was the unexpected winner of the 1999 Miss France Pageant, a woman of dark complexion and of African origin who, during her reign, became another symbol of the new multiethnic France. In contrast, the selection of an earlier Miss Italy by pageant officials caused an uproar in the country because, though she was beautiful, she supposedly did not reflect the authentic Italian woman, because of her visibly mixed Italian and African origins. Youths of African origin growing up in this context receive mixed messages about belonging from such controversies, which imply a type of national unity yet to be realized at the societal level. Indeed, the notion of *E pluribus unum* (Out of many, one) resonates differently in the French context, where the *pluribus* destined to become the *unum* are selectively and inconsistently identified.

Again, such belonging hinges on questions of culture that are informed by assumptions that Muslims are incapable of assimilating into French society, and that Muslim girls, in particular, are the antithesis of French ways of being and knowing. Though the headscarf has come to symbolize their difference, the issue of forced marriages clinches it, as do other forms of violence deemed "Muslim" by a public conditioned to see Muslims in deficit terms. And yet forced marriage looms large not only in reality but in legend among girls, as a price they may pay for having violated some expectation that provokes shame. Participants described the fate of girls labeled *putes* (for reasons ranging from open defiance of masculinity and patriarchy to wearing short skirts and tight shirts or having boyfriends) as a one-way ticket *au bled* (to their parents' home country); girls might be sent away and not heard of again. For some, their French nationality is their only protection against forced marriages, though sometimes only after the fact. During an interview on this topic, Mariama captured sentiments expressed by others that reflect a "here-there" dual frame of reference similar to the one described by Marcelo Suárez-Orozco in his studies of Central American immigrant youths in the U.S. (1987, 1989). That is, "there" refers to their parents' countries, which they see in negative terms, while "here" is home, or France.

> Over there, it's miserable, and she'll understand the opportunity she had being born in France if she ruins it. Her life is wasted in one shot. And don't bother to protest; they will believe you deserved it. They'll send you over there. You'll have to marry someone, have babies, and that will be your life, and you won't have any diplomas. It's too bad. You won't be able to go to school then.

The high-profile case of Fatoumata Konte, a high school student of Senegalese origin, perfectly exemplifies this fate. Not only did her abduction spark an international incident between France and Senegal, it also became a lightning rod that drew attention to the issue of forced marriage in France, much as Madame Gréou's indictment did to excision (detailed in chapter 5). The broader implications of these cases reside in the culturalist comparisons made between what gets constituted as an atavistic "African" practice—forced marriage—and what is considered modern—French culture.

The Issue of Forced Marriage

The issue of forced marriage seemed somewhat insignificant to my participants until the media frenzy over Fatoumata's disappearance in April 2000. Like Fatima, whom I introduced earlier, Fatoumata was described by her teachers as "a young woman with a great deal of personality," someone "totally integrated in France," indeed a gifted student. She was in her final year at the Lycée Colbert in Paris, expected to pass her *baccalauréat* without much difficulty and planning to pursue university studies. Reluctantly, and at the behest of her father, this young woman agreed to spend part of her vacation in the Haute Casamance region of Senegal, where her family was originally from. She had no idea that this short visit would become a four-month ordeal, during which she was sequestered in her father's village, accused of having a relationship with a French man, and destined for a forced marriage.

Fatoumata is one of several young women whose families have attempted to decide their matrimonial destiny, even when they are nationals of other countries. Challenging this expectation can be catastrophic for girls of African origin born and raised in France:

> their sexuality and marriage can be the most problematic vis-à-vis familial customs, themselves in contradiction to the examples that they encounter every day . . . a woman marrying a non-Muslim calls into question religious continuity, since it is understood that children are supposed to marry according to their father's religion. (Quiminal et al., 1997, 8)

Traditionally, as Catherine Quiminal and her colleagues argue, Muslim women are expected to marry Muslim men, while men need not marry Muslim women, since the father typically bestows a child's religious identification. Some parents use a forced marriage as a preemptive strike to avoid having a daughter marry someone outside of her community or a non-Muslim. For such young women, on the other hand, remaining students as long as possible becomes the best protection against what some (like Naïma, quoted above) feel to be their unavoidable fate.

Fatoumata, unlike others in this situation, turned out to be one of the fortunate ones, owing to help she received from friends and teachers at her school, as well as the Senegalese and French governments. As reported in the media, hundreds of students from her high school mobilized in an effort to have her disappearance investigated and to galvanize support for her immediate return to France. So determined were her classmates that they even drew into this cultural melee the minister of education and the president of Senegal, Abdoulaye Wade (whose wife is French), both of whom pledged that they would do everything in their power to bring the young student back to France. And so they did. With a great deal of help, Fatoumata returned to her high school, passed her *baccalauréat*, and entered university. It was also reported that she returned to her non-Muslim French boyfriend, much to her family's dismay. And while relations within her family were strained by this entire affair and the media attention it received, Fatoumata remained optimistic, stating in the press, "I'm sorry things turned out this way. I would have liked to remain on good terms with them [her parents]. I hope that they'll understand."[3]

Such cases are increasingly coming to light in a number of Western European countries where these young women, as nationals, are protected by the law, and some are using the law to defend themselves against gender-based persecution. Clearly, the issue of forced marriage is not limited to Muslim girls of African origin, or to Muslims in general. The high-profile stories of Narina and her two sisters in England and the case of a non-Muslim sixteen-year-old in Utah in the United States reveal striking similarities. For Narina and her sisters, an unanticipated trip to Pakistan turned out to be nothing more than a clever ruse to force a marriage on Narina, a British citizen. The deathbed wish of a grandmother was used to lure the sisters back to their parents' village, where their parents seized their passports and informed Narina that she was to be married to her cousin. Facing death threats should she not comply, Narina and her sisters managed to disguise themselves and escape to neighboring Islamabad to seek asylum with the British authorities, who intervened and forced Narina's mother to return her daughters' passports, allowing them to return to Britain.[4]

In 1998, the Mormon teenager accused her father, John Kingston, of taking her to a remote location and beating her for fleeing from a forced marriage to her uncle. Not only was this teenager expected to marry her father's brother, she would have been wife number fifteen in a family where polygamy was a long-standing tradition. And while Utah's constitution bans polygamy, a vast number of people in the state practice it, many of whom anticipate challenging Utah's law on this issue. However, the entire subject is a thorny one, entangled as it is with questions of religious freedom and the realities of forced marriages that sometimes involve minors. "Women don't have any say as to what's happening with their daughters in the first place," reported a woman interviewed about the Kingston case who, herself, was wife number six in a polygamous marriage. "These decisions are made by the men . . . and often the men will trade their daughters with each other," she concluded.[5] And while numerous cases of forced marriage are reported internationally, the sensational case of Nadia, an eighteen-year-old Norwegian citizen of Moroccan origin, also deserves attention, because of its similarity to the other cases highlighted and the controversy that it raised in Norway, a country awakened to its own multicultural diversity and Muslim population by this case.

As reported by anthropologist Unni Wikan (2000), Nadia, like the others, was held against her will while awaiting a forced marriage. Having been threatened with this prospect on more than one occasion, Nadia, anticipating the worst, confided in fellow employees about her home situation. When she failed to show up for work one day, her co-workers feared that those threats had materialized. During a telephone interview about Nadia's disappearance, one fellow employee stated, "She was in a terrible state, telling how she had been drugged, beaten, and forced into a van that had transported her, in handcuffs, with her family to Morocco" (55). Like Narina's and Fatoumata's, Nadia's parents kept her passport, thus thwarting any attempt to escape or even prove her nationality. But Nadia's father ignored a critical point, while the Norwegian government ignored another. In the eyes of the Norwegian judicial system, Nadia was Norwegian (she and her parents were Norwegian citizens), and the victim of an alleged crime committed in Norway. Consequently, Ministry of Foreign Affairs officials demanded her immediate return. Further complications arose over the issue of guardianship. While Nadia was an adult by Norwegian standards, since the Norwegian age of majority is eighteen, by Moroccan law, however, she was still a minor, since the Moroccan age of majority is twenty. Thus, Nadia was under her father's authority, according to Moroccan jurisprudence, and Morocco was where they were. But Norway was not giving up so easily, because Nadia's case had created a national uproar over citizenship rights and had become a *cause célèbre* for girls in similar situations, who saw in Nadia a means of increasing public awareness of their plight, as had happened with Fatoumata in France.

After a series of pressure tactics by the Norwegian government, including the threat of cutting off her father's pension and social assistance, Nadia returned to Norway. Surprisingly, however, in a twist of events, Nadia retracted her original story and said that she had willingly gone to Morocco to visit an ailing grandmother, though evidence suggested that this story was a cover-up to protect her family from prosecution. All the same, her recantation was felt as a betrayal by other girls who had rallied to her support. In the end, Nadia confessed that her parents had in fact abducted her, parents who were described as "being of a prominent and cosmopolitan Moroccan family" (59). She was also reported to have helped the police gather evidence after they charged her parents with her abduction, though she did so at a great personal cost. After her parents were found guilty her family rejected her, she received death threats, and her father died shortly after sentencing. Moreover, the Muslim community and others who had initially supported her now denounced her for sullying her family's honor and that of Muslims everywhere. They felt that it was not only Nadia's parents on trial, but also an already stigmatized community that saw itself, through this highly publicized case, being condemned as law-breaking, culturally barbarian, and identified with forced marriage. But Nadia was determined to take a stand, not only for herself but for her young sister, who she feared would be subjected to the same treatment by their father. Nadia described him as abusive and testified that he believed her to be "too Norwegian." "Too Norwegian" translated into not being a virgin, wearing pants and makeup, and "drinking and smoking and staying out late at night" (65). Because of this, her parents removed her from the source of this presumed debauchery: Norwegian society. And for that act, her parents were given a one-year suspended sentence and a stiff fine of roughly $10,000. Wikan, who was brought in as a "cultural expert," documents how the affair boiled down to cultural wars, or perhaps politics, politics about Nadia's "wish to be Norwegian versus their [her parents'] insistence that she 'become Moroccan' and 'become Muslim'" (62).

Though these cases received a great deal of media attention in Europe and forced the public to become more aware of this continuing problem, Wikan correctly asserts that these cases raise a number of important questions. The most pressing and obvious one is, how can human rights be balanced with respect for and tolerance of cultural differences? And while forced marriage is neither unique to

Muslims nor a new phenomenon, the practice persists in a number of countries, often clandestinely, and girls and young women can pay enormous prices—sometimes their lives—for defying it. Moreover, these young women's experiences illustrate just how tenuous their status can be in countries where they are assimilated to ways of being that are in conflict with their upbringing. In such countries, their rights as citizens can be a means of self-defense. Indeed, forced marriage can become an issue of international intrigue and law, a site of controversy over those very rights and how they are interpreted in their families. Yet the attention given these cases in the European media is not without its negative effects. These stories, when cast as "Muslim problems," often further the misconception that the practice is unique to Muslims, though international human rights organizations such as Human Rights Watch, Amnesty International, and the United Nations have documented it among non-Muslim populations across the globe. More importantly, when measured against cultures in Western countries a sense of cultural supremacy emerges, suggesting that these practices are displays of Muslim values deemed pernicious in Western societies, as are its practitioners.

Many of the girls in my study feared the possibility of forced marriage; the instances they are aware of have taken on the dimensions of urban legend. As they reasoned, such cases serve as warnings in their communities about what can happen to disobedient daughters who succumb to "Western" ways. And while school may be a refuge or a way to stave off marriage, failure within that system further complicates matters in the lives of those young women, whose lives are already so utterly complicated. For the most jaded among them, life becomes a cruel joke, and at the heart of that cruelty is their neighborhood, where their ways of being, expressed in their self-understanding, are also fashioned, often in contradictory ways. It is to that "other France" that I now turn, indeed to the site where the "x" in their assertions that they are "French of 'x' origin" is both made and unmade.

2   Structured Exclusion

Public Housing in the French Outer City

> I am the voice of the ghetto. I am the voice of
> the hood. I'm not talking about the Bronx or
> Soweto—Ghetto, children of the ghetto—but
> about our neighborhood . . . We've suffered
> enough in these projects.
> —**Pit Baccardi and Jacky Brown,** *Enfants du
> Ghetto (Delabel Records)*

> Without their parents and France knowing
> it—seemingly astonished by their existence—
> they are here. Their screams, their violence
> are the most extreme expression of a
> legitimate claim: "I belong to this society!"
> —**Yamina Benguigui,** *Mémoire d'immigrés*

What is life like for young people growing up in the French outer
cities? Why do some feel so betrayed by the high principles of human rights, equality, and freedom taught to them in their homeland? In many ways, social context at its most local level plays an essential role in explaining how such young people become locked
into conditions of exclusion and misery that extinguish their hope
and circumscribe their life chances. For some, the variables in their
complex calculus of being are reducible to a simple equation: youth
of color + public housing = delinquency, insecurity, and violence
against the general public. Yet what is ignored by such simplicity and
prevailing arguments of "excuse-abuse" and "personal responsibility
discourses" (examined in this chapter) are the critical ways that public housing and neighborhood impact the oft-overlooked and less
visible dimensions of their lives: their expectations, their thresholds

of tolerance, their health, their emotional well-being, and their sense of security. The neighborhood, like the schools, socializes these young people in seemingly contradictory ways, particularly when their living conditions are themselves an expression of violence, albeit of a different kind. And while such young people are taught that France is their country, indeed their homeland, this idea becomes a metaphor for hypocrisy when home is an immense, multistory housing project known as *la cité des Courtillières*.

Entering the Zone

La cité des Courtillières is located in part of France's famed "Red Belt," the city of Pantin, which has been the stronghold of the French Communist Party since the 1920s (Stovall 1990). Pantin is one of several boroughs in the economically disadvantaged department of Seine-Saint-Denis, an area reputed to be dangerous and overrun by "immigrants."[1] And while Pantin and especially the Courtillières are perceived similarly, the last census classified 83 percent of Pantin's 49,919 inhabitants as "French," and only 19 percent of the more than 6,000 residents of the Courtillières as "foreign."[2] However, the Courtillières was not always so stigmatized. At its inception, it not only symbolized modern living, but it additionally responded to the 1950s housing crisis following the Second World War, which left many urban dwellers homeless or living in squalor (De Jesus Vaz 2002). Its initial inhabitants were mainly working-class French families who saw in their new homes a sort of "worker's paradise," as it was characterized. Conceived by the avant-garde architect Emile Aillaud, the Courtillières was designed not merely to offer new comforts and conveniences to those unaccustomed to modern accommodations, but also to represent a different way of living, one that implied replacing old habits and practices with new, modern ways of being. Recalled one former resident, who had moved in in 1958, "What luxury to have a three-bedroom apartment with a toilet and separate shower," one that belonged solely to oneself or one's family.[3] Residents found their apartments luminous, spacious, and pest-free, and with all the cherished conveniences that were typically lacking in their former homes, such as indoor plumbing, consistently working electricity, adequate heat, and multiple rooms.

Pristine buildings, flourishing markets, grassy grounds, and a sense of grandeur became the signature of the Courtillières, which stood in contrast to the pauperized conditions of residents' former dwellings. Mere seconds away was a beautiful nursery nestled within the heart of the complex, where children could play comfortably in rooms bathed in warmth and sunlight passing through the nursery's generous windows. In this neighborhood, one could picture a French working-class version of Ozzie and Harriet Nelson as one's neighbors, as the Courtillières was indeed a type of "paradise" when compared to the dank, dimly lit, and overpriced apartments where the underprivileged had resided. To migrants and their families living in shantytowns (*bidonvilles*) north of Paris, these dwellings appeared miraculous by comparison.

It is difficult to describe what I have observed and learned about the Courtillières without recalling a term frequently used by both residents and non-residents when describing this place: *sale* (dirty). And some feared that I would only see and write about that perspective. I struggle, nonetheless, to imagine a pristine Courtillières, or at least to see it as something grander than the blighted public housing project that it is today. Some of its current residents see few signs of the Courtillières' former glory, which has been overwhelmed by a certain barren, abject poverty that has come to define the public housing experience in the French outer cities. This complex is but one example, though by no means the worst.

I was introduced to its inner sanctum by participants who were only in middle school at that time. They had a certain youthful inquisitiveness about everything, typical of those who lead segregated lives. This became apparent to me during our outings together, during which I discovered that, though they lived on the edge of Paris, some had never visited the Eiffel Tower nor entered Notre Dame, nor had they stood on the old observation deck at the Beaubourg Center to see the panoramic view of the city—that is, until I took them there. In fact, we traversed a great deal of the City of Light together, which prompted Rima to say on one occasion, "It's weird, Madame, you come from the United States and it's you who shows us Paris!" At that time, Rima and the others had no real motivation to leave their neighborhood, given that school, friends, and family could all be found there. If Paris was a distant, mythical land, it was no loss, since what they knew well was their world, the Courtillières. As my guides, the girls revealed to me an existence that I knew only from my own childhood memories. Ten years of living in Jim Crow's cabins in northern Ohio, punctuated by summer visits to cousins living in Chicago's projects, were transformed into a metaphor for the African Diaspora as a whole when I was confronted by the Courtillières. In 1995, when I arrived on the scene, only a few basic services were available to people living there, which were succinctly captured by two local middle school teachers in their study of the neighborhood's youth culture:

> One bakery, one pharmacy, one laundromat, one grocer, one newspaper stand. Zero markets. Zero post offices. No local offices for public utilities. One city hall annex all the same. One middle school and two elementary schools. (Seguin and Teillard 1996, 3)

This neighborhood, like the boroughs that border it, was profoundly affected by deindustrialization, which accelerated during the economic crisis of the 1970s, the period when immigration was officially halted in France, in 1974. As scholar Catherine Rhein (1998a, 443) asserts, "Deindustrialisation hit these communes more severely and much longer than their south-western counterparts; service jobs replaced industrial jobs, and only partly compensated for the loss in jobs and fiscal wealth." As the factories that provided work for families living in places like the Courtillières closed, demographic shifts ensued, including "white flight" from the projects. The population was largely replaced by underskilled workers, increasingly of African origin or descent. Looming large on the complex's horizon is the smokestack of one of these now abandoned factories. It serves as a constant reminder to the current residents that jobs were once plentiful in this area, where the unemployment rate is 20 percent, twice the national average.

Both fame and infamy are attached to the Courtillières: fame for its having been the subject of an acclaimed documentary, and infamy for the way young people living in the neighborhood were depicted in a separate, commercial film, both released in early 1999. January saw the arrival of filmmaker Nicholas Stern's eagerly awaited documentary *De ce côté du monde: 33 parc des Courtillières*. Stern, a long-term resident of the development, received high marks from Courtillières residents for his attempt to show the transformation of this area from its heyday to its present condition of neglect and disrepair. In stark contrast is the perverse, commercially oriented film by Jacques Doillon, *Petits frères*, whose cast included children from the Courtillières. Although Doillon claims to be working in their best interest, his film conveys a familiar combination of exploitation and paternalistic possessiveness through his images of young people who, already stigmatized, are portrayed as gun-toting, destructive little gangsters. Interestingly, during a televised interview with Doillon and his handpicked cast, the director spoke with great sincerity about the authenticity of his film, which he argued accurately reflects life in the "other France." However, when asked if that statement was true, several of the young people responded, "It was all just an act," much to Doillon's visible chagrin.

Sadly, this same television program, in its quest for "reality TV," took a camera crew into the apartment of one of the cast members, a young person of West African origin whose parents were away at the time. Enjoying his newfound celebrity, this youth, without his parents' consent, allowed the crew free access to his home. Cameras zoomed in on his younger brothers running around half-dressed, while other siblings were seen idly watching television in their unkempt apartment. This scene was amplified by the high-pitched squeals of other children dashing out of camera range, which underlined the glaring fact that the children had been left unsupervised. This program and Doillon himself not only succeeded in manipulating these young people, but also reinforced the very thing that they supposedly sought to combat: stereotypical representations that further disparaged people already so vilified. These events recall Jacques Chirac's insulting and dismissive characterization of African families in 1991 (before he became president of the Republic), families he described as having "three or four wives and twenty-odd children, who receive fifty thousand francs in public assistance without, of course, working . . . If you add to that the noise and stench, the French worker living on the same floor becomes crazy."[4] Such descriptions elevate one group while downgrading another, without explaining the causes of the social conditions that poor people endure, often across generations.

While African immigrants and their children are denounced in France, it should be remembered that France has historically invited Africans to its shores according to its needs, initially men and subsequently their families through reunification programs (Haute conseil de l'intégration 1993). Nor should it be forgotten that scores of African conscripts (*les tirailleurs*) fought and died for France in the French army during both world wars, and many more toiled on French soil as exploited manual laborers afterward.[5] After France's African colonies gained independence in the 1950s and 1960s the number of immigrants steadily increased. These men were recruited by the construction and automobile industries, industries that overworked and underpaid them. Many of them (and, later, their families) lived in shantytowns dotting the periphery of northern and eastern Paris. Sociologist Abdelmalek Sayad vividly captures the deplorable housing reserved for African workers encouraged to come to France in his penetrating study *L'immigration* (1991). Almost confrontational in style, his photographs document the tragic reality of migrant workers' living conditions, and are complemented by his critical and reflexive analysis of immigration and its emotional costs to families ghettoized in France's *bidonvilles*. Sayad's photographs shocked my young participants, as they were largely unaware that such conditions had existed not far from their neighborhood and, worse, that people of African origin, like themselves, had lived that way. Equally powerful are Yamina Benguigui's documentary *Mémoires d'immigrés* (1997) and her book of the same title. Her footage shows disturbing aspects of the recruitment process used to select men who would eventually labor in France's industrial sector, and who would also inhabit those same shantytowns. Not only were men sought who had little or no formal schooling, their hands were also inspected for calluses and sores to confirm that they were familiar with the type of work they could expect upon arrival in France.

Some of these men did escape the horrors of the *bidonville,* but only to find themselves in somber and isolating *foyers,* or workers' dormitories, controlled from the 1950s to the 1970s by the National Company for the Construction of Housing for Guest Workers. As scholars Moustapha Diop and Laurence Michalak describe it,

> The foyer is a ubiquitous aspect of the French urban and architectural landscape wherever there are high concentrations of foreign workers. The term foyer, or "home," with its domestic connotations, is ironic, in that the foyers rarely house families and typically forbid couples and children. The migrants in the foyer are frequently married, but they have left their families in their countries of origin. The foyer is a social universe of non-French males, an island of workers, usually unskilled or low-skilled, away from their homelands and isolated from their families. In fact, foreign workers have had high rates of unemployment in recent years, so that the foyer has become a kind of reservoir of cheap foreign labor. The function of the foyer is to provide sleeping accommodations and common facilities for its inhabitants. Several workers may share a room or a group of small individual bedrooms, grouped around a shared kitchen/dining facility and a bathroom. (1996, 74–75)

In the 1960s, an urbanization plan was launched permitting workers and their families to relocate from the shantytowns and foyers to *cités* like the Courtillières. It was presumed that they would appreciate living in the comforts of public housing after the horrors of the *bidonville* or the isolation of the foyer. But over the years relocation has turned into segregation, in that public housing located in the most disadvantaged outer cities of major urban areas has become a dumping ground for the least desired populations.

Take the Courtillières as an example. The city of Paris, through its office for low-income housing, was the principal lessor of more than eight hundred apartments in the Courtillières (and many other buildings in adjacent boroughs) for forty years. And for a number of years, the city has been accused of having "warehoused" African families in these neighborhoods in an effort to keep them from occupying public housing in the center of Paris, where the city also controls several low-income buildings.[6] The result of such social engineering is places like the Courtillières, where only a small number of original inhabitants remain, with a larger population of families of African origin who end up in these neighborhoods when they request support and qualify for low-income housing. It is important to keep in mind that, unlike in the U.S., there is little stigma attached to seeking governmental assistance, though this is changing under the weight of neoliberalism in France.

To find out more about how African families might have been disproportionately placed in the Courtillières, I interviewed one of the city officials charged with allocating low-income housing in that area. While she contended that her office manages only a few of the twenty-plus buildings in the complex, she said that the real culprits behind the increased presence of families of African origin in the Courtillières were the public housing authorities in Paris:

> If there is a high concentration of African families—the statistics, I believe, are that 3/4 of the families are African—it's because, well, these people were living in deteriorating conditions, in apartments that were falling apart, in Paris. They couldn't put these people in the street, and so the city of Paris used Pantin's housing program and placed them here. So the high concentration of large families and African families is due to this policy, not our office.

However, although the city of Paris manages more than six thousand low-income apartments within Paris proper, officials in Pantin maintained that these apartments are not usually made available to low-income African families or others deemed undesirable.

During this interview, I also inquired about the placement of large families, such as Fatou's, in apartments that were clearly inadequate for them. In response, she stressed that the majority of the apartments handled by her office had three bedrooms, which meant that officially only a family with four or fewer children could be placed in them. She insisted that her office would *never* place a family of more than four children in such housing, but that the public housing authorities in Paris would and did. When I told her that I knew larger families who lived in those buildings, in the very apartments that her office managed, she countered by saying that the sizes of the apartments matched the family sizes indicated on the original applications. She earnestly added that if the family reported an increase in household size and asked to be reassigned to "more suitable housing," they would try to comply. Sociologist Patrick Simon documents in his studies of public housing allocation in France (2001) that Maghrebin, sub-Saharan African, and Turkish people presumed to be immigrants make up the largest populations in public housing in France. According to his findings, they typically encounter multiple forms of discrimination when applying for such housing in more coveted areas, including within or near to urban centers. That is, Simon found that they are coded as "undesirables" and housing officials sometimes refuse to see them, or treat them with hostility or disregard when they do see them; they experience greater delays in having their applications processed, if processed at all. "More suitable housing" could, then, be situated farther from Paris in more desolate, isolated, or underprivileged projects than the Courtillières, places reserved for groups deemed pariahs of the nation, whom some would have leave France or in some other way disappear altogether.

Because of the Courtillières' affordable rents and its proximity to Paris (to which there is good public transit), residents are reluctant to lose their place in the development in exchange for unknown conditions, especially since the turnover rate in the Courtillières is low. Complicating matters more, public housing authorities overseeing the Courtillières have received upwards of six hundred requests for housing, according to the official I interviewed, of which only twenty or slightly more were fulfilled. Pantin has received more than 2,200 requests annually, of which less than 10 percent are filled.

During one phase of my fieldwork, I lived in an economically depressed, yet increasingly gentrified section of the nineteenth *arrondissement* (district) of Paris, not far from my participants' neighborhood. In this area, a studio apartment rented for roughly six hundred euros, though this amount excludes the very expensive basic utilities in France, whose cost spikes during the winter, when there is a dire need for vital heat. Heat is even more precious and expensive in poorly insulated or constructed buildings such as mine was, in which warmth dissipates before it even reaches a corner of the room. This was all too frequently the case in the worst apartments in the Courtillières as well. One consequence of poor living conditions is a perpetual flu and a general feeling of fatigue, making daily tasks and work seem all the more daunting. Rents are, nevertheless, lower in the nineteenth *arrondissement* because the area is classified as *un quartier difficile,* a dangerous neighborhood. But danger is relative to a person's perception of it, and according to my building manager, this danger was defined in terms of young people who were "hanging around with pit bulls," an image that has come to typify the run-down public housing that dots the periphery of this area. And yet, in this area of lived and realized cultural diversity, one easily finds low-income housing adjacent to newly constructed condominiums. Indeed, in this strangely eclectic district, one finds the homeless side by side with people of various African origins dressed in billowing boubous of iridescent hues. *Hijab*-wearing Muslim women cross paths with Hasidic Jews, merchants of various Asian origins, and recent Eastern European migrants. And although this area is considered dangerous, in the two years that I lived there I never encountered a single problem. In fact, people were extremely civil, including the supposed delinquents.

There are emotional costs to these lived conditions that echo through French society, especially its outer cities. During my fieldwork, I asked my core participants to record the songs that best reflected their experiences in France. Among them was a popular song about outer-city youths' sense of exclusion in their contested homeland. Entitled "Parisiens du Nord" (Parisians from the north) and performed by Cheb Mami, Imhotep, and K-Mel, raï and rap artists of Maghrebin origin, its very title expresses tensions inherent in the politics of French identity and its content poignantly speaks to the rejection these youth face on all levels of their life-worlds:

> because of my looks you called me a foreigner.
> I thought this was my country, that I could die here.
> that's how you played me . . .
> that's how you betrayed me.

An assistant principal I spoke with addressed some of the underlying factors that contribute to a sense of being "played" and "betrayed," as the song says. One is urban planning:

> Within our school district, there is a great deal of cultural diversity, people who find themselves in an extremely difficult situation, people uprooted from their homes and who are concentrated in a highly dense area, like the Courtillières, which is right next door to us. Even the police don't go there anymore. That said, there remains a lot of work to be done so that this area can be like any other. Personally, I feel that urbanization plays a

big part in this because from the moment that you live in public housing, on the periphery and near the freeways—you can't convince me that the experiences of people living there are the same as for someone who lives in a quiet, residential neighborhood. And our district is like that, a mix of all of that, but it was poorly conceived. We don't have the same situation to the west of Paris or the same situation to the south. And it's often connected, in many cities, to the north and east.

Although the conditions of the area are indefensible, this place, with all its horrors and inequities, is nonetheless home—with all that this notion connotes—for many families, and my participants are aware of the debilitating effects of their neighborhood. They are also aware of how others perceive it—and them. Yet they tenaciously resist becoming yet more casualties of the outer cities, though admittedly some are already hardened by their conditions.

"This is not a ghetto?"

This area is often described as a "ghetto"; in France, close associations are drawn between the French outer cities and U.S. inner cities. However, these projects, and the neighborhoods in which they are located, did not emerge historically to serve the same purpose as did ghettos in the U.S. That is, the Courtillières and other public housing projects were not built with the intent of enforcing racialized boundaries, quarantining a stigmatized population.[7] Nonetheless, Kenneth B. Clark's penetrating and provocative work *Dark Ghetto: Dilemmas of Social Power* (1965) strikes a familiar chord in his powerful depiction of the forced containment and segregation of Black Americans in the United States. His observations begin to take on transnational dimensions when juxtaposed with the contemporary outer cities of Paris. "The dark ghettos," Clark writes, "are social, political, educational, and—above all—economic colonies. Their inhabitants are subject peoples, victims of greed, cruelty, insensitivity, guilt and fear" (11). If these are the conditions that define ghettoized segregation, then France is well on its way to duplicating the worst aspects of the U.S. model, as has already been done in other European countries (Small 1994; Wrench and Solomos 1993). What's more, the process of ghettoization, as Douglas Massey and Nancy Denton assert, "supports other racially discriminatory processes and binds [individuals] into a coherent and uniquely effective system of racial subordination" (1993, 8). Further, Massey and Denton define a ghetto as exclusively populated by a single "racial group." This is not the reality in French public housing complexes in the outer cities, though they are fast approaching this same distinction with the increased placement of families of African origin in projects like the Courtillières.

Other striking similarities exist as well, illustrating a type of French-U.S. connection related to perceptions of youth of color from public housing. Crime, for example, has been given a "face" in France, that of young people from the outer cities, who hold center stage in televised news reports of increased fundamentalism, violence, delinquency, and incivility in the country. Media images of attacks described as "Islamic terrorism" and reports on drug users highlighting people of African descent, coupled with imports of U.S. television programs like *Cops,* encourage the French public to see youths like those depicted in these broadcasts as responsible for crime and terror. These programs reinforce a generalized representation of these young people as prowling about in gang-like formations throughout urban centers, like Paris, where few positive representations of them are found.

At the other end of the spectrum, one finds very few people of color in French films and television shows, beyond certain stereotypical roles. Rarely are French people of non-European origins depicted in positions of influence and authority or as outside the "underclass" trope or featured as entertainers in music videos and variety shows. This lack prompted the novelist Calixthe Beyala, the musician Manu Dibango, and others to form a coalition demanding more, and more positive, roles for "Afro-Metropolitan" people—the coalition's term—in French film and television. Undermining this effort, however, is the continual juxtaposition of the discourse and imagery of violence with one-dimensional, negative images of youths of African origin, who become narrowly, yet powerfully, defined as something to be controlled and contained.

More damaging is the statistical evidence of catastrophic increases in juvenile delinquency and violence, evidence produced and interpreted by the police and "crime experts." These statistics have had a powerful effect on public opinion, even though a range of scholars have shown that such increases, when more closely scrutinized, turn out to be specious. And while serious acts of delinquency and crime must be acknowledged, the amplification and generalization of crime in the media, which is itself informed by those (mis)interpretations, fail to capture or acknowledge some highly relevant facts.

For example, according to police reports, the number of offenders between the ages of thirteen and eighteen in prison and detention centers tripled between 1993 and 1997. The French prison population continues to swell under the influence of "zero tolerance" policies imported from the U.S. (Wacquant 1999a). However, sociologist Laurent Mucchielli (2000) effectively demonstrates that most of this increase results from the frequent arrests for minor drug possession (which in France usually means derivatives of hashish), not violent crime as is often indicated. Yet the inflammatory rhetoric of increased delinquency and violence, suffused with fears of terrorism, fuels the public's insecurity. In response, the police have been given carte blanche to target these youths (Bonelli 2001). Stricter policing of them is legitimized by that very rhetoric of "insecurity" and codified by France's homeland security laws (i.e., *La plan vigipirate*), which gives the police unrestrained search, seizure, and detainment authority. These activities become a type of theater played on a public stage at places where these youths gather, such as the metro station at Les Halles and the adjacent shopping mall. The carnival-like atmosphere is animated by music and youth of all origins dressed in the latest hip-hop attire who have seized this space, which offers a bevy of social activities and services not found in outer-city neighborhoods. This area is also heavily patrolled by police, increasingly of all origins too, whose station is located seconds away. I commonly saw the clash of these two groups, as youths were stopped, questioned, and taken away by the police under the angry gaze of other youths.

According to police reports, pickpockets and dealers in everything from pirated goods to hashish are ubiquitous in the area. These, along with other factors, have led to a general crackdown on youths identified with these activities at other such sites around Paris as well. Sociologists Stéphane Beaud and Michel Pialoux show in their analysis of urban violence in France (2001) that youth of color from the outer cities, particularly boys, are constantly profiled and harassed by law enforcement agents who randomly demand to see their identification papers, though they have committed no crime. Moreover, these scholars argue that such young people typically come from neighborhoods where unemployment is as high as 30 to 40 percent, an unemployment that "transmits itself from the eldest brother to the youngest; even the possession of a degree of higher education is no protection [for those who are] tracked into 'rotten' vocational high schools in their neighborhoods, where they feel trapped in the fate of 'losers'" (18). Their attire, or "uniform," tags them as deviant to the general public—their ways of speaking, baggy clothes, designer insignias, and cornrowed or closely cropped hair serve as the visible confirmation of their irrevocable outsider status. "One part of the population," Beaud and Pialoux insist, "is openly hostile to anything that resembles the Maghrebins" (19), and sub-Saharan Africans should be included in their observation. These sentiments translate into racist acts experienced by people of color, in particular these youths, who face employment and housing discrimination, are refused entry into bars and night clubs, are routinely followed by security personnel in stores, and are treated with hostility because of their appearances, as I have witnessed and experienced myself. These findings parallel data collected by the antiracist group SOS Racisme. Its annual report notes that most of the acts of discrimination and racism reported to their office were related to employment, law enforcement, and public sector services, such as the post office and city hall.[8]

Of course, poor relations between law enforcement and youth of African origin are not unique to France; one finds similar problems throughout Western Europe and the United States. And residents of the "other France," particularly teenagers, can recount numerous stories of police brutality or express feelings of being put upon by law enforcement officers, who in turn see themselves as besieged by youth violence. The unfortunate result is mutual animosity, or even hate, and distrust that can culminate in death, as happened at the Courtillières in January 1999. Lionel Obadina, a twenty-nine-year-old man of African origin, was shot and killed not far from Fatou's and Mariama's building. The police officer who fired the fatal shot insisted that he acted in self-defense when Obadina confronted him, brandishing a rifle. Unsurprisingly, police, media, and local accounts of these events differ, as do the explanations of why the officer used deadly force. The media described Obadina as a drug dealer and said that he had drugs in his possession at the time of the shooting. His mother and friends had a different image of Lionel. Indeed, their sentiments echoed those expressed by Kadiatou Diallo over the murder of her son, Amadou, who was shot repeatedly and killed in a disadvantaged area in New York City by police (Diallo and Wolff 2003), and those of many families who have lost their young in similar ways. That is, Lionel was beloved by them, but a "suitable enemy" in France. It is critical to remember, however, that in France these types of shootings hardly approach the alarming rates that one finds in the United States.

Left unaddressed, however, are the root causes of what is being described as *la violence* in France. Too often the explanation simply begins and ends with these young people. Mucchielli (2000) and others have shown, nevertheless, that reported increases in violence are directly linked to greater policing of outer-city youth. Rather than an increase in actual violence, what one sees is "the deterioration of relations between the two principal parties involved" (363–364)—youth of color and law enforcement. The latter is backed by the state, which has no plan or policy for dealing with the outcomes of the violence it itself directs against such youth—their poor education, their high unemployment, and their contained social exclusion in the outer cities.

The wheels of this vicious cycle began spinning with the anti-immigrant campaigns during France's economic crisis of the 1980s. The extreme right and conservative politicians pressed for changes in the naturalization laws that made it more difficult for the children of immigrants to attain French nationality. With this intensified xenophobic rhetoric pushing for the ousting of "non-French French" from the country came a self-imposed public blindness to the conditions of their exclusion in the outer cities, particularly in the schools. On the one hand, immigrants became scapegoats for high unemployment, because they were supposedly taking jobs from the "real French." And on the other hand, crime and the ongoing crisis in public education were blamed on the children of immigrants, who, being social outcasts, fit nicely in the category of violent delinquents, a category once held by the working-class, unemployed *français-français* youth. Although the latter are no longer associated with these problems in the public mind, they, too, are failing educationally and commit crimes.

During the 1990s, crime became increasingly associated with foreigners, or those perceived to be foreigners. Their numbers dramatically rose in French prisons, because of so-called immigration violations. Sociologist Loïc Wacquant argues that "the cells of France have grown distinctly 'colored'" over the past years because of an "over consumption [of] . . . nationals perceived and treated as foreigners by the police and judicial apparatus, such as the youth born to North African immigrants or others who come from France's predominantly black overseas dominions and territories" (1999b, 217). Further, people imprisoned for immigration violations are commonly given sentences rivaling those meted out for felonies. "Far from resulting from a hypothetical increase in their delinquency, as some xenophobic discourses would have it," Wacquant continues, "the growing share of foreigners in the prison population of France is due to the tripling in 20 years of incarcerations for violations of immigration statutes." Under French immigration law people convicted of such violations can also be deported to their parents' countries of origin, to places as foreign to them as to anyone who has never set foot off of their home soil. But more importantly, the lingering question is this: Will France's prison system become a "peculiar institution" used to neutralize undesirable groups and condition them to a "new economic and racial regime" where they will remain marginalized, as Wacquant (forthcoming) demonstrates has been done in the U.S.?

As France's "suitable enemies," the most excluded of these young people are also the ones least likely to claim its "national identity," since they have long ago abandoned—and been abandoned by—one of the principal institutions that shape their self-understandings: national education. Seeing few alternatives and filled with anger, some come to see informal economies or crime as a viable alternative to the cumulative effects of social exclusion to which they have acquiesced. But these activities, seemingly profitable in the short term, ultimately only lock them more securely in those very conditions of exclusion. Enters, then, a "dark ghetto," or places like the Courtillières, as feeders to the prisons. Even worse, criminal activity, particularly by stigmatized young people, winds up providing ideological justifications that allow those conditions to persist. That is, to a public that believes they are being preyed upon by delinquents, or supposed "terrorists" in the making, segregation and confinement become, in their view, not only justifiable, but also desirable. And when this belief is reinforced by the politicized rhetoric of individual responsibility, there is no need to search for the causes for, or explanations of, these youths' actions. Everything else becomes a mere excuse. But if we remain at the superficial level of "excuse-abuse," we remain blind to what creates and fuels that behavior in the first place. Consequently, it becomes impossible to offer more than a bandage solution, which eventually comes undone. It is easier, and more publicly appealing, to make these youths into "savages," to use the words of French hip-hop artists KDD (Kartel Double Détente), and lock them in cages, thus absolving society of its responsibility for contributing to social violence. It is all well and good to demand that individuals be responsible and held accountable for their acts. But who holds society—that would be us—accountable for our indifference in allowing, year after year and generation after generation, the sustained marginalization of children, who become hardened teens and adults?[9] This cycle only continues, and therein lies the brand of violence that indifference typically breeds, and that comes back to bite those who remain indifferent. Some consider prisons or cages excellent solutions to violence, but removing people from society does not remove the violence that shaped them, or prevent others from following them down that same tragic path. The Courtillières is perhaps not a ghetto in the U.S. sense, but its effects are omnipresent, and most visible at the lived, more personal levels, that is, within this complex social process of exclusion.

The Courtillières: "I love it, and I hate it!"

During one of our initial conversations, I asked Aïcha if she felt "integrated" in France, given the much touted discourse of "integration" prevalent at that time. "I can't tell you," she bleakly responded, "because I live in the suburbs [the outer cities]. I can't tell you for sure, but I feel integrated in France, but more with people who live around me, people I've known for a long time . . . I don't see myself integrated with a group of French people." And yet she was surrounded by "groups of French people" in that very neighborhood, though they were of African origin. Perceptions of such neighborhoods and their residents are integral to identity politics because they symbolically reinforce group boundaries against a broader discourse of integration that these places contradict. And while the Courtillières exemplifies this fact, it lies at the intersection of an old-world, ethnic neighborhood of communal living tied to residents' origins and modern urban blight.

There have, however, been improvements to the area since 1997. During that year a community center was opened, designed to respond to the many needs of residents that were ill addressed by the small city hall annex that had previously stood in that site. Housed within its walls are a small modern library, a revamped version of that annex, several computer terminals with access to the Internet, after-school tutoring programs, and a number of associations and workshops focusing on social issues and artistic interests. Also within the building is the only café in the neighborhood, in a country where "café culture" is significant. The community center provides space and resources for local organizations such as Les femmes médiatrices sociales et culturelles, a women's support group directed by Marie-Clémentine Bendo and Sara Miangu Mas that helps women with issues ranging from illiteracy to domestic abuse.

Many women who are recent immigrants, especially those from rural areas, find that the Femmes médiatrices and the community center cushion their transition into a society in which their customary ways of operating have been drastically altered. For example,

Madame Bendo spoke at length about aiding women who have never used electricity or a gas stove, or women who are unprepared for the European winters and lack warm clothing for themselves and their children. The center also has a social aspect, which is cherished by residents used to living within a community of family and friends. The center plays an exceptional role in attenuating the isolation and fears experienced by women living in a foreign context whose laws and traditions may conflict with their own customs, discussed in chapters 1 and 5. Other issues mediated by the association include those pertaining to the seclusion of women who have traditionally been house-bound homemakers. On migrating to a new country, such a role may be difficult or even impossible to maintain, especially since economic pressure may require women to work outside the home. As Egyptian scholar and woman's rights activist Nawal El Saadawi explains it,

> Women migrate to escape the hardships of life in the countryside. They seek jobs, education, or are willing to provide services or be part of a migrant family. A female migrant will suffer much more than a male because she is much more vulnerable. She is a victim of tradition, of male exploitation and sexism, of concepts related to honor and virginity which clash with the changing moral fabric in urban societies and the development of different social and cultural patterns. Nevertheless, a woman in an urban area will enjoy a greater degree of freedom than her sister in rural areas even if she lives within the framework of a nuclear family. (1982, 196)

The center fulfills a variety of needs, and provides essential services to the neighborhood. And while the lack of services has been a long-standing issue, in September 2000 a new post office opened in the area, as did a technical institute, housed in a refurbished section of the abandoned factory that looms on the horizon of this neighborhood. While a positive addition, it is marred by broken windows, gutted rooms, and gaping holes in the parts of the factory that have not been restored, which dwarf the institute itself. Moreover, these types of institutes are considered second-rate community colleges, not rigorous, and their degrees are devalued in the job market. In Bobigny, the adjacent borough, there is a smaller branch of the University of Paris XIII, though some of the classrooms are in trailers, and it faces the worst side of that abandoned factory. Nonetheless, these institutions provide some access to higher education to youths who typically would have none.

Courtillières: student protestors and middle school before renovations.
Photograph © Ville de Pantin (France).

Courtillières: middle school after renovations.
Photograph by Trica Keaton.

Courtillières, exterior view: condition of buildings.
Photograph by Trica Keaton.

In April 2004, the middle school in the Courtillières was completely renovated. During the mid-1990s, it had had the lowest test
scores in the nation. Residents now describe this once somber structure as modern, clean, and beautiful, and its radiant colors remind
some of Gorée Island off Senegal, a point of no return for enslaved
African captives. Habiba and Su'ad positively gushed at the mention
of their old school during my last visit, and over the other impending
improvements in their neighborhood. "You'll see, in a couple of
years, everything's going to be totally fixed, almost like new," said
Habiba, expressing an optimism, in many ways simple hope, about
what they see as home, despite its being so visibly marred by long-
term neglect. Indeed, surrounding this renovated building where
children are schooled are the buildings where they live, which are
still falling apart at the seams and appear not to have been painted
since their erection. Stained by pollution, marked by visible holes,
broken railings, falling shingles, old non-weatherproof windows,
and graffiti, these buildings offer little reason for optimism to those
living within them. Other residents indicated that these improvements hardly compensate for years of neglect, the consequences of

Courtillières, exterior view: poor maintenance of
apartments in the complex. Photograph © Ville de
Pantin (France).

which they continue to endure. Many looked on the changes with
pessimism and suspicion, such as Fatou: "This area still has an image
of being dirty and run-down, and even though things are changing
here, people still think that we're just like this place, dirty, because
we live here. But some people are making it, you know, not a lot, but
some." One of those making it was Fatou's elder sister, a nursing student, who gave me a tour of the neighborhood on my last visit.
When I asked how she felt about the renovations, she remarked,

Courtillières: overview of the complex.
Photograph © Ville de Pantin (France).

Above right: Serpentin, side view: exterior conditions.
Photograph © Ville de Pantin (France).

Below right: Serpentin, side view: exterior conditions.
Photograph by Trica Keaton.

"They really haven't done very much; OK, they've changed the outside, but the problems are deeper than that." And on that tour she pointed out what she and others see as the most egregious aspect of the Courtillières, the building in which she and Fatou grew up, the Serpentin.

Lying at the heart of the complex is this building, the oldest and most imposing in the Courtillières. Reputed to be the longest building in Europe, it comprises nearly eight hundred apartments, of which almost forty are classified uninhabitable. Among the buildings in the complex, it is the most in need of extensive repairs, many of which were identified during a class action lawsuit brought against the city of Paris for mismanagement by a coalition of residents and concerned citizens. Their complaint cited a general lack of maintenance and false billing for phantom repairs, services never provided, and groundskeeping not carried out. Documents showed

Courtillières, exterior: walkway under the Serpentin.
Photograph © Ville de Pantin (France).

that residents had been charged for sand to fill children's sandboxes that never seemed to materialize and for the removal of graffiti on walls with gaping holes and fallen siding and shingles, themselves not repaired. And as the Serpentin encircles a large grassy area, people were supposedly hired to maintain this area, which was all too frequently overgrown, unkempt, and abandoned-looking.

Equally outrageous were charges that the city added to residents' rents to cover increases in water costs due to leaking pipes that the city failed to repair. Though residents continually demanded a hearing from public housing authorities, their written complaints were ignored. The city's attitude changed radically, however, when the regional courts intervened after reviewing some rather alarming evidence suggesting that officials managing the Courtillières had embezzled city funds. One had purchased a Chinese statue worth nearly €5,000 in today's currency, and scores of dinners in upscale restaurants, vacations, and other fiscal anomalies were discovered. Of course, these funds should have gone toward the maintenance of the Courtillières, toward, that is, the homes of the poor and their children.[10]

Visible signs of degradation are everywhere, from the boarded-up windows to the dismantled balconies—relics of former years—to

Courtillières, exterior view: condition of buildings.
Photograph by Trica Keaton.

Courtillières, interior view: entryway of one building in the complex.
Photograph © Ville de Pantin (France).

the walls covered in graffiti inveighing against these pernicious conditions.

The Serpentin is pink on one side and painted pale blue on the other, but both sides are grotesquely stained by grime from air pollution. One side is masked by a tree-lined boulevard that actually makes the area look inviting, until one gets much closer and sees what lies behind those trees. In the architectural miscue of his day, Emile Aillaud, the architect, designed the structure with subterranean cellars that have become breeding grounds for roaches and rodents that find their way into people's homes. When confronted about these problems, local media reported, officials responded, "What good does it serve to exterminate when people don't clean up after themselves?"[11] This attitude not only indicates the general indifference shown to the neighborhood, but also illustrates a lack of knowledge about the people living there. Families are almost fanatical about cleanliness, despite the poor conditions in which they live, something the bleach- and chemical-damaged hands of certain mothers and girls painfully reveal. Such hurtful slights and disparaging assumptions equate poverty with slovenliness as though the first were naturally followed by the second. The truth, however, is that infestation follows from neglect and poor maintenance, for which city officials were responsible.

The broken and loose handrails in poorly lit stairwells are the first dangers one encounters in some buildings, stairwells only refurbished once in forty years. Many of the apartments lack reliable water heaters, and some lack both hot water and heat, in a country where winters are seldom mild. Electrical installations are not up to code, and in some cases wiring has been left exposed in hallways and apartments whose walls are stained with mold and mildew. All of these conditions pose health risks and were cited in the lawsuit. This building is, again, Fatou's and Mariama's home. Although the city of Pantin is already the landlord of nearly two thousand apartments in the complex, it recently fought to take over the management of the buildings controlled by the city of Paris. A major stumbling block was the cost of repairs. That is, the city of Paris was delighted to have Pantin take over the buildings that it had mismanaged, provided that Pantin financed the repairs that years of neglect had made necessary. In addition, Paris also insisted upon retaining the authority to allocate apartments once improvements were made, which could mean a continuation of the same policies that relocated African families to such areas.

After walking the grounds of the *cité*, being invited into the homes of some of my participants, and interviewing or informally speaking with anyone who was willing to talk to the *américaine*, I came to a clearer understanding of this sprawling housing project and its inhabitants. At best, the Courtillières is an example of poor urban planning, being couched between a cemetery (which serves as the backyard for one section of the development) and other economically depressed areas of East Pantin: Bobigny, La Courneuve, and Aubervilliers. Each area is marked by long-term unemployment reaching 20 percent and higher, and these boroughs have similar public housing woes. At worst, living conditions are as a child described them when asked to write about his neighborhood for the now defunct newsletter of his middle school. He entitled the piece "Life."

> I have lived 15 years in Courtillières. Life here is hard. There is unemployment, delinquency, and too much failure in school. I live at [XX] in Courtillières in front of the elementary school. In the hallways the walls are dirty because there is so much graffiti. In my building many people of different origins live together: Moroccans, Algerians, Senegalese, and to finish . . . my family. We are Kabyle. Every day, every weekend, children continually cry and fight on the stairs. My mother does not work, like many mothers in the building, and to fill her day she takes care of my niece and cooks every afternoon. The life I live, I like . . . I was born here and that's how it is. I like my *cité* and that's why I'll stay here all my life.

The ambivalence expressed in this piece reflects both the affection and the scorn that residents seem to have for this neighborhood. On the one hand, it represents an egregious contrast to what they see on television, in the cinema, and in Paris if they venture to the city. On the other hand, it is home; they have known no other. Thus, to reiterate the words of the student above, "that's how it is." In fact, when I used this excerpt as stimulus with participants as a way to invite them to comment on its content, a common response was that it was accurately entitled "*Life.*"

When I visited the homes of my participants, they often immediately pointed out graffiti on the walls and the need for paint and repairs in their buildings. The playground equipment, now broken (some replaced), recalled another time. One student was extremely apologetic about the fact that we had to walk up several flights of stairs to get to her apartment because the elevator in the building was broken. This climb can turn into training for the Olympics when one must carry groceries or other items up and down those stairs. True, I have seen worse, and I too have lived in deplorable housing, even in the center of Paris. Yet the difference is that the living conditions of these and other disadvantaged urban youths in effect circumscribe their options, which are constrained even further by a poor education in a society that venerates degrees and credentials. All of these collectively work against them. Yet these young people are expected to abstract these differences, pass the same national examinations, and become un-angry, model *"citoyens"* like children in more advantaged situations. Again, no one I spoke to could contest the existence of this silent violence. More often than not, it was described as one of the many by-products of the current social woes plaguing France, of which the Courtillières is but an example.

On January 1, 2000, the city of Pantin was officially awarded ownership and control of the buildings formerly managed by public housing authorities in Paris. To inspire a bit of hope among families who have seen hope dashed in the past, some critical repairs were made. Weatherproof windows were recently installed in the Serpentin, and two of its uninhabitable apartments were refurbished (with furniture donated by the upscale Ikea) and displayed as models of what lies in the future. These apartments astonished those who visited them, leaving them with a feeling of awe and optimism, not unlike the reactions of the Courtillières' first inhabitants in the 1950s. But the repairs needed are so extensive and costly that other critical renovations are not expected to begin until 2006, and another winter is fast approaching. Some problems, however, cannot be fixed by hammers and nails. They include broader social problems pertaining to intergenerational economic precariousness and structural exclusion that circumscribe the life opportunities of the poor in general and especially poor people of color, who are also subjected to racism and racialized hostilities. It is these social ills that underpin the indifference toward the decaying material conditions in places like the Courtillières and their effect on residents' total well-being. As a former director of the community center noted,

> Well, first of all, the living conditions are a problem. You see, people are often in apartments that are not adapted to the size of their families. Then there is the problem of unemployment, I don't have the statistics, but I know it's high, especially among the youth. Then there are the problems that are a consequence of the first problem, the environment here: for example, with trying to do homework. We also have a parallel economy that exists in the neighborhood. We have [drug] dealers, and with all of that, we have health problems, school failure, but again, all of this is linked to the very first problem—living conditions—I feel. But the housing problems and housing not adapted to a family's size are due to the housing policies

that bring a disproportionate number of ethnic groups to the neighbor-hood. By that I mean the policy that relocates families to the neighborhood essentially relocates Africans here, which means that sometimes we have exchanges between people that are not so positive. It's not always easy.

Nor is it easy to be a child growing up in these conditions, particularly when there is insufficient space or elevated noise levels in the homes that prevent young people from doing their homework. And while the community center receives a high percentage of the middle and elementary school population each night in its tutorials, there are not always enough tutors to accommodate everyone. For example, Fatou and her sister told me that sometimes they sought refuge in the hallways of their building to study, insisting that this was not unusual for them. Sometimes they stayed at home, since they were "used to the noise." It cannot be ignored that the size of Fatou's household, within these conditions, negatively impacts their schooling, and by extension their life chances. And it is these types of issues that get racialized as African or Muslim, despite numerous examples of African and Muslim households to the contrary. One teacher described the noise problem her students face:

> They have a hard time concentrating; they're always working in noise. It's not only secondary noise—some study wearing a Walkman over their ears —but sometimes they live in conditions at home that aren't always that easy, in particular Muslim girls. When they are the eldest in the family, they have additional responsibilities. Also there isn't always a room where they can study by themselves. And it's true, we expect a great deal of effort from them.

The noise is not only due to the size of the family, even when there are many young children. The sounds of neighbors' daily lives penetrate thinly constructed walls and enter into the homes of all who live in these buildings, making noise also a structural issue.

The center's former director also worried that fundamentalism might take root within the outer-city communities, echoing a general concern of French society. As he explained,

> We have an association here which asked to use a room at the center to have Koranic studies. Well, the board, they reacted, as they should have. Since the center is in a public building, it's secular, which means that we don't allow religious activities here. The board felt that they had to respond quickly to this type of request, especially from such a group, because it could lead to religious fundamentalism. We know that there is a rise of this in the neighborhood. It exists here, but I think it's found a bit everywhere, more or less.

Interestingly, when the city of Pantin surveyed residents of the Courtillières in 2001 in an effort to give them a voice in decisions pertaining to renovations in their neighborhood, more than 60 percent of the seven-hundred-plus respondents indicated that "the creation of worship space for the Muslim community" should be a priority. Though the center is supposed to respond to the needs of the community, and though everyone believes that the largest population in the neighborhood is Muslim, the center, as public space in a secular country, does not permit religious activities. So an abandoned nursery in the Serpentin was recently transformed into a small mosque, and a cellar into a prayer room.

Again, it is difficult to determine accurately just how many people are Muslim in the neighborhood, since this information is not documented by the state. The tendency is to make elevated guesstimates of the Muslim population in France and in the schools. For example, I often heard that more than 80 percent of the student population at one high school in my study was Muslim and Maghrebin. To support this figure, people cited the number of students absent on the day of celebration following Ramadan. But in fact, many non-Muslim students had been invited to friends' homes for the celebration, while others simply did not show up, since this day has become a *de facto* holiday in schools attended by Muslim students. As concern grows over a purported connection between ethnicity and school performance in France, certain schools now unofficially try to determine the ethnic background of their students, usually by categorizing their surnames and certainly their faces (Varro 1992; Poiret 1996). Surnames are not sufficient in themselves, as people from the French Antilles also have French names.

It is essential to reiterate that these youths' national status and lived experiences have been affected by reforms to the naturalization laws, in effect between 1993 and 1998, that permitted the parents of a minor to request French nationality on their child's behalf. Many men who had immigrated from Africa intended, or at least hoped, to eventually return to their country of origin, and some therefore did not seek a status change for their children, not recognizing how useful their being naturalized French citizens might someday be. But their children can encounter a number of problems, including in something as seemingly simple as a school field trip, as a friend of my participants discovered. One day while doing observations, I noticed some of my participants comforting a girl who was crying uncontrollably. As I learned, her hopes of accompanying her classmates on a field trip to Italy were quashed because she did not have French nationality, as she had thought. When the school tried to obtain a visa for her as a national of Côte d'Ivoire, her application was denied. In tears, this student explained that she thought that her parents had already completed all the necessary paperwork for her naturalization. Apparently, this was not the case.

As political scientist Patrick Weil argues (1997), one important reason for having had young people formally declare their desire for and intent to pursue French nationality was to avoid the recurring problem of their not knowing with certainty if they were actually nationals of the country. The paperwork involved has been described as daunting, even in a country famous for its bureaucracy.[12] However, this argument becomes moot in the Courtillières and in French society, where such young people are not perceived as French. Possession of papers stating Frenchness becomes, on the one hand, a form of defense. On the other, it becomes a reminder of outsider status when authorities target certain people because of their "tête" (or appearances) who are forced to prove what they feel should be obvious: that people with their "looks" can be French too.

This mis-recognition is inseparable from the perception of these young people's neighborhood, which a young man of African origin describes in Nicolas Stern's documentary on the Courtillières:

> When you live in the suburbs, you wouldn't even think it's France; you wouldn't even think that we live in Paris. It's another world. Really. Ile de la France [i.e., Paris], I don't see it, really . . . and Paris is only two metro stations away. When you go to Quatre Chemin [one metro stop away], it already starts to deteriorate, and when you go to the Courtillières, you're in another world. It's the zone.

As disheartening as the Courtillières is, it is indeed home to all who live there, especially the young ones, and it subtly fashions the "x" that some articulate as "French of 'x' origin." Perhaps this neighborhood, with its complexities and colors, reminds them of those origins and how important family ties can be in a world in which they must continually battle to prove they are French, or even that they are worthy of civil treatment from those who claim to fear them. All too often ignored is the fact that forms of violence and incivility are not attributable solely to these youths, who are, themselves, the victims of both symbolic and material aggression by the *français-français*. Incidents occur daily, while they are walking down the streets and in service contexts, such as the post office, banks, and even the bakery (*boulangerie*). These incidents go beyond stereotypes of French aloofness or abruptness. As I have seen and experienced, they can be trials of endurance that erode people's levels of tolerance when they are treated so often and so routinely with hostility and rudeness, as a nuisance or an annoyance, and discourteously as a matter of course, as happened often to my participants. I am also reminded of an Algerian colleague (his self-representation) who, when walking on the sidewalks, would systematically descend to the street to yield the path to approaching French people, only to return to the sidewalk after they had passed. "It's a self-imposed conditioning," he said, "to avoid problems and that look of annoyance." Having lived in various parts of France since the mid-1980s I understand that "look" and have often encountered French people who refuse to yield the right of way, which can drive one to the streets, narrow sidewalks and accusations of imagined treatment notwithstanding. In the absence of clear evidence, however, it is difficult to determine whether one's "looks," and the meaning attached to them, decisively and unquestionably play a role in such behavior. Nevertheless, lived experiences have taught racially inferiorized groups that "race" cannot be discounted in such encounters. Not knowing with certainty if treatment is "race"-driven attests to the insidiousness of the social reality of race.

The difference between my colleague and me and these youths is that they are excoriated by politicians, the police, and the media, or are generally demonized and criminalized for exemplifying some of the same behavior and attitudes as the *français-français*, who are not condemned as a group for them. As Su'ad said, "When he [a French person] sees an Arab do something, they say, 'yeah, all Arabs are like that!' And when a French person makes a mistake, it's *a* French person!" For the *français-français* who have been taught to see such young people and their parents as the cause of their own unemployment and a threat to their way of life, it is just a small leap to create and support discriminatory structures that sustain a country's intolerance of difference. Enter places like the Courtillières.

More to the point, how people are taught to see each other has much to do with how they treat one another. Indeed, the expression *Je suis français(e), c'est mon pays* (I'm French; this is my country) is a long-standing shibboleth in France used by a people who were convinced that with time, with segregation, with violence, and with the law—with exclusionary, shifting naturalization legislation—the non-*français-français* would eventually leave. What all have failed to grasp, however, is that the world, including France, belongs to no single people—despite popular perception to the contrary—and the cry of *je suis français(e), c'est mon pays* now opens the gates of fortress France to its children of various African (and Asian) origins: opens the doors, that is, to these "beings perceived." As Jean-Paul Sartre argues in the preface to Frantz Fanon's powerful text on the psychology of colonization, *Les damnées de la terre* (*The Wretched of the Earth*), no one person or people (though he is speaking specifically of Europeans) will ever become more human or righteous through "creating slaves and monsters" out of others (Fanon 1961, 26). Yet rejection and stigma have become convenient weapons against a racialized "other," who must live within the climate of strained nationalism and racism prevailing in France (CNCDH 2000, 2002, 2003). But let us also remember that rejection is painful, however it may be expressed, as is life lived in these conditions, a point poetically captured by a participant in her journal:

> My neighborhood, I love it and I hate it. It makes me happy and sad, and I have so much against it, my poor neighborhood . . . When I was young everything was green and now everything is somber . . . Practically all the boys I grew up with are on the streets, not in school, without work, and some don't know how to read or write. When I was little, they were my friends, we worked together and had fun together, but today, we dare not even speak to each other.

She goes on to write about the glaring transformations to her community that have affected not only the physical structures within which she and others live, but also the emotional well-being of her friends, whose misery motivates her to *s'en sortir*, or "make it," as is often said. But making it depends greatly on succeeding in the national system of education, wherein these youths' self-understandings are also forged. The schools can become critical avenues toward social inclusion and upward mobility, but in the urban outer cities, they amount to an experience of structured inequality. The lived experiences of French-born and -raised youths of color and immigration growing up in places like the Courtillières cannot be entirely understood without considering their connection to the educational system. It is to that subject that I now turn.

3 Transmitting a "Common Culture"

Symbolic Violence Realized

We are told that we are supposed to take children and turn them into citizens. The school is there to make you a citizen, to make you French.
—High school literature teacher

I think that our society has arrived at a point where it seems that our standards for a common culture, so that they harmonize, must go through a de-Christianization, and a de-Islamization, among other things. I mean that this deculturation, or acculturation if you will, can lead to that common cement that binds us.
—High school history teacher

To mold a teacher: can one conceive of a more noble and certain way to contribute to the glory and greatness of the homeland?
—Jules Ferry

The French school is the site *par excellence* of contradictory yet simultaneous movements—cultural assimilation[1] toward the "national identity" and the social reproduction of inequality—both of which are historically rooted in the system of national education. Schooling became a means of bridging cultural and class differences in France to unite a fractured society, and this hinged on the removal of all religious authority from the educational equation, namely the Catholic Church. Championed by the nineteenth-century statesman Jules Ferry, this effort led to the development of secular compulsory schooling whose mission was to transmit a "common culture," understood as both academic knowledge and historically accumulated and embodied ways of being, knowing, and perceiving. This objective is as firmly embraced today as it was at its inception and inheres in contemporary educational policies, discourse, and practices. The transmission of this reified entity is carried out perforce by the purveyors of national education's "common culture" idea, that is, educators at all levels, who are themselves products of this system. Once it has been brought to bear through people, policies, rules, and regulations, the idea of "common culture" becomes a form of symbolic violence, an expression of authority (exercised with the complicity of those subject to it) that goes unrecognized. This chapter describes how the nineteenth-century mission of promulgating a "common culture" remains fundamental to French national education. The French school functions not only to "franco-conform" (enforce conformity to French cultural forms and norms), but also to advance the representation of itself that the nation seeks to preserve: its "national identity." In this analysis, I highlight two foundational academic subjects constituted with that purpose in mind: history and French literature.

Crisis and Culture in French National Education

At the beginning of the 1998 and 1999 academic years, a new generation of disenchanted French students, instructors, and parents took to the streets to protest the appalling inequities and archaic conditions in France's most internationally lauded institution—its system of national education. While smaller strikes and protests continued through the early 2000s, they paled by comparison to the thousands upon thousands of demonstrators in 1998.[2] In scenes reminiscent of the May '68 student revolution and the university student strikes of 1995, the 1998 protestors demanded satisfaction from the state for placing their educational and professional futures in jeopardy. Ultimately, what enraged them most was the realization that they had been fed many empty promises. That is, though national education is vaunted as a great social equalizer in France, the schools reproduce social inequalities, largely because of the failure of the French state to fully democratize education. What has been democratized is educational access rather than life chances; the latter are critically linked to academic tracking and the real and imagined value placed on students' degrees or certifications. While every child in France has the right to a free secondary education, irrespective of nationality, this right is greatly circumscribed for disadvantaged students, who enter into the educational arena already stigmatized by presumed cultural deficits, and they are presorted according to their socioeconomic backgrounds. Once in school they are sorted and selected again, relegated to the most disadvantaged schools in disadvantaged areas, where schooling can be more punitive than productive.

During the course of these strikes and demonstrations, protesters trenchantly described factors contributing to the crisis in French national education. These included inferior facilities at their schools, inadequate resources, crushing course loads, high teacher turnover, low salaries, and the elimination of critical teaching positions even as classroom sizes had doubled and tripled. While the gravity of material conditions differed across schools and districts, a unifying issue among protesters was their rejection of the minister of education's policies, felt to weaken national education's fundamental mission: the transmission of a "common culture." Protestors argued that to reduce, for example, the number of teaching hours in history (i.e., the nation's patrimony), as had been proposed, or in French (the "medium through which values, how people think and behave, are communicated," as Habiba's French teacher characterized it), was to tamper with that mission. And while youths of African origin were highly visible in these strikes and protested vigorously against the inequalities in their schools, they did not raise their collective voices in opposition to the "common mono-culture" woven throughout their schooling. In fact, they did not seem even to consider it an issue. And yet this "common culture" is problematic in an ethnically diverse French society of color distinctions.[3] That is, it references an illusion, termed a "national identity," from which those student demonstrators and their families are excluded owing to their origins and how they are perceived. Hostile to multiculturalism, the French school seeks rather to assimilate youths to the cultural norms and forms of French society (Bleich 1998), an aim that Habiba's literature teacher further explained in the following way:

> We are told that we are supposed to take children and turn them into citizens. The school is there to make you a citizen, to make you French, which means speaking the language and knowing French culture. This is what we try to convey through education.

Addressing this point, sociologist Gérard Noiriel shows in his studies of immigration that the secular school has played a crucial role in re-

Striking students and teachers from Seine-Saint-Denis, protesting against deteriorating conditions in French schools. Photograph by Trica Keaton.

More striking students. Photograph by Trica Keaton.

Surveillance of demonstrators against educational inequality by
French police in riot gear. Photograph by Trica Keaton.

making immigrants into French people, which becomes a condition
of immigration and eventual membership in the society:

> The school was a powerful factor in the abandonment by the children of
> immigrants of their culture of origin; for their generation this stigmatiza-
> tion was a fundamental psychological incentive, which filled them with a
> fierce determination to integrate within French society by ridding them-
> selves of the slightest trace of any difference. (1998, 20)

This process of cultural incorporation occurs, however, less consciously than Noiriel suggests, since the very objective of the French
school is "education in French culture," as political scientist Patrick
Weil aptly conveys:

> The French Republic therefore responds to the requirement for a common
> identity, necessary for the unity of any human group and therefore any
> nation, with symbolic republican values: you are French because you ad-
> here . . . to republican values; those same values which give French citi-
> zens the desire to live together. (1996, 81)

Youths of African origin on the roofs of buildings in a
neighboring borough. Photograph © Pascal Sacleux.

Nonetheless, not all students simply acquiesce in this process. As discussed in chapter 2, those most removed from the educational system are those least likely to succumb to its acculturating forces. Further, rejection and stigma are powerful weapons of persuasion, convincing youths that they do not belong. Aïcha discussed this in her journal, using her sister as an example:

> My sister who was born in Morocco is doing everything in order to be French. But it's not because she's trying to integrate herself into French culture, because we know full well that we could never truly become French.

And yet what Aïcha and others do not realize is that they are already *of* and *in* that culture, itself enriched by their very presence. Yet to teach socially stigmatized children of African or other origins that they are French, only to have this understanding short-circuited once they walk out the school's door and back to their neighborhoods, sends a damaging message to these young people that keeps them constantly teetering between social inclusion and exclusion.

As historian Antoine Prost posits in his analysis of the development of educational reforms in France since 1945, access to schools and success in the educational system depend on understanding how education functions and the explicit and implicit purposes it serves in maintaining class divisions in France. Educational inequalities, homologous to class inequalities, persist in the national educational system, wherein scholastic failures come to be interpreted as "natural intellectual differences . . . The harm resides in the moral attitudes that the school engenders more than in the realities of inequalities: the worst is not that there are the rich and the poor, but that the rich despise the poor" (Prost 1992, 49). And the despised of the despised, according to the CNCDH report on racism and xenophobia, are those identified as "Arab Muslims, blacks, and Jews."

To understand how education reproduces social exclusion and cultural conformity, it is critical to grasp how its concealed purposes interact. As Pierre Bourdieu and Jean Claude Passeron argue (1977), education has three interlocking functions. Its essential function is to impose and inculcate a cultural arbitrary, which it does not produce, by an arbitrary power; its external function is to maintain class divisions through processes of socialization and selection; and its ideological function is to conceal this relationship and to perpetuate social divisions by making them appear normal, thus legitimate. The school works well for those most adapted to its essential function; all (especially those who need the school and its credentials the most) fall prey to its external function, while the entire process is maintained by its ideological function. The social exclusion of the most vulnerable members of the society is the outcome of this entire process of education, and although they resist it, all are ultimately affected by the various forms of violence that these functions engender within French society.

Acceptable progress in the school system is measured not only by the acquisition of knowledge, but additionally by students' capacity to assimilate the dominant behavioral forms and cultural norms that are presented to them as their own. As the literature on the formation of the French nation-state shows, the school serves to incorporate differences in the national interest, because a central aim of the nation-state is to foster a love of the homeland and its culture. The process of incorporation occurs subtly through the day-to-day experience of simply living in a country where values and customs are unconsciously transmitted and assumed. And while culture is a slippery concept subject to multiple interpretations, it is neither static nor coherent, as French national education portrays it. All the same, students are franco-conformed, assisted by the national program that teaches them to be French with the implicit understanding that French culture is superior to the cultures that they are presumed to have.

Through Bourdieu's Lens

In this analysis, I draw frequently on the work of Pierre Bourdieu because he exposes the mechanisms perpetuating multiple forms of domination, and shows how those forms are legitimized through social structures. Moreover, Bourdieu effectively demonstrates that the school, as an extension of the state, is the site for the imposition and elaboration of the dominant culture and its categories of perception. Although he is criticized for being derivative, Bourdieu reminds us that we work through and against existing epistemologies in carrying out the work of social science. That is, as he argues, "you can think with a thinker and against that thinker . . . with Marx and Durkheim against Weber, and vice versa. That's the way science works" (1990a, 48–49). And, as a social scientist, I am particularly drawn to his analysis of symbolic struggles over classifications and representations indicative of identity politics, that become naturalized once they are institutionalized.

Implicit within descriptive classifications of self and "other" are prescriptive understandings of culture, ranked and reified, that mark the distinctions and differences used to maintain social distance or class divisions between human beings, whose selves and opportunities become structured around those categories. The motivations for residential and educational segregation (and separation) exemplify this point: such segregation is driven by a belief that people, measured according to some classificatory scheme, are undesirable or unacceptable, indeed inferior in some way. Bourdieu argues,

> Symbolic struggles are always much more effective (and therefore realistic) . . . The relationship between distributions and representations is both the product and the stake of a permanent struggle between those who, because of the position that they occupy [within power relations], have an interest in subverting them by modifying the classifications in which they are expressed and legitimated, and those who have an interest in perpetuating misrecognition, an alienated cognition that looks at the work through the categories the world imposes, and apprehends the social world as a natural world. (1990b, 140–141)

By the conditions in which this "vision" is ideologically imposed—for example, the family and national education—classifications and categories of identification become perceived as universal or normal, thus "misrecognized," since the forces guiding their use remain largely concealed. But human beings are also "knowing beings," as Bourdieu points out, and thus entirely capable of recognizing these forces and understanding how and toward what ends they operate. Yet ruling ideas permeate our lived understandings and inform our actions, and we overcome them only with difficulty, and often against considerable resistance. As an example, consider the ideology of "race" and the enduring belief that "race" is biological (as opposed to a social construction) or that racial classifications reflect natural differences beyond the discourses that make them so. Already founded on a fiction, these classifications are prescriptive rather than descriptive, but more to the point, they reduce the diversity of humanity to physical differences (real and imagined) that are ultimately posited as the causes of social disparities and inequality between groups that have been racialized. Bourdieu and Passeron reason that "every power which manages to impose meanings and to impose them as legitimate conceals the power relations which are the basis of its force" (1977, 4). Such meanings, when defined in terms of a legitimized culture or dominant cultural representation, thrive through systems of learning where they are made and remade by people *of* and *in* social institutions (teachers, parents, unions, editors and publishers of textbooks, etc.). Such persons, through the *system* of education, become then the purveyors, if not arbiters, of cultural formations that are stakes in relations of power involving those who seek, at varying levels of society, to preserve or transform dominant representations and to whom those formations refer, and to whom they do not. And while cultural formations do not derive from any natural law or universal principle, they are perceived to do so, and are perpetuated through institutions of learning (families, schools, the media, etc.) that shape young people's minds and bodies.

The existence and expectation of standards, both linguistic and behavioral, exemplify this point. As imposed models of cultural correctness that indicate propriety or that one was "well raised" (*bien élevé*) (e.g., accents, pronunciation, syntax, lexicon, and mannerisms), they are expressions of a dominant cultural arbitrary. The imposition of a cultural arbitrary generates, as Bourdieu asserts, its own symbolic effect when its arbitrariness "is never seen in its full truth" by socialized beings (Bourdieu and Passeron 1977, 11). Underpinned by commonsense knowledge that blinds and binds people to this institutionalized understanding, recognition of a cultural arbitrary and its symbolic effects is the first step toward delegitimizing the violence that ranks one way of being above all others in ethnically diverse societies. And while it may appear axiomatic that "French culture" is the content of schooling in France, we must investigate how the monocultural curriculum became legitimized in multiethnic schools, and how this culture became the model to which students of differing origins must, and do, adhere.

Muslim youths of diverse African origins have, nevertheless, effected certain changes in school practice at the micro-level, such as the *de facto* acceptance of their holidays and the relaxing of the test schedule during the fast of Ramadan.[4] Yet very little substantive change has occurred as a result of their presence in French public schools and the schools' occasional accommodation of their ways, despite the opening of one private Islamic high school in Lille in 2003 (the Lycée Averroès). If anything, the system has rigidified, as evinced by policies and the law enforcing secularism in the schools. This law was spurred largely by the aggrandizement of the "Islamic veil" as a symbol of fundamentalism by politicians and the media.

Cultural assimilation remains the means of fostering national unity in France and sustaining a "national identity" that is coming apart at the seams. The national educational program and teaching approaches are geared toward that end, intended to produce a test-passing French citizen, not hybrid variations on this theme. This goal is not readily challenged by a public whose understandings and practices have been shaped by the embedded institutional structures that they reject or defend as French citizens. The national educational system, as an extension of the state, exerts its own symbolic force, through discourses and policies that foster a "common culture." This is in keeping with the long-standing adaptation of the young, beginning often in their early, most impressionable years.

Franco-Conformity and the "Common Culture" Idea

Ideologies are measured by their effectiveness and the degree to which they are apprehended as just or normal. The educational revolution giving rise to the national system of free, compulsory, and secular schooling in France was born of ideologies inspiring a passion for patriotism, national interests, and modernity. The late nineteenth century was an age when ideas of progress and a belief in European cultural superiority exercised tremendous influence over political and social life. Jules Ferry (1832–1893) sought to align French schooling with the ideas of the Enlightenment rearticulated through aspects of Jacobinism. Human reason, rather than religious doctrine, would combat ignorance, superstition, and inequality, forging a prosperous and modern French nation-state in which the school would play an integral role. Implementing those ideas would also necessitate unshackling the French school from the tight reins of the Church and ending its influence over the minds of French citizens (Talbott 1969; Gaillard 1989). Schooling in France had to be both national and entirely secular, reasoned Ferry, who saw the Church as "mental incubators designed to breed anti-republican and anti-modernist ideas" (Wright 1987, 236). The elite and bourgeois statesmen driving this transformation considered the general public unenlightened and not ready for self-rule; national education would become the means of morally and intellectually developing them. It would assimilate and transform the masses into a uniform national culture "without God or King." "Ferry wanted the school to raise generations imbued with the national spirit, citizens invested in the important and noble traditions of the French Revolution" (Guilhaume 1980, 424).

The ideological and political dimensions of these events are extremely important, as national education would not only further national unity on French soil, but it would also play a fundamental role in French colonization. That is, while the school would build "na-

tional unity over the diversity of regional cultures and social conditions in the country" (Guilhaume 1980, 78), it was also intended to
elevate the "inferior races," as Ferry argued when promoting his
colonial policies (Gaillard 1989; Wieviorka 1995). Indeed, in Ferry's
day the idea of "race" was already an established, pervasive social
fact (in the sociological sense of the term), and justified cultural
hegemony and racialized oppression. Implicit, unconscious racialist
thinking fit well with the views of the day as structured by Enlightenment writings. Philosophers of earlier periods who influenced
modernist thinking, such as Voltaire and Kant, viewed non-whites
as inferior even while championing critical reasoning and freedom
(Omi and Winant 1994; Eze 1997; Banton 1977; Bernasconi and
Lott 2000). Moreover, men such as Ferry were very much taken
with Protestantism, Comtian positivism, and a range of ideas cloaked
under the name of science, including the fiction of biological race.
For example, the influential texts of this period included Arthur de
Gobineau's *Essays on the Inequalities of the Human Races* (1853) and
Paul Leroy-Beaulieu's *De la colonisation chez les peuples modernes* (1874),
a text that celebrated colonialism and its economic benefits. Opinions like these helped legitimize increased territorial occupation and
expansion into a number of countries, and in France the principal
architect of this was Jules Ferry.[5]

The influential and well-educated men of Ferry's time believed
firmly that theirs was a modern, industrial society, a democratic society, and a superior society in which the "higher races" were presumed to have the clear and righteous "duty to bring science and
industry to the inferior races and raise them to a higher level of culture" (Wieviorka 1995, 6). Such reasoning legitimized colonization,
dressing it up as social benevolence, when its actual purpose was the
permanent occupation of Africa for capital gains at any cost, including human. By the 1850s, France's infamous policy of assimilation—
its "civilizing mission"—in its occupied territories was well established, assisted by imposed educational institutions that endure to
this day in parts of North and West Africa and the Antilles. Ferry fervently supported this policy, and earnestly pleaded in its favor in the
Chamber of Deputies while defending the economic aspect of his
colonial policies, then under fire:

> Today, as you know, the laws of supply and demand, freedom of trade, the
> effects of speculations, all of this radiates its influence in a circle that ex-
> tends to the ends of the earth. This is a an extremely serious problem, gen-
> tlemen . . . Nothing is more serious . . . and these problems are intimately
> linked to colonial policy . . . We must find markets . . . There is also a sec-

ond point that I wish to address . . . and this is the humanitarian and civilizing aspect to this undertaking . . . The superior races have a right over
the lower races. I repeat that the superior races have a right because it is
their duty. They have the duty to civilize the inferior races. (Gaillard 1989,
540; cf. Robiquet 1893–1898)

This "duty," however, was not merely a colonial policy. It was additionally a national policy according to which the school, as an instrument of the state, would assimilate the masses into French citizens, as the interests of national unity dictated. In addressing the
Deputies of the Assembly in his capacity as minister of public education in France in 1885, Ferry asked,

If the school is education, if it is an important national institution that pro-
poses not to watch over a child in order to teach him to sign his name, but
to shape his soul and his mind for the patriotic and national cause, can it
remain narrowly restricted in a way that, until this moment, you have
considered adequate? (Gaillard 1989, 540)

The state's responsibility to families, indeed to the national family,
was "to raise their children well and make them honest people,"
through schooling (Gaillard 1989, 464). This was to be accomplished
by a finely crafted common-culture curriculum, one intended to
bind young republicans morally and civically to their homeland.
Rather than religious exegesis, it would be scientific methods and ra-
tional thought that would underpin Ferry's national program. So
important was it to him to have national education serve as the
moral compass for young people that he placed great emphasis on
civic education, designed to replace religious instruction, while the
study of language would form the common basis of all education. Of
equal importance would be the study of French history, which, according to Ferry, would demonstrate the grandeur and magnanimity
of the nation. All this would be illustrated in textbooks designed to
develop "a general culture" (Gaillard 1989, 473). In other words, the
Ferryian project was intended to mold the mind, body, and soul of
French and non-French youths alike. This project remains powerful
because its goal is not just the imparting of academic knowledge, but
specifically franco-conformity, designed to level regional and cultural differences. This is as true now as it was during the nineteenth
century. The difference is that today the target population is non-
Catholic.

Scholar Edgar Morin articulates this project in a report to the
Ministry of Education on the state of cultural literacy in France,

highlighting "a need for a culture that integrates the various disciplines and allows children to situate themselves within their human identity, their French identity, and their history" (Morin 1998, 5). Moreover, this point is reiterated in another national study conducted by the Ministry of Education, which emphasized the importance of a "common culture"—"an ensemble of knowledge and know-how . . . an ensemble of cultural information." The report's authors argued that a "common culture" would allow children to make reference to "their history . . . the common culture constructs the constitutive elements of a genuine citizenship. It contributes to social cohesion and participates in the struggle against exclusion" (Comité d'organisation 1999, 5, 7). The state has long battled social exclusion and educational inequality, but what has endured across space and time is the "common culture" ideology and its aim to "franco-conform" everyone who experiences schooling in France. Indeed, heritage shaping and citizenship making are goals not only articulated in the discourse of national education; teachers have also clearly stated that doing so is their role in French society. This view was strongly asserted by Rima's and Naïma's relatively young history teacher, for example. After having taught in an at-risk middle school for several years, he had requested a transfer to their high school, where he believed that he could perform his "social function," as he termed it, more effectively. During an interview, he expressed a common perspective that may shock the proponents of multiculturalism, but that is in perfect keeping with the educational project of conforming young people of non-European origins to the "national identity" and making them into French citizens. Describing himself as "profoundly attached to the values of the French Republic," he advocated a process of "deculturation," as he termed it, through French schooling in order to make the non-*français-français* more French:

> I asked myself, is a common culture, which is transmitted largely by the school and by national education, is it, in fact, deculturing those who have their own culture? Personally, I think the answer is yes. But I'm not sure if it's good or bad. But I believe with all my heart that it's a good thing. It's good because I am profoundly Republican and *laïque* [secular], through my education, through the way I function as a citizen and as a human being in our society. What I'm saying is debatable, but I think that our society has arrived at a point where it seems that our standards for a common culture, so that they harmonize, must go through a de-Christianization, a de-Islamization, among other things. I mean that this deculturation, or acculturation if you will, can lead to that common cement that binds us.

Not all teachers agreed with this view; some felt it was necessary to recognize students' cultures of origin and fuse them with French culture. But deculturation is consistent with the aim of promoting a "common culture." Once institutionalized, it is a formidable weapon in the battle to level rather than embrace differences among young people whose diversity and diverse ways of being are neither understood nor particularly valued. And this is not a new issue, nor one restricted to youth of African origin; the republican school has always sought to level difference, linguistic difference in particular, such as regional languages and accents (Bourdieu 1991; Djité 1992).

To look more deeply into this matter, I asked all participants during interviews what a "common culture" meant to them. Either it was an un-interrogated given or a desired objective, a fundamental purpose of French schooling that they deemed necessary in some way. This is how symbolic violence and power works: through ideological saturation of dominant ideas that structure practices and beliefs toward a specific understanding of reality that goes unquestioned. The power to dominate or absorb a specific group is expressed not always in brute force, but rather in sustaining a legitimized ideology, such as a "common culture," whose existence has yet to be proven beyond the discourses that make it so. Youth who witness (and live) the intergenerational effects of social exclusion, as described in chapter 2, easily see a "common culture," or anything that appears to include them, as socially beneficial, a view that Leïla captured in all its simplicity:

> A common culture is the culture that is shared by everyone, like for all the kids at school. So it's a subject, like history and geography, but it's also a culture that applies to everyone. For me, a common culture is a culture that's open to everyone. And the way I see it, this culture is right for everybody.

In principle, Leïla's understanding has driven "common culture" ideology, but the content of that culture and its person-forming intent is more exclusive than inclusive, and erases more than it embraces differences. On the one hand, as Leïla correctly notes, a "common culture," understood as a shared fund of academic knowledge, was intended to minimize educational inequities amplified by class differences. On the other, presumed cultural differences are leveled in the interest of sustaining a national culture and a national representation. And what is often overlooked is the simple reality that the *français-français* and non-*français-français* do share a cultural foundation and common views, owing largely to French schooling.

To understand, then, this process of incorporation, it is necessary to return to the 1970s in France, a watershed period in French educational policy because of reforms established by the 1975 Haby Law, which reconstituted the middle schools into a comprehensive school, a *collège unique*. In the wake of May '68—the violent student revolution that emerged in response to social and economic disparities within educational structures—the Ministry of Education set out to expand educational opportunities for disadvantaged youth who were failing in secondary education. In the highly selective educational system, youths had previously been assigned to academic tracks geared toward different careers, in keeping with their socioeconomic backgrounds and perceived intellectual capacities. This process meant that students were not exposed to a common core curriculum, the foundation of the Republican school and the engine of national integration (Prost 1992; Cacouault and Oeuvrard 1995). To rectify this problem, ministry officials sought to reestablish this curriculum, considered essential to advancing the "common culture" and to full participation in French society. French literature and language, history, geography, civic education, math, natural sciences, foreign language, art, physical education, and, in high school, philosophy became the content of French schooling, which was carried out by uniformly trained teachers who had experienced a similar education. The tools of their trade would assist in this process, in particular comprehensive textbooks that legitimized France's cultural ideas.

Both the content and the structure of teacher education were essential elements of this scheme. As teacher education was seen as a weak link in the educational system, the Instituts universitaires de formation des maîtres (IUFM; institutes for teacher education) were established by the state in 1989 to consolidate teacher preparation within one national institution. Prior to that point, teachers had come from various universities, where they had had little or no student teaching experience or pedagogical instruction. The IUFM were intended to temper the distance and differences between prospective teachers by providing them a common curriculum within a single teachers' college, thus allowing them to more effectively carry out their "social function," as Rima's and Naïma's history teacher described it.[6] More importantly, the IUFM were believed to be critical to advancing a "common culture" among teachers and thereby their future students.

School reforms during this period were not without their drawbacks, since the ways of being and knowing fostered in the new

French school assumed that incoming students possessed the intellectual and cultural knowledge held by advantaged groups, a fact
that has not changed since. These issues are not unique to the
French context, as they surface in schools where multicultural students with varying levels of preparation find themselves, that is,
schools in which certain cultural forms are elevated while others are
downgraded. As educators often say, communicating the knowledge
and know-how expected by the national program is a daunting task.
This is not because the cultural content of French schooling is deficient or lacking; rather, as Fatou's case illustrates, some of these
educators see the public to whom schooling is directed as deficient.
In fact, educators and non-educators alike frequently claimed that
these young people had cultural, and more specifically language,
deficits. For those who labor in the crisis-stricken French educational system, these deficit arguments become causal explanations
for low student achievement and test scores. This sentiment was
powerfully articulated by a literature teacher who, in voicing the
concerns of others interviewed, explained this problem in the following way:

> In France there is a problem linked to, well, children of Maghrebin de-
> scent. It's our culture; it's Greco-Latin. We, in France, are the heirs of a
> Greek and Latin world; our language stems from Latin and our writers,
> they all were educated to manipulate Latin as easily as Greek, which is
> where our cultural references come from. They're Indo-European. It's
> clear; you need only take the writers of the sixteenth, eighteenth, and
> nineteenth centuries. They were all educated by the Jesuits. Let's be clear
> about this; it's a cultural foundation that is carefully and clearly defined.
> You see, we are in a system that is relatively closed, and only Indo-Euro-
> pean. Therefore, for our students, well, they would rather make reference
> to the Muslim world, and it's not possible because we don't operate in that
> system, and when we tell them that they have to understand *this* system,
> understand *its* values, they think we're making religious propaganda, that
> what we're trying to tell them is cultural propaganda.

This puissant understanding is institutionalized in the educational
system and shared by many, though certainly not all. Yet, as former
students themselves of "a system that is relatively closed" who are
now on the front lines of national education, a number of educational professionals expressed heartfelt agreement with it. More importantly, this understanding, in the French context, is in keeping
with the cultural objectives of schooling.

It is important to note that difference-deficit propositions are not
applied only to Maghrebin (North African) youths; young people

from the "other France" are generally viewed in similar terms, and their language varieties are taken as an immediate indicator that they are more "other" than French, particularly when Frenchness is narrowly conceived. A former assistant principal at the general studies high school clearly articulated this idea during an interview, in discussing how language difficulties derail the full integration of students of African origin into French society:

> The first difficulty is that we require a great deal of written work at the high school level since the *baccalauréat* is a written examination. Our students are not ready for that. The deficit is a deficit at the level of written French. Written! You know, sometimes I have conversations with students, and I'm not shocked by their language. They speak French, even correctly sometimes. But they are not able to write it. It's absolutely necessary because all the qualifying examinations are written. So someone who doesn't master French has little chance of succeeding . . . The first obstacle to integrating in French society, I would say, is educational excellence, because that is also a French tradition.

Although these outcast youths do (and often only) speak French, it is not always the prestige or standard variety, which is then interpreted as a deficiency in the eyes of the educational establishment. Boris Seguin, a teacher at the middle school in the Courtillières, readily acknowledges that language mastery is crucial to academic achievement in France (as elsewhere), and that language difficulties are a major obstacle in schools such as his:

> Language is at the heart of the process of exclusion . . . If many children from the Courtillières are failing academically, it is the duality between their language, spoken at home, and the intellectual language of the school that poses a profound problem for them. So it often happens that I must correct a student for a misused expression, and he responds, "But that's what my father says; he says it like that." How do I suggest to him that his father is wrong? (Seguin and Teillard 1996, 114)

"Some students," said one librarian interviewed, "speak French, but with an accent from the suburbs. It's the language that they use in class. And I don't know if they realize it, but it's not the accent that, well, you hear on television. In any case, it brands them; it shows that they're from the suburbs." Another teacher described this issue the following way: "These students just don't have the same relationship with the culture that French youth have. On the other hand, they are the ones who create libraries in their homes because, as first-generation middle school and high school students, they are often the first ones to bring French literature into their homes, thanks to their textbooks. But, in the beginning, there are just so many cultural gaps." But as another teacher put it, "We need to have common references and knowledge, but for me, a common culture doesn't come from one culture dominating another." Nonetheless, that is exactly what does occur. Maintaining a narrowly defined national culture in multicultural classrooms and societies is a national interest in France, and is done through schooling, the mechanism for franco-conformity. More to the point, these views and aims do not exist independent of the social structures in which they are embedded.

The issue of language, both verbal and written, signifies a great deal in a country where language has been used to construct a nation (as happened in the Revolution of 1789) and dismantle others (as occurred in the nineteenth-century colonial "civilizing missions"). Furthermore, it is important to note that the Académie française has enjoyed a particularly powerful place in the promotion and production of prescriptive language. It is, therefore, unsurprising that the educational system plays a decisive role in legitimizing that standard, which is an integral aspect of nation-state formation:

> The [Jules] Ferry Educational Laws (article 13 and 14) of the early 1880s instituted free, compulsory and secular education—the *école laïque*. French therefore became synonymous not only with education, freedom and equality but also and especially with patriotism. Speaking French became a tangible measure of one's adherence and commitment to the nation. The French language was the monument of the Revolution, the language of the Law and State, and a new equation—"One Nation = One Language"— was put forth. (Djité 1992, 165–166)

To force an institutional recognition of "language varieties" in this context is to miss how much the official or standard language is bundled up with power and perception, and how deviation from the standard is considered tantamount to illiteracy or cultural deficiency in France (Bourdieu 1991). In the U.S. context the "ebonics" controversy clearly illustrates this point.[7] In France, even the country's rich regional linguistic diversity is measured and evaluated against the standard. For example, regional accents and varieties can be the stuff of mockery and ridicule, as I learned upon returning to Paris after having studied in the southwest of France (Pau), where I picked up some of the local accent, as Parisians readily pointed out to me. But my point here is that certain members of the educational establishment view the failure of students such as Fatou to master standard

French as one of many deficits linked to their home cultures, while ignoring the fact that they are also culturally of France.

And while some students need help in French, the issue is ideological and institutional, not cultural. Yet this is not the prevailing understanding among French educators. A teacher interviewed at the vocational school in this study reinforced this point is discussing the importance of standard French to academic and occupational success, an opinion that reveals entrenched value judgments about language and culture as inflexible. At the same time, I must stress that when speaking with her, I sincerely felt that her observations were not intended to disparage students. They are, rather, a reflection of how she has been taught to perceive these young people and their ways of being in relation to what she understands being French to be, or not to be. Her views mirror broader public understandings, frequently heard in French society. They also illustrate the extent to which the belief in a standard language variety (which, in fact, no one truly speaks) is bound up with power and perception:

> These are students from Seine-Saint-Denis. [*Which means?*] Well, it means that they are students who have their own language, well, the language of the *cité* [public housing]. So my role is to make them understand that there is a place where you can speak like that and other places where you must not speak like that, where you cannot. I have to show them continually that they can express themselves, but that they don't have to be taken for a fool, if they speak normally and not like they do in the *cité*. And this is very difficult because they're not aware of it. They let themselves get carried away by their culture. So I have to make them understand that they are not going to find a job if they continue to speak like that. You see, it's not only a question of vocabulary, if you will, it's also a question of attitude, clothing, the way they dress.

As elsewhere, the courts of public opinion will condemn them for speaking in ways that are interpreted as substandard in a linguistic market that has little tolerance for variations on the prescribed language. Certainly, the attempt to eliminate English words from the French language during the late 1980s and 1990s exemplifies another form of this intolerance.

In the remainder of this chapter, I focus on the role played by the official curriculum, canon, and textbooks in French and history classes in the elaboration of the "common culture." As they are closely associated with intellectual culture in France, these subjects powerfully articulate cultural assumptions that remain largely implicit in the process of schooling itself. A striking example is the silences and distortions surrounding the history of colonization, decolonization, and the Algerian War. Further, the representations, contributions, and even presence of people of color and of women were problematic, despite some cosmetic changes, during the period of this study. Moreover, the choice of textbooks by teachers and school officials as well as the actual textbooks that end up in the hands of students derive from the politics of culture and publishing.

The Politics of Textbook Selection

In France as in other countries, textbooks must satisfy Ministry directives that outline the educational canon, policies, and guidelines. While textbooks are not intended to constrain teaching styles and methods, those charged with selecting textbooks are expected to choose books that are "best adapted to the needs, capacities, and interests of [their] students," a policy that seems sound on the surface.[8] However, competing interests, stakes, and strategies exist in the selection process, which is heavily influenced by a range of people and forces that meld national education to the world of textbook publishing (Choppin and Clinkspoor 1993; Choppin 1992). Unlike in certain European countries, where teachers must choose textbooks from state-approved lists, in France school-based committees comprising administrators and teachers have some freedom in that regard. This freedom is, however, relative, influenced by who authors and edits the books that teachers and students come to use in their courses. In keeping with Ministry directives, textbooks are produced and published by fiercely competitive private-sector institutions that vie for the largest market after literary sales, the schools. Often textbooks are embellished with photographs and maps to make them more appealing to this market segment. However, the cost of such enhancements is prohibitive for those presses operating under financial constraints, and for schools having fewer resources. Thus, a common strategy used by publishing houses to gain a competitive edge is to hire school district inspectors as the principal authors and editors of textbooks. District inspectors are appealing not only because they supervise the pedagogical and administrative realms of secondary education, but also because they represent a small population within national education, which heightens their name recognition. The implicit appeal of inspectors as authors and editors lies in one of their other official duties: they also evaluate teachers. In that capacity, they have also been known to lord their authority over textbook selection committees, and some teachers have expressed fears of being sanctioned for not choosing a textbook authored or edited by the person who evaluates them. Though documented and known among educators, this practice essentially remains concealed from the public and persists because of the very power that inspectors wield.[9] This is but one factor at play in the politics of textbook selection, as all other roads lead back to the issue of educational inequalities.

While textbooks are reissued every four years, it is not uncommon to find schools in disadvantaged districts with textbooks that are much older. Two separate, yet interrelated issues arise from this practice. Not only are older textbooks less likely to have cultural references pertaining to students of non-European origins, but students using such texts find themselves competing on national exams with students from more privileged schools and districts who have access to the latest and greatest educational textbooks. In those districts, parents influence the quality and types of textbooks used in such schools. Though committees select textbooks, parents are given a voice in that decision, and when parents belong to powerful parent associations or unions, they can ensure that their children and their schools have all the performance-enhancing materials and books to assist them in preparing for their national exams. It is also in the interest of advantaged schools and districts to ensure that their students perform well on those exams, as a school's reputation and ability to draw a more elite student population are highly influenced by its ranking, which is determined, in part, by test results (a topic to which I'll return).

Educators have decried publishers' practice of reissuing costly texts as "new editions" with only minimal changes, in order to induce schools to purchase expensive books unnecessarily. Moreover, some educators viewed certain texts, particularly in the natural sciences, as so overly complex and technical that a child would need a university degree just to understand the material. Citing this as one of many problems contributing to academic failure and educational inequalities, in 1998 the minister of education, Claude Allègre, announced that a committee would be established to inspect textbooks, which would receive a stamp of approval from the Ministry of Education. Although this idea has not been entirely shelved with the dismissal of Allègre, who was one of the casualties of the strikes and demonstrations of the late 1990s, it is clear that if such a committee were formed, the state would exercise another level of already considerable power to control the content of schooling materials.

Again, some teachers do not strictly follow the textbook recommendations issued by the state, but they are, nevertheless, required to teach the official curriculum in order to prepare students for the national examinations, and these exams refer back to those texts and the cultural canon they presumably embody. Clearly, textbooks are not mere pedagogical tools; they are also political ones, subject to multiple interests (both ideologically and economically driven) whose stakes include young people's minds and what gets presented to them as truth. As historian Alain Choppin argues, in French national education, these works are expected to "transmit a system of values, an ideology, and a culture . . . the traditions, the innovations, indeed the pedagogic utopias of an era" (1992, 20). Within a broader nation-state framework, philosopher Étienne Balibar critiques nineteenth-century ideas upon which national education was founded to show that the French school continues to provide a "privileged space" for "institutionalizing the utopias of citizenship" (2004, 18). Those "utopias" inhere in the "common culture" idea that shapes youths' self-understandings, yet stand in contradiction to the reality of educational inequality. Nonetheless, "teaching the national language and literature [and history] has always helped to diffuse the national idea and develop attachments to France, and this tendency was particularly strong up to the late 1960s," and continues to this day (Bleich 1998, 86).

The Transmission of a "Common Culture": French Literature

"Is the French school, compulsory for all until the age of sixteen, still in a position to transmit [a literary] heritage, this precious element of the common patrimony?" ask researchers Danièle Manesse and Isabelle Grellet (1994, 5). In echoing views held by Jules Ferry and Emile Durkheim (1938/1977), these scholars take the position that "literature contributes to cementing the community," and is fundamental in fostering a "common culture." While this view informed their study, they sought to determine the forces guiding middle school teachers' selection of and tastes in French literature, teachers who taught in both economically advantaged and disadvantaged areas (including one borough in Seine-Saint-Denis). Using surveys and interviews of more than 350 teachers, they examined the degree to which teachers adhered to or deviated from the literary canon outlined in the official curriculum. The canon is an essential guide for teachers, especially those new to the field, and it reflects the traditions of schooling that these teachers themselves have experienced. Further, Manesse and Grellet sought to determine whether teachers' literary selections were influenced by their students' class and ethnic backgrounds. Students' cultural capital figured prominently in this study in light of the greater class distinctions and ethnic diversity in contemporary schools, whose students, these researchers reasoned, are "more deprived of [French] cultural references" than those of a former era (Manesse and Grellet 1994, 22). Manesse and Grellet's study is instructive for its effort to reveal the ideologies that French schooling seeks to transmit.

Is the school still transmitting a French literary heritage? According to Manesse and Grellet, the answer is a resounding yes. That is, they found that 94 percent of the literature used by teachers was by French writers of European descent, reflecting France's literary traditions as outlined in the canon, which consisted almost entirely of French authors. More revealing of identity politics is the fact that teachers selected such authors irrespective of their students' social and cultural origins. Although there is a large body of literature written in French by people from countries once colonized by France, such works were nearly absent from teachers' selections. In fact, only one was mentioned, a classic published in 1953, Camara Laye's *L'enfant noir* (The African child). Between 1985 and 1999 the official canon for French literature, again designed to articulate France's literary heritage and cultural traditions, remained essentially unaltered in the official program, and this has remained true even after the reforms of 2001.

In a separate study of French literature textbooks used at the high school level, researchers frequently noted the glaring lack of "francophone" African writers and writers of African descent as late as the end of 1990, which is as consistent as it is shocking (Fouet 1998; Joubert 2000).[10] Women authors are also so rare as to be almost invisible. When non-European francophone authors are mentioned, a few names recur repeatedly, becoming emblematic of this literature to the exclusion of other voices and faces. So Léopold Senghor, the first president of Senegal, exponent of Negritude, and a member of the Académie française, represents West African experiences; while prizewinning novelist and activist Tahar Ben Jelloum stands in for all literature from the Maghreb. The canon outlined in the official high school curriculum makes the point. Authors to be read in the first year include Montaigne, Corneille, Flaubert, Ionesco, and Malraux; however, only three on the list are women—Colette, Marguerite Duras, and Natalie Sarraute. Further, the curriculum for the second year, which culminates in the national examination in French, lists only one woman writer, Marguerite Yourcenar. Certainly, instructors can choose to include more literature by women and people of non-European origins in their lessons. However, as the curriculum is quite comprehensive, covering a wide range of genres and periods, innovation is difficult, especially since students will be tested on that material. Ultimately, literary culture in France is unequivocally French, concluded Manesse and Grellet: "The middle school continues to overlap the national culture. A very strong tradition encourages it to do so, and teachers' choices clearly reflect the education that they received themselves" (1994, 31). These researchers also found a striking homology between the teachers' sociocultural origins and the complete works that they taught in their classrooms, teachers whom they identified as "French."

As was the case with the CNCDH reports on racism and xenophobia (discussed in chapter 1), these researchers also failed to problematize one of their essential categories—"French." As they did not indicate the ethnic background of the teachers in their study, it is unclear whether some of them are French of non-European origins. The ethnicity of teachers is an interesting dimension; one wonders, for example, whether teachers of African origin or descent are among those adhering to the canon issued by the Ministry of Education and see authors of European origins, to the exclusion of others, as reflecting their heritage. This study does, however, illustrate that the educational system seeks to "franco-conform" students (including teachers, who are former students) through a critical element of national education, French literature.

In those schools where I conducted fieldwork, the majority of the teachers appeared to be of European origin. I asked middle and high school teachers if they taught literature that corresponded to their students' cultures of origin, given the large and visible presence of youths of African origin in their schools. In response, teachers confessed that time and the need to prepare for examinations did not always permit experimentation, which was more feasible at the lower levels of middle and high school when tests were not pending. These findings are borne out by Manesse and Grellet. Yet, interestingly, Manesse and Grellet found that even when test preparation was not an issue, teachers still preferred literature written by authors whose heritage reflected their own, writings that they knew well and felt comfortable using. And make no mistake, preparing students for high-stakes tests whose content draws from the official curriculum is no easy matter. The most life-defining of these exams—the *baccalauréat*—presumes coverage of that material and is also a rite of passage and line of demarcation in French society.

The *Baccalauréat*

People outside of France typically do not fully appreciate the symbolic value of the *baccalauréat* (*bac*) for the French. Initially administered in 1803 to boys and in 1861 to girls, the *bac* is an undeniable sign of academic achievement. Although its value in the job market has decreased, with access to employment increasingly dependent on the possession of higher academic degrees and credentials, there remains, nevertheless, a prestige in having one's *bac*. Without it, career opportunities diminish drastically. More than a mere test, the *bac* is both a diploma, marking the completion of high school studies, and the minimal requirement for enrollment in a university. The examination is grueling and the content has been described as university-level. For example, the math required is often compared to graduate-level studies in engineering, and the history component is nothing short of western civilization. This means all the information covered during one's high school tenure is fair game. Students and their parents fret for days waiting to learn the results, and for many, failing the *bac* carries great shame, though it can be retaken.

The exam includes both written and oral components, so that students must demonstrate factual knowledge while being evaluated for the quality of their arguments that demonstrate their mastery of the cultural, methodological, linguistic, literary, artistic, and historical material on which they are tested. The French component of the exam is given at the end of eleventh grade (*1re*), while the remaining subjects are tested at the end of twelfth grade (*terminale*). While the Ministry of Education has set its sights on an 80 percent pass rate, this goal has only recently been achieved and does not reflect the state of affairs across the nation, or the other forces affecting those scores, such as attrition rates (detailed in chapter 4).

Although the Ministry has encouraged greater leniency in grading the exam, nearly 20 percent of those who take it fail, and for them, employment prospects are limited. As more and more students are passing the *bac*, there exists also the risk that the job market will not be able to absorb the increase in job seekers, or that the exam will be devalued, since the scarcity of the diploma enhances its importance. Yet informed parents and students also understand that the market is credential- and title-driven, so they pay great attention to the various high schools' test scores and the access that they allow to more prestigious universities. Moreover, such parents and students also understand that prolonged studies are often a foregone conclusion, something that delays entry into the job market. Thus, in France, the *bac* represents more than a mere exam; it is most certainly a highly valued French tradition. It is also a form of convertible symbolic capital, especially the most coveted of *bacs*, that is, the one attached to general (non-vocational) studies, the very one that has eluded Fatou. More than this, the *bac* is predicated on the acquisition of "facts" presented as truths, that is, facts and fictions that attest to dominant groups' influence on and control over ideological institutions and the realities they constitute.

Historical Facts and Fictions: Colonizing the Mind and Constituting Memory

The "common culture" idea is nowhere more present and more powerfully experienced by students than in the history curriculum, in which a society's patrimony is presented to young people as their own. History, like French literature, plays a fundamental role in shaping youths' self-understandings by structuring their collective memory of events and facts in a way that contributes to making them French citizens, invested with the ideals of France. In light of the present student diversity in French schools, does French national education continue to fulfill its role, indeed its mission, in that capacity? This question lies at the heart of the two Ministry reports previously mentioned concerning the role of the school in fostering a "common culture," an aim the Ministry considers even more critical in light of that diversity (Morin 1998; Comité d'organisation 1999). In many ways, these reports harken back to views espoused by Ferry, who made the school central to the process of heritage shaping and citizenship making, in which history instruction played a pivotal role. History is

> not merely integration into the complex totality that constitutes the homeland, but [also] fundamental in adapting the children of immigrants to a French identity . . . What does one discover in this history? A progressive Gallicizing force that has endured over several centuries . . . This powerful Gallicizing force, now Republican, facilitated in one century the integration of children of Italians, Poles, Africans, and Portuguese. (Morin 1998, 10)

But what does one discover in this history presented to these youths as their own? What messages are transmitted through this "progressive Gallicizing force," which has also historically taught the children of slavery, colonization, and immigration that their ancestors were Gauls (in the infamous phrase *nos ancêtres les gaulois*)? Some clues lie in the Ministry directives for 2000, which state that the purpose of the history program is "to construct a culture and not merely [have students] accumulate factual knowledge."[11] The broader interest implicit in this goal entails shaping a consciousness of the past that promotes patriotism and a sense of pride in the nation, a patriotism that preserves young peoples' idealism and attachment to their homeland: a seemingly worthwhile objective. History instruction, like French instruction, is a basic constituent element of the culture, conveyed through national education in which textbooks, imbued with their rhetoric of certainty and truth, play an integral role. However, the content of history textbooks has come under fire in France, as has happened in the United States, though the debate is relatively recent by comparison. At issue in France is the problematic treatment of colonization and decolonization in textbooks used at the middle and high school levels, in addition to the impoverished representation of people of varying African origins and women in the presentation of French history itself. The same can be said of the Asian experience, a rich area in need of further excavation. The most polemical and taboo of all subjects is the Algerian War, whose depiction, according to critics, all too frequently amounts to a type of propagandistic campaign of misinformation aimed at perpetuating a feel-good history. However, a feel-good history is essential to the process of franco-conformity, mediated as it is by national education that is designed to "adapt the children of immigrants to a French identity," as stated in the Morin report.

First and foremost, there is a dearth of scholarly studies critiquing the treatment of these topics in French history textbooks, suggesting that they are non-issues for the educational establishment.[12] This throws into sharp relief how privilege and power ensure that a dominant narrative is taken as universal, that one reality is *the* reality, thus the norm. Filling the void are prominent antiracist watch groups (e.g., SOS Racisme and Human Rights Watch) and authors who publish in alternative forums, such as *Le monde diplomatique,* who have written critiques of French history textbooks' silence and implicit messages about African colonization, decolonization, and the Algerian War.[13] While they are neither comprehensive nor officially sanctioned by any governmental body, these analyses shed some light on watersheds in French history that warrant further and continued investigation.

History instruction in French national education has been designed to furnish young people with a foundation of knowledge that
will allow them to understand their contemporary world, according
to the Ministry directives. A traditional pedagogic approach has been
to emphasize chronology (often mirrored in the textbooks and
tests), with an eye toward fostering a broad understanding of the totality of history in relation to the events situated within it. But the
price of breadth is the sacrifice of depth in coverage of significant historical events that could advance the understanding of that totality.
What is ultimately lost in the process is the oft-ignored fact that history itself has its own history, and French history is far more intertwined with a number of African countries and the Caribbean than
the textbooks would lead students to believe.

Historical misrepresentation is not unique to France. Sociologist
James Loewen, in his controversial bestseller *Lies My Teacher Told Me:
Everything Your American History Textbook Got Wrong* (1995), identifies
a number of myths that continue to surface as historical truth in the
teaching of American history in the United States. Loewen's analysis
is instructive because the end results in many countries are quite
similar when it comes to the glaring omission or distortion of pivotal
and critical historical facts from the textbooks, and history instruction in general. That is, the "official" account of history becomes *History* itself and serves to sustain a sanitized version that the realities of
(de)colonization and the Algerian War (or, in the U.S. context, of
slavery, Jim Crow, and the Vietnam War) shatter. In France, nevertheless, a few dirty secrets have been let out of the closet over the
years. "With the arrival of [President François] Mitterrand, we managed to liberate a few historical facts that had been hidden away,"
stated one teacher, who credits Mitterrand with a type of *glasnost*
about taboo issues such as the Algerian War. One must bear in mind
that the war was not explicitly acknowledged in the history curriculum prior to his administration. In fact, it was not until 1986 that the
final high school exam even posed a question about the war's
chronology (Stora 1991, 1999). In other words, it has taken France
nearly forty years to break the silence over what has been called
"the war without a name." In fact, it was not until 1999 that what
occurred between Algeria and France from 1954 to 1962 was officially called a "war." It had been called "a maintenance operation."
This absurd euphemism failed to signify the gravity of human loss
and of the hatred entrenched and unleashed during this period,
which continues to this day. France, like other countries, is not
quick to air its historical dirty laundry or acknowledge its own mis-

conduct. Consider, for example, the anti-Semitic conspiracy against Alfred Dreyfus in the now infamous Dreyfus Affair of the late nineteenth century. Though Dreyfus was innocent of the crime of treason for which he was twice court-martialed, and though he was granted a presidential pardon in 1899, it was not until 1995, nearly a hundred years later, that the French Army publicly declared Dreyfus's innocence and admitted that he had been framed (Cahm 1996).

On a related topic and one that warrants further study, several eighth-grade (*3e*) textbooks published in 2003 (by the Hatier, Hachette, and Delagrave companies) have been denounced publicly for their depictions of the Israeli-Palestinian conflict, which have been described as so decontextualized that their highlighting of violence ultimately invites it. Anti-Muslim and anti-Semitic violence is on the rise in France, and these textbooks are accused of contributing to that violence and discouraging critical thinking about these problems, the very opposite of what textbooks are intended to do.[14] Critiques of middle school textbooks published by the major presses and used in the national curriculum have also noted their deemphasis of slavery, a crucial historical step toward colonization (SOS Racisme 1999).

It is not surprising that France tiptoes around the subject of the Algerian War, an emotionally loaded topic fraught with political intrigue. And it is unsurprising, too, that national education is reluctant to include more than just its veneer in the history curriculum and textbooks. As it stands, the war, and indeed the whole era of colonization and decolonization, are often reduced to chronological blips on a timeline of European history, a history in which women and Africans appear obsequious, secondary, or altogether invisible, despite historical facts to the contrary. The entire process works to colonize the mind and constitute the collective memory of those to whom this history is presented as truth, namely the young. In his passionate and polemical treatise on the politics of language in African literature, *Decolonising the Mind,* scholar and novelist Ngugi Wa Thiong'o (1986) writes that language is culture, a powerful and intimate vehicle that transmits a cultural "identity" in the form of images projected through the written or spoken word. Ngugi underscores the centrality of African languages to the cultural imagery embedded in African literature. I find that his argument is insightful in an analysis of the representation of African colonization and decolonization in history textbooks now used in French schools by the descendants of these twin forces, youths of African origin.

In examining a textbook used by my participants (published by Hatier and intended for eleventh-graders [*1re*]), I found that only about a dozen pages out of more than three hundred are devoted to colonization, and the images depicting it present colonization as devoid of human costs. For example, featured in this text are striking images of paintings that show smiling colonized people gathering their wealth and resources for the colonizers, and these images are buttressed by detailed maps illustrating the expansive French colonial empire that together reinforce the economic defense of colonization more than its violence. Although these images are intended to illustrate the views of that era, they are, nonetheless, powerful and leave students with a false sense of Africans' responses to the occupation of their homelands. Counterimages are available and could have also been included to invoke critical thinking that may not occur in the classroom. In fact, the opening line of the chapter on colonization is "The End of the European World," and this world is described in loaded terms, such as "European supremacy" and "European superiority." Indeed, in this world the continent of Africa is reduced to mere European territories, and this representation, unanalyzed in the text, may remain equally unanalyzed in the classroom. Students are shown no representations of African resistance to colonization or even exposed to the idea that Africans had their own civilizations prior to European occupation. Yet as historians of French colonization acknowledge, the French encountered stiff opposition during the colonial wars, wars not mentioned at all in this textbook. Not mentioned as well are significant African historical figures, such as the renowned Mandinka military leader Samori-Touré (c. 1830–1900), who, with his armies, fought some of the fiercest battles against African partition and French forces in the 1890s. The pitched battles from 1849 through the 1870s against permanent colonial occupation of Algeria are also omitted. The lack of such consequential information in French history textbooks leaves students with the impression that Africans did not seek to defend, nor had any attachments to, their homelands. Worse, it leaves the lingering impression that they had no homelands in the first place. The message continually transmitted to students is one of African inferiority and passivity vis-à-vis French, indeed European, might and magnanimity. Again, such symbolic violence inheres in the identity politics of which these youths are part and parcel, a violence that elevates an idealized Frenchness while downgrading all things African. Reinforced year after year in French schools and society, this message subtly yet assuredly weaves its way into the self-under-

standings of some youth, who learn to shun their origins and succumb to an ideology of French and European supremacy.

This representation of France inheres in the new revisionist view
of colonial history enacted by the February 2005 legislation, which
mandates that school curricula, indeed national education, must
recognize France's "positive role" in the process of colonization.[15]
Documenting colonial history in this fashion also promotes a positive image of France's "civilizing missions," a France presented to
students of diverse origins as their "common culture." The textbook
that I examined was used as late as 1999–2000 in a high school
where students of African origin appear to be the majority.

In its examination of colonization and racism in textbooks that
were released in 1999, SOS Racisme notes a paucity of material devoted to colonization. Further, people of color, when present, were
represented stereotypically and frequently identified in terms of
their national origins. This analysis further notes a lack of women
and people of color in historical themes related to both political and
tertiary sectors. The absence of women in positions of authority or
their objectification in history textbooks has been a long-standing issue in French national education (Rignault and Richert 1997). This
was apparent in certain twelfth grade (*terminale*) textbooks whose final pages are devoted to the biographies and photographs of world
rulers from the nineteenth century to the present. Of the three textbooks that I examined, only one (Nathan) included a woman, Margaret Thatcher.[16] Although there has not been an abundance of
women in such leadership roles, Thatcher is not the only one. More
importantly, what message does this omission convey to girls about
their potential contribution to and leadership in "the world," the expressed focus of the history program? Interestingly, these texts were
released on the educational market during a time when France was
being hailed as more open and multicultural. In some schools, they
may still be in use.

The SOS Racisme study also found that only a few pages of middle school texts were devoted to decolonization. It also noted that
struggles for independence were sanitized, particularly the Algerian
War, as well as the violence suffered by Muslims. In fact, the former
minister of education, Jack Lang, spoke about the need to modify
textbooks to include this topic and atrocities committed by "certain
military officers" and governmental officials.[17] Frequently cited examples include the massacre in the Algerian city of Sétif by the
French military. This pivotal event galvanized Algerian support for
independence, though it is rarely mentioned in French history text-

books. And in light of growing demands to have the French government investigate allegations of war crimes and crimes against humanity committed by the French in Algeria, this part of history becomes all the more relevant for students who are supposed to learn about their "contemporary world."[18]

But this subject, or rather the question of whether and how to teach students about it, is as contentious and conflict-ridden as is the topic of the War itself, or even whether it should be officially called a "war." Moreover, educators feel it unseemly, even repugnant, to expose young students to these heinous aspects of French history, even though history textbooks are rife with other instances of violence and mayhem. For example, the atrocities of the Holocaust are graphically depicted in high school textbooks, even the hangings of the young German resistance fighters Sophie Scholl and her brother Hans in 1943. The difference, however, is that the "bad guys" are not French. And while the textbook published by Nathan, for instance, gives one sentence to the Sétif massacre, it mentions only the 103 Europeans who lost their lives, while saying nothing about the thousands of Algerians killed. "We cannot give credence to the idea that our military systematically behaved disgracefully," stated a politician on the subject (Stora 1999, 133). But it is quite a leap to equate "disgraceful behavior" with mass killing; it is like equating throwing a drink in someone's face with beating and maiming him or her. Students are left with a sanitized history far removed from the reality and complexities of the Algerian War and what it symbolized to the countries involved.

When the textbooks remove the opportunity for students to understand those complexities, they also remove the necessary link between the historical past and the immediate present, those critical issues that would help these young people understand the conditions that led to their presence in France. But no less important are the silences maintained by certain teachers who remain reluctant even to broach the topic. As one bluntly put it, "It's still too early to talk about it." But the war is out of the closet, and its offspring are in French schools and society. After forty years, is it still "too early" to confront in depth this pivotal struggle that led to the demise of the Fourth Republic and to the controversial de Gaulle presidency and the Fifth Republic? In many ways, the subject remains taboo and difficult to discuss in French society, as Laamirie and Le Dain show (Laamirie et al. 1992). Reflective of that difficulty are other factors that contribute to the climate of silence surrounding the Algerian War. For example, while the endings of the world wars are commemorated in France, the end of the Algerian War is not. The war's tragic loss of life goes unacknowledged in the country and in many of the textbooks issued to its young citizens of Algerian and other African origin.

When I asked the participants in my study what they had been taught about the Algerian War, they knew some dates, names, and places, but not very many details, and they added that they never discussed it with their parents. One history teacher who attempts to cover the war in depth explained that he includes it in his lessons precisely because of the silence concerning it in the official curriculum, textbooks, and families of France. But then one faces the problem of what version of events to present, and how romanticized that presentation can be:

> I teach them the true history, but from my perspective also; but, all the same, the true facts. I tell them two things. First that the Algerian people fought for their independence. OK. That's part of the historical evolution of things; it's how it was. I'm clear about that with them. And then I tell them the rest of it. I tell them that the situation in French history at that time was also affecting—really try to follow me—it was also affecting the French people during that period. That is, Algeria was France! I try to make them understand that the French who were in Algeria hadn't just arrived fifteen years ago, that they were born there, them, their parents and their grandparents. And yes, it's true that it was a colonial situation in the beginning. I don't deny that. But what you must understand is the French in Algeria were French people from Algeria, and that it was out of the question for them to be French people from France. It was their land, taken from the Algerians and Muslims. OK, I agree, it was historical theft, but I tell them also to try and understand what happened.

Understanding what happened is not only important, but essential to the learning process, but the Algerian perspective must also be included in that understanding. Otherwise, students are left with a seriously biased historical subjectivity that fails to explain this extremely tension-filled period and the antagonisms and population demographics that the war engendered. Yet including this perspective could impede the assimilation of these youths; they might reject France as a homeland after learning about this chapter in French history.

Historiography is a discursive process, subjective, and often messy when it concerns racialized relations, antagonisms, and moral evaluations of war. But history becomes mere myth when critical information is treated superficially or vacillates between fact and fiction such that "the entire pedagogic arsenal is used to ensure that the students . . . know the least possible about [the Algerian War]" (Maschino 2001, 8). The obfuscation of the war is, however, in keeping with the general treatment of it in the textbooks and in the national program. Another startlingly odd omission is that of the French West Indies, even though discussion of them would be instructive since they remain French territories to this date.

Teaching the "unofficial" history, however, can be daunting in schools where most students are of African origin and the teachers are of European origin, as is typical in the "other France." Teachers who attempt to subvert the program and the images presented in the textbooks should be applauded, because they do so at their own peril, particularly if they are unprepared to respond to students who may ask the difficult questions that teacher training and textbooks fail to address. Among these questions are why Sétif is not discussed while the killing of Europeans by Muslims is highlighted, and why African resistance and women are largely excluded from French history. One new teacher whom I interviewed was well aware that her students might ask difficult questions. She further stressed that as a first-year teacher, she felt uncomfortable deviating from the prescribed curriculum, especially in a classroom where students of African origin were the clear majority. Even her students commented on her nervousness when I asked them about what they had learned about this period. However, judging from my observations, students did not question or contest this curriculum either—especially when a test was in the offing.

At the same time, enormous pressure is placed on teachers to complete the national curriculum, and they may face sanctions for teaching against the textbook. Such teaching can easily be construed as criticism of their school's textbook selection committee and especially of the school district inspectors, who may have written the text in question and who evaluate teachers. If the goal is to assimilate students to a "national identity" through an image of France that inspires patriotism, indeed respect and love of homeland, rather than contempt for their country, then the official history transmitted by the national history curriculum, textbooks, and educational politics effectively works toward that end.

The distortions in history textbooks are not limited to the treatment of colonization. Similar problems appear in the texts' treatment of decolonization, which is a bit more relevant for students of African origin, since many of their parents were directly affected by the struggles for independence from colonial France. Further, the period of decolonization offers them a context for explaining some of the racialized barriers that persist, such as patterned segregation in public housing and the schools (Van Zanten 2001). When I explored the principal textbooks that were to be assigned to my participants during their final year of high school, I found that (with some notable exceptions) the representations and images of decolonization were as problematic as those of colonization.

Further, the contributions of the diverse African conscripts during both world wars, the *tirailleurs,* are absent from the history textbooks beyond archetypical photographs that define the entire contribution of these infantrymen. These men, many of whom were Muslim, who died in service to France and the war effort, remain, for the most part, erased from the textbooks, even though Africans had been serving in the French military as early as the eighteenth century. In fact, historians have documented the participation of hundreds of thousands of African soldiers who died along with French soldiers while fighting in Europe. Historian Myron Echenberg stresses that

> Only France brought about an intense militarization of its African colonies. Only France instituted universal male conscription in peace as well as in war from 1912 until 1960. To be sure, some functional similarities did exist with the colonial units of the British and the Belgians, for instance. All colonial systems have understood the practical advantages of recruiting part of their coercive police and occupation force from among the local population . . . [but] France was the only colonial power to bring Africans by the thousands to the trenches of northeastern Europe in the First World War, and to form a key element in the continental defense of France in the late 1930s. (1991, 4–5)[19]

And while Echenberg acknowledges that Britain used colonial troops as well, he maintains that the British avoided using African conscripts for home defense. The French, asserts Echenberg, "did what other colonial powers dared not do: arm and train large numbers of potentially rebellious colonial subjects," many of them Muslim, who fought and died for a country that had enslaved them (5). French history textbooks either ignore or downplay this integral dimension of French history. Ironically, including it could promote franco-conformity by illustrating to young people that diverse Africans and Muslims fought in defense of the "motherland" that is now their homeland too. But more to the point, excluding this information from the historical texts signifies that it has little or no value in French history, though all the historical evidence of African conscription suggests just the contrary. Further, such an obvious omission seems to contradict one of the key objectives of the history program: again, understanding the contemporary world and a contemporary France, which includes people of African and Asian ancestry. Instead, it aims to structure students' collective memory toward sustaining or preserving France's utopias and ideals. But, as Jules Ferry proclaimed, "if France wants to remain an important country, she must display everywhere that she can her language, her values, her flag, her genius" (Lefeuvre 1997, 32; see also Gaillard 1989). But what values are those, and at what future costs? Certainly, these questions warrant further examination, as I have only scratched the surface of profound social issues. For the moment, these are seemingly irrelevant questions in national education, in which the school remains the most efficient means of promoting a "common culture," even if that sustains national myths. And clearly France is not alone in this construction of history. The treatment of Reconstruction and the Vietnam War in textbooks in the United States are obvious examples (Loewen 1995). Neither is France alone in reproducing other fictions, such as equal educational opportunities. This is the subject to which I now turn.

4

Counterforces

Educational Inequality and Relative Resistance

> When your name is Modoud or something
> like that, it brands you and makes it hard
> to find an internship. It's true. It's difficult,
> but not impossible.
> **—Vocational school teacher**

> When we got to high school, we had to do
> three times the work . . . my grades really
> changed from junior high to high school; it
> was a total change! So I failed the first year.
> **—Naïma**

The French educational system, as I have argued, reproduces social inequality and culturally assimilates outer-city youths of immigration and color in particularly detrimental ways. This chapter examines how schooling operates as a counterforce to assimilation when youths are failing in that system or resist the content of schooling. Indeed, the same school that levels differences also creates it, despite twenty years of affirmative action measures in secondary education and, more recently, in higher education. And while these measures have provided youths in the most disadvantaged schools with some indispensable resources, they have had little impact on those mechanisms that select and sort them toward downward mobility. A critical factor is racialized discrimination, couched in terms of differences and deficits belonging to these youths. As the state does not produce data pertaining to French students' "ethnicity" or national origins, such discrimination is not easily documented. There is, all the same, resistance to the forces of social exclusion. Battling to earn at least minimal certifications is one way to resist, though such battles do not necessarily lead to greater emancipation. In fact, they can have the opposite effect. The same can be said of certain Muslim girls' resistance to the assimilative forces of French schooling, which I explore in relation to two tension-ridden courses: natural sciences and physical education. Although the content of these courses can challenge both fundamental beliefs and modesty, these girls are not without their own resources.

Situated Inequality and the Politics of French Schooling

In chapter 1, I introduced Fatou, one of several representative cases of patterned downward mobility in French national education. Young people like Fatou are conventionally viewed as having cultural deficits that are both inferred from academic failure and used to explain academic failure. In his numerous writings, sociologist Pedro Noguera examines how such presumed deficit arguments become independent explanations of low academic achievement. His insights into the U.S. context accurately apply to France as well:

> explanations for the achievement gap focus on deficiencies among parents and students. Dysfunctional families, lazy and unmotivated students, and the "culture of poverty" in inner-city neighborhoods are all frequently cited as causes of the gap. Left overlooked and unaddressed are the conditions under which children are educated and the quality of schools they attend. (Noguera and Akom 2000, 29)

Extreme disparities continue to plague schooling in France, particularly at the middle school level. These disparities make apparent the external function of schooling: maintaining class divisions through processes of socialization and selection (Broccolichi 1995; Trancart 2000; INSEE 2000; Van Zanten 2001). Two processes working in tandem sustain this function: students are tracked by real and expected ability, which fixes their educational trajectories for the future, and parents and students try to avoid lesser tracks and unsatisfactory schools, particularly in disadvantaged areas such as Seine-Saint-Denis (Broccolichi and Van Zanten 1997). Moreover, teachers in disadvantaged areas find themselves trapped within a proverbial double bind, as sociologist Franck Poupeau describes it in his study of the teacher strikes in Seine-Saint-Denis. That is, they see themselves confronted by a "new public"—youth of non-European origins—and caught between their belief in a system of which they are a product and the lived reality of its failure, between their faith in the values of equality and justice and the repeated observation that they can do nothing to change the system, between their hope for freedom through the school and their feeling that they are ultimately doing nothing more than "policing" or pacifying this "new public." (2001, 83–95)

Affirmative Action *à la française*

In the early 1980s, the state initiated a number of affirmative action policies (*la discrimination positive*), directed at the most disadvantaged districts in the country and its overseas territories. Initially, these policies affected 15 percent of elementary and middle schools in France. Operating under the motto of "giving more to those who have less," the *zones d'éducation prioritaires* (ZEP, priority education zones) were created to target the critical early years of schooling during a period when striking numbers of primary and middle school students were failing in the system. For example, only 26 percent of high school students passed their *bac* at that time.[1] Although there were heated debates about these concerns, the ZEP initiative did not initially encounter the kind of opposition that affirmative action policies did in the U.S., because the sociohistorical context of French affirmative action was drastically different. That is, *la discrimination positive* did not emerge from a civil rights movement, a revolution against the legacies of slavery and the realities of legalized segregation of indigenous peoples and people of African descent. French affirmative action was framed in terms of poverty rather than "race," and thus was not interpreted as "reverse discrimination" because the *français-français* working class benefited from it as well. The ZEP initiative sought to redress "social inequalities by selectively reinforcing educational initiatives in areas (*zones*) where failure rates are the most pronounced . . . and where the social and cultural conditions are an obstacle to the academic advancement of children."[2] By 1999, nearly 18 percent of French schools were ZEP, and more than 30 percent of the middle schools in Pantin's school district were ZEP, compared to 18 to 24 percent of those in the school district that included Paris.

While poverty became a criterion for ZEP classification, a combination of extreme poverty and school violence was held to warrant additional state assistance beyond what was provided through ZEP. A parallel intervention was created, the *réseaux prioritaires* (REP), to promote academic excellence, while schools identified as having critical levels of poverty and violence were classified as *écoles sensibles* and eligible for additional support. While the ZEP, REP, and *écoles sensibles* programs showed some positive returns, they were also sharply criticized for not reaching enough of the public they were intended to benefit. Their failure to do so was one of several factors contributing to the academic failure of the Fatous in the outer cities.

At the beginning of the 2002 academic year, 20 percent of the middle schools in France were classified as ZEP or REP, the programs now combined under the rubric of *education prioritaire* (EP). However, this overall statistic does not reveal the situation at the district level, which highlights the human dimension of the crisis in French national education. In fact, 35 percent of the middle schools in the district that includes Seine-Saint-Denis are EP, the second highest percentage in the nation (after Corsica, 41 percent). For comparison, the figure for Paris is 29 percent. In Seine-Saint-Denis itself, the figure is even more dramatic: 62 percent of middle schools were EP in 2002–2003, according to district figures. At a more local level, all the middle schools in Pantin were classified as ZEP during my fieldwork, and the one attended by my participants was classed as both ZEP and *sensible*.

While these measures have responded to the desperate need for additional resources in disadvantaged districts, determining which schools will receive them can be highly subjective and motivated by interests other than the needs of at-risk students. This proved to be the case at the general high school in my study, whose administrators had decided against accepting ZEP subsidies because of the stigma associated with the ZEP label, a label deemed more subtractive than any benefits gained from additional state support. When the school's reputation and its potential to attract a more desirable student population are the stakes in the politics of education, the decision by these administrators, spearheaded by the principal at that time, is misguided, though not completely unfounded.

A school's reputation reflects upon its administrators and teachers, and can confer considerable prestige when it is stellar. And that reputation is determined officially by test scores and unofficially by the make-up of the student body, whose social and cultural origins translate into their own currency when such origins are non-African and non–working class. On both counts, this school fell short, but the principal reasoned that by trying to improve the former (test scores) he could eventually change the latter (student demographics), thereby restoring the school to the standing it once enjoyed. By all established criteria, this high school qualified for such assistance, and its absence frustrated teachers on the frontlines of a crippled

educational system, as one fervently conveyed in an e-mail correspondence:

> The profession that I'm trained for is science education, but I often feel like
> I'm a social worker in this school, a profession for which I have no train-
> ing. There are considerable money problems at this school that prevent us
> from buying the necessary materials to teach, or to organize school outings
> that would be extremely beneficial to our students and would allow them
> to make connections between textbook and real world knowledge.

The monies that could address some of the problems identified by
this teacher are weighed against the label attached to those funds. In
the final analysis, that label was considered more important. Already, the school is stained by the negative perceptions of Seine-
Saint-Denis and of the neighborhood where it is located, both considered dangerous and overpopulated by "immigrants." However,
middle-class *français-français* live there too. As happens elsewhere,
parents, already armed with information capital, commonly consult
annual Ministry and popular reports ranking schools in order to
avoid schools classified as "low-performing." These rankings are
based on actual and potential *bac* scores, the latter determined by
parents' socioeconomic status (SES) and the demographics of a district and school. Factors such as students' age and the number of foreign students are taken as negatives when both are elevated, something that the ZEP classification amplifies. A teacher summed up the
problem in the following way: "The high school has an unfavorable
reputation, and you have to admit that the area is not particularly
pleasant either. But, what counts, as so many of my colleagues say,
are the test scores!" And indeed the test scores, like a school's reputation, count a great deal in French national education and in the
French collective conscience, factors driving parental strategies aimed
at avoiding ZEP, REP, and *sensible* schools at all costs.

But what these efforts have produced is a ghettoization effect,
resulting in the concentration of disadvantaged students in the most
disadvantaged schools. Moreover, these young people's parents are
typically less aware of how to play this avoidance game: parents, that
is, who may not have experienced schooling themselves and who
may interpret any schooling as good schooling provided that employment expectations are met upon its completion. It is also important to remember that ghettoized schooling can be disadvantaged in
ways other than monetarily. These schools sometimes have high
rates of teacher turnover and absenteeism without substitute instructors taking up the slack, leaving youths fending for themselves

in core courses. And there are real tensions between students and teachers, born of mutual misperceptions and mistrust, which are exacerbated by patterns of inequality and such issues. I am not suggesting that surface incivilities between students and teachers are not an issue, but they are inherent in a dysfunctional educational system that reduces learning to relations of force.

French affirmative action, if properly implemented, could respond to the needs of at-risk youths. However, it cannot address the ideologies underpinning educational inequality, experienced by the poor and outsiders. Ideology, argued Gramsci, is a site of struggle, indeed a battleground over competing versions of reality. As historian John Talbott rightly asserts, "Education has always been an intensely political matter, for to ask who should be educated is to ask who should rule" (1969, viii). The striking homology in France between the captains of power and privilege and the elite schools they attended speaks to this assertion (Bourdieu 1996). In short, French affirmative action can only do so much when there is resistance to or a subversion of these resources, or when the problems are greater than the means to redress them.

Interestingly and unexpectedly, an additional affirmative action experiment is underfoot in France at one of its most elite universities, Sciences Politiques, colloquially called Sciences Po. Students from seven ZEP high schools were recruited to Sciences Po for the 2001 academic year, admitted not on the basis of test scores alone, which were viewed as inadequate predictors of long-term academic potential, but according to more flexible criteria. As one of the architects of this initiative argued, the goal is not to impose "quotas," reflecting an array of "colored faces," but rather to provide access and hopefully opportunities to those traditionally excluded on socioeconomic grounds from the elite institutions of higher learning.[3] But make no mistake, this measure encountered great public opposition and sparked heated debates over questions of merit, which culminated in a lawsuit filed by some students (with their parents' backing) that aimed to prevent these ZEP students from entering the French "Ivy League." Moreover, these students have been denounced as unqualified and as receiving unearned advantages, despite their achievement and progress at Sciences Po. Interestingly, however, the privilege that accrues to those who benefit from a society structured toward their class advantages and origins goes unquestioned. As the students participating in this initiative are predominantly of non-European origins, they risk facing the same backlash and charges of inferiority as their counterparts in the U.S.

They risk, too, internalizing this discourse of inferiority, believing it on some level, which is how it wreaks the most damage. Surviving and succeeding in such institutions is a question not only of access and preparation, but also of acceptance and support within the culture and traditions of the French Ivy League, something that mere access alone does not guarantee. And while the French version of affirmative action is intended to redress rampant inequalities and the attendant social exclusion, the consistent problem that emerges is that the very inequities that national education seeks to eliminate are all too often reinforced and reproduced in other ways. These ways include the sorting and selecting of undesired students away from better schools and opportunities.

Sorting and Selection Practices

Since the 1980s, high school students have not been required to attend a school within their catchment area. One unanticipated result of this policy has been student flight from lower-ranked schools to those reputed to be of higher quality. Such schools find themselves in the enviable position of being able to select students whose profiles correspond with the reputation that school officials endeavor to maintain or elevate. Highly regarded schools can receive, for example, two hundred applications for only a few slots, which activates the supply side of the market, dictating access to more valued or prestigious institutions. To maintain their reputation and rating, school administrators carefully vet applicants in order to identify undesirable students (Broccolichi 1995). Having certain "ethnic" names or addresses in stigmatized areas lends itself to this practice, along with photographs when required. In this way, applicants identified as the "new public" tend to be overwhelmingly rejected by schools catering to parents (some of whom may be teachers) who use all their powers to separate their children from students they see as deficient. In so doing, they contribute to the educational segregation that even they claim to deplore.

Another twist in the selection process has to do with the acceptance of students based on their requests for certain high-prestige courses, courses that disadvantaged schools do not typically offer (e.g., Latin, Greek, or advanced art or music). These courses are understood by informed parents and students to be gatekeeper courses to more distinguished schools and prestigious universities. Such requests have also been used by school officials to reject students who do not meet their student profile, or to explain their practices when their admissions criteria are called into question. In other words, the rejection of a student's application is attributed to the student's inadequate preparation in those subjects rather than, obviously, how the student is perceived. Educational selection becomes, then, another means of perpetuating the system's external and ideological functions, which become lived realities within a school, such as the one attended by my focal participants.

An Outer-City High School in Focus

As one approaches Henri III, the general high school in my study, the first obstacle that one encounters is the security gate and iron fence that encircles the entirety of the school's grounds. This once dormant relic of years past was resurrected by a former principal in response to what he described as "increased violence" in the neighborhood and to prevent "exterior elements" from entering the school. Although the general opinion of the school and neighborhood is negative, students and teachers commonly view Henri III as a relatively calm *lycée*. The security gate is, nevertheless, a symbol of order, control, and security, visibly demonstrating to staff, parents, and students alike that the school grounds are safe, as is everyone within its confines, from any real or imagined danger lurking about the neighborhood.

From the students' perspective, the gate symbolizes yet another barrier to overcome, since entry onto the school grounds often depended on the mood of that day's gatekeeper. On several occasions I observed students locked out of the school when, for legitimate reasons, they returned late from their off-campus physical education class. And on bone-chilling winter mornings students were forced to wait for the first bell outside, where they were subjected to all the elements, rather than in the lobby, as had been the case prior to the reactivation of the security gate. This situation engendered tension between the students and the gatekeeper, which degenerated, at times, into screaming matches that become the stuff of reported youth aggression and incivility. All the same, the gatekeeper ultimately controls access to Henri III, and even I have been mistaken for a student and denied entry. Though the reactivation of the gate was a sign of changing times and of feelings about those changes, the students also saw it as representing a need to control and confine a population deemed dangerous, a need to control and confine *them*.

The gate, in many ways, amplified the already penitentiary-like appearance of the school, which aesthetically lacked much. Inside most classrooms, there were little or no educational accoutrements, such as books, posters, globes, or anything that could enhance the learning environment. The few posters that I saw in classrooms were sometimes tattered and dated and, in some rooms, there was a need for paint and a patching of small holes in the wall. Hung on the walls in the hallways were framed posters of various European countries as well as the school's rules and regulations. However, despite its austerity, the school was kept nearly immaculate by a lively cleaning and maintenance team of people predominantly of African descent who, along with the cafeteria staff and a handful of teachers, were the only visible adults of color in the school. As is the case at the Courtillières, a sense of community existed within these walls, especially within the few comfortable spaces, dwarfed though they were by the school's bareness. These included a makeshift café operated by students and a small student lounge that contained vending machines. Here students socialized and studied between classes, as they also did in the library and in front of the school's entrance. The main artery of social life at the school, however, was the reception area, where students congregated during breaks and at the end of the school day, when access was not restricted. It was here that I could talk with students informally and witness their interactions, which clearly illustrated that they were "typical" teenagers and not monsters in the making. Discussions of fashions, music, boys, homework, teachers, and a number of other topics circulated among students, who often approached me to confirm or dispel stories and information from their television-generated version of "America." That is, I became the one who could tell them if Tupac Shakur was "really dead," since new remixes of his music were on the market, or if one of the many hair relaxers from the U.S. advertised in magazines and billboards in Black Paris "really straightens your hair," a somewhat curious question to ask me since I always had my hair in braids.

Like other schools in the Parisian outer cities, Henri III is a cornucopia of visible diversity, "enriched by 25 nationalities, 20% of which are foreign," according to the 1998–1999 teacher-student handbook. Most of the student population (486 of the 599 students) were classified as French, and this has generally been the case at this high school. In Pantin roughly 80 percent of the students in the public high school were also French, and nearly 86 percent of the high school students in all of Seine-Saint-Denis between 1999 and 2004 were so classified. Again, ethnicity remains a huge unknown in student demographics, and when I attempted to learn which students were "French by acquisition," the statistical division of the Ministry of Education responded, "'French by acquisition' is not a concept that we use . . . a student is French or foreign . . . we do not distinguish them by nationality."[4] Nor did the division generate data on their parents' or grandparents' national origins. However, popular perceptions fill this void. In educational discourse, coded terms are used to imply ethnicity, such as "new public" and "heterogeneous classrooms," connoting disadvantaged students from "dangerous neighborhoods" and/or the presence of youth of non-European origins. Again, this combination becomes lethal when administrators are preoccupied with the school's reputation, as was the case at Henri III when the former principal rejected resources offered through ZEP initiatives. Students had their own opinions on that score. Aïcha noted in her journal, "Our principal is nice, but he wants to make this high school like one in Paris. I don't think that's possible . . . how are we supposed to act like exemplary students when we live and go to school here?"

During its heyday, Henri III was a classical French high school catering to the stable, working-class *français-français,* who, in a phenomenon of "franco-flight," left the neighborhood as immigrants from Africa moved in. The children of these immigrants are not only the majority population in this school, they are also likely to be the majority in vocational studies, and in that track one in two of them is at least two years behind. This means that these students may be older, in an educational structure in which the state is under no obligation to extend their schooling beyond the age of sixteen. Further, Ministry statistics show that their chances of obtaining their *bac* diminish with age. In other words, the chance of passing the *bac* is determined not only by how schools are classified (i.e., their performance ratings and ZEP standing) but also by two other critical factors: a student's socioeconomic origins (implying the presence or absence of cultural capital) and age. The combination of a disadvantaged background and being twenty or more years of age in high school, classified as disadvantaged or at risk, converts into low or no probability of obtaining the *bac.*[5]

As an example, consider Fatou, who in 2004, at nearly twenty-four years of age, was attending a vocational high school in Pantin, where she was attempting to obtain a devalued certification, inferior to a vocational *bac,* itself a stigmatized diploma signifying minimal qualifications suitable only for low-wage labor (Moreau 2003; Lévy 2003; Caillaud 2002). Or Su'ad, who was almost twenty-four years of age as well and held minimal vocational certification. Su'ad's sister, Habiba, who had great potential to pursue higher education, completed one year of college and told me that she did not intend to return. Fatou's sister was completing nursing school in Belgium, and Fatou admired her and aspired to emulate her example. Habiba was working in a secretarial pool, while Rima had been working and studying for a degree in management since completing her *bac.* Others were in college, working, married, or unemployed. Then there are quite different cases: Fatima was completing her law studies at an elite university, while Aïcha was finishing her master's degree in clinical psychology at a less prestigious university while working part time as an aide (*surveillante*) in a high school for at-risk students.

Yet the reality for many students is that even stigmatized schooling is better than none at all, especially when the alternatives are their parents' low-wage occupations or unemployment, unwanted marriage, or a one-way ticket to their parents' home countries. For some, the alternatives are prison or life on the streets. Perseverance and determination to stay in school become instruments of resistance in the hands of such young people, who see their futures dependent on possession of their *bac.* At Henri III, *bac* scores lag significantly behind national figures, and in 2003 only 51 percent of the students passed this critical exam (see table 1). Although national test scores have climbed, and scores at Henri III have spiked upward at times, these figures should be taken with precautions, as they may not reflect improvements in schooling or the superiority of national education. These scores can conceal high attrition rates that remove students from the test-taking population, often early in their educational careers, and who are not part of the test-taking population reflected in those scores. This would include in France the thousands of students who never make it beyond middle school and those who leave high school with no or minimal qualifications.

The class of 1999 at Henri III illustrates at the micro-level what generally happens to underprivileged young people attending disadvantaged schools in France, even though test scores at those schools have supposedly improved over the years. That is, the class of 1999 would have entered Henri III at the beginning of the 1996 school year, at a time when only 57 percent of the students passed their *bac.* After three years of high school, nearly 40 percent of the class of 1999 had never reached the *bac,* and were therefore not reflected in that year's passing rate of 64 percent, already a low figure. The point is that an improvement in test scores can mask what lies behind it, and does not necessarily indicate that a particular school has improved the way it educates its students.

Table 1. Rates of *Baccalauréat* Attainment: France, Paris, Seine-Saint-Denis, Pantin, Henri III (1995–2003)

Year	France	Paris	Seine-St.-Denis	Pantin	Henri III
1995	74%	77%	65%	63%	61%
1996	73%	76%	68%	60%	57%
1997	75%	76%	66%	59%	59%
1998	76%	77%	68%	61%	63%
1999	79%	75%	66%	61%	64%
2000	80%	77%	67%	69%	78%
2001	79%	75%	65%	59%	66%
2002	79%	77%	66%	60%	64%
2003	80%	78%	68%	52%	51%
Average	77%	76%	67%	60%	63%

Sources: Académie de Créteil and DEP.

Left overlooked as well is the fact that such students often fail a grade and repeat it, sometimes several times, or are eliminated from the system altogether. Between the 1995–1996 and 2003–2004 academic years nearly 20 percent of students repeated the first year of high school in Seine-Saint-Denis (compared to nearly 16 percent in Paris). "For the city of Pantin," the DEP emailed me, "we only have students 'behind' in the first year of high school."[6] In actuality, about half of the students who made it to high school in Pantin were at least one year behind, and nearly a third of them were two or more years behind.

And while some struggle to avoid vocational studies, indeed resist the forces of social reproduction, such resistance can also further entrench them in their conditions of exclusion. The cycle of failure and repetition can lead to the very thing they dread: vocational studies or dismissal altogether. Moreover, their resistance does not emancipate them or lead to greater freedom; often it results in their being older students in an age-conscious society of dwindling opportunities. The educational structures, on the contrary, remain intact while purging from their midst undesirable, low-performing students who, in failing or being eliminated from the system, seemingly fulfill a tragic destiny of living the "fate of losers," as discussed in chapter 2.

For those in vocational studies and specifically in vocational schools, attending the university and, more importantly, completing

Table 2. Pantin: Public High School Students in General and
Vocational Studies (School Years 1993–1994 to 1998–1999)

Type	93–94	94–95	95–96	96–97	97–98	98–99
General	878	728	661	663	666	688
Vocational	620	729	828	860	895	919

Source: Académie de Créteil.

Table 3. Pantin: Public High School Students in General and
Vocational Studies (School Years 1999–2000 to 2003–2004)

Type	99–00	00–01	01–02	02–03	03–04
General	734	732	823	894	912
Vocational	893	777	739	751	736

Source: Académie de Créteil.

university-level studies is not impossible in France. Rather, it is unlikely. University studies—perhaps once a dream—were no longer
even contemplated among the young people I interviewed at Su'ad's
vocational high school. The number of high school students placed
in vocational studies in Seine-Saint-Denis increased steadily between 1993 and 2000. In fact, in Pantin between 1994 and 1999,
there was a striking reversal in the number of high school students
in general versus vocational studies (see table 2). Interestingly, this
trend reversed again between 2000 and 2003, when there was a
steady increase in the number of students in general studies and a
decrease in the number in vocational studies (see table 3).

Social promotion policies, decentralization initiatives shifting
decision-making to more local levels, parent's and students' avoidance of vocational studies, and the changing availability of courses in
both tracks help to explain this phenomenon. For a time, it seemed
that conditions had improved at Henri III on a number of levels, as
indicated by the 78 percent success rate on the *bac* in 2000. Compared to previous years, this represents an astounding improvement.
However, according to district records, not all students who showed
up to take the exam were admitted, and some are therefore missing
from the test-taking pool. A common reason given for their non-ad-
mittance was that they did not present acceptable identification.
Moreover, during the very period when the number of students in
general studies in Pantin began to increase, *bac* scores began to plum-

met. At Henri III, they went from 78 percent in 2000 to 51 percent in 2003.

Pantin is not the worst-case scenario. The neighboring borough, Bobigny, has well over half of its high school students in vocational studies, and this proportion is climbing. Moreover, it reflects only those who are still in school. Do keep in mind that, as Maria Vasconcellos argues, "[t]he French educational system, constructed on an intellectualist and elitist model, has always demonstrated a certain disdain for activities manually executed, for the people who carry them out, their social status, and the mentality that they supposedly have" (1993, 64). Moreover, Vasconcellos shows how early tracking often locks students into a near irreversible trajectory that structures their future educational and career opportunities. In 2002, for example, 70 percent of those with a professional *bac* were employed in precarious low-wage service sector jobs (e.g., hairdressing, sales, hotel service, or tourism), and nearly 18 percent were unemployed (DEP 2003).

Once in vocational studies, students of color face additional obstacles when seeking the internships (*stages*) that are required to complete their practicums. Su'ad's accounting teacher, who had more than twenty years of teaching experience, openly discussed the dual forms of discrimination that such youths confront, due to both the stigma of vocational studies and those aspects of their person over which they have no control: their color, their name, and the perceived dubiousness of their membership in French society:

> They live this situation terribly because they've already experienced a double failure . . . In reality, there is a type of hierarchy among schools and subjects. There are the ones that are "noble" and the ones that are less "noble." And so the vocational school is felt to be less "noble" than a classical high school. So these students experience it as a failure . . . And it's true that it's difficult for them. When your name is Modoud or something like that, it brands you and makes it hard to find an internship. It's true. It's difficult, but not impossible. The proof is that they all ultimately find one, and it's just as hard for a black, a white, or a beur. But, with that said, it's even more difficult if you're black or beur. That's certain.

While all students attending the vocational school in my study did ultimately find a *stage,* the students I interviewed, both informally and formally, took it as a matter of course that they would encounter discrimination in the workforce because of their origins and how they are perceived (Simon and Stavo-Debauge 2002). Catherine Raissiguier addresses the issue of workplace racism in her study of identity formation among youths of Algerian origin attending vocational schools in France. She found that such students were discouraged from pursuing studies and internships that would bring them into direct contact with the public: "it was very common for principals not to recruit North African and black students in those sections because they had too many problems finding them internships," a district inspector told her (1994, 101). Aïcha expressed a common sentiment regarding work-related discrimination in her journal: "You have to be a hypocrite in life because honestly if you tell people your origins you won't get hired, that's what you get for being honest."

Long before they make it to the doors of a high school, far too many of these young people have already been written off, as the test scores and theories of deficiency show. The untold story has to do with parents who have had little formal schooling and actively support their children's education. The parents of most of my focal participants do, in fact, fall into this category (the exceptional cases are noted in chapter 5). There are, however, a host of internal factors contributing to their children's failure in French schools, children who are already hamstrung by substandard education and social stigma. Among them are a failure to diagnose students' academic (and emotional) difficulties early and to provide them with organized, sustained, and individualized assistance. Other factors affecting achievement are overcrowded classes in core subjects, and a lack of resources, will, and know-how in treating students who do not respond to a teacher-centered, transmission-response pedagogical approach that requires all students to master the same knowledge at the same time. Moreover, middle school teachers in disadvantaged areas have been accused of inflating grades and oversimplifying material in order to bolster students' self-esteem, or simply help them make it through the year:

> Sometimes, despite our best efforts, we have a tendency to oversimplify material or lower the level. It's a catastrophe because our students end up with grades that don't very often reflect their true level . . . And it's often these students who leave school without their *bac*. It's such a betrayal.

A betrayal it is indeed, especially for students in general studies who may never make it to their *bac*, like Fatou.

Clearly, educational inequality cannot be disconnected from broader social structures, nor disconnected from the living conditions in which these students all too often wither rather than thrive.

Henri III is located in "an entirely urban area where natural land-scapes are almost nonexistent[, in an area whose residents are] poor, unskilled workers, foreigners or descendants of foreigners living in public housing" (Fosset 1991, 168). In these conditions, what has been allowed to fester is the very real anger and frustrations felt by people who are expected to consider themselves fortunate to be allowed to stay in France and have their children attend French schools, even if those schools are substandard. But it is the children who are most affected by these conditions, as it is they who are, by and large, French nationals and who believe that the school represents their only opportunity for a better life. "Today, an education is more and more important in society, and personally I want to have my *bac* so I can attend the university, which will make my life and future a lot easier," wrote Khadija in her journal. After failing her senior year, she ultimately obtained her *bac*, and while she had intended to pursue medical studies, she is now married and lives with her husband in the Courtillières.

In the remainder of this chapter, I examine some of the school-based interventions, designed to disrupt patterns of low academic achievement, that focus on what educators identify as "language handicaps" among outer-city youths. Again, the issue of language is salient in the French schools, where multiculturalism is rejected and where the form of French enshrined by France's language academy is the only accepted or recognized norm. These interventions relate directly to national identity politics in France, because the efforts to better educate youth of African origin are also efforts to better assimilate them, albeit culturally and not structurally. The impact of the affirmative action policies discussed earlier on the upward mobility of at-risk students has yet to be fully assessed. Yet every student who completes her or his terminal exams and enters higher education thanks to these policies embodies resistance to the dictates of social reproduction, to the cyclic perpetuation of exclusion and inequality, though clearly these students are not turning the system on its head. However, these measures have had only a minimal impact at Henri III, where there was resistance to them, resistance by teachers in a system of education in which things either fall apart or fall together. Unfortunately, at Henri III, the former was more the case than the latter. In this section, I also explore certain Muslim girls' reactions to two tension-ridden courses, natural sciences and physical education, that challenged some of their core beliefs and ways of being.

School-Based Interventions

In an effort to respond to students' academic difficulties, school-based plans of action were developed, called *le projet d'établissement,* that focused on basic skills remediation. Despite the noble intent of this measure, it is a challenge for high school teachers constrained by the expectations of the national curriculum, geared as it is toward the national examinations. Through these measures, teachers are expected to redress the prior failings of the educational system, including the social promotion of students to rigorous general studies for which some are not prepared. Naïma, who repeated her first year of high school, captured this dilemma faced by such students: "In junior high [*au collège*], I was with Assia; we were the best students, but when we got to high school, we had to do three times the work. You see. So my grades really changed from junior high to high school; it was a total change! So I failed the first year." In this context, a great deal was expected of teachers, who must educate students and prepare them for critical tests, or face being held accountable both for the students' poor showing on those tests and for the negative effects of their scores on the school's reputation. Further, teachers readily averred that the fundamental difficulties experienced by their students at Henri III required far more than these cosmetic reforms. I heard repeatedly that students were not up to grade level, and high school classes were thus little more than tutoring sessions spent covering material that should have been addressed in middle school. This often meant that teachers could not complete the high school curriculum, which presumes a model student steadily progressing through the system. As one teacher confessed, "I always finish my program when there's the *bac* at the end of the year. But for the tenth-grade students, I don't, because I'm spending a great deal of time teaching them how to work, techniques, etc. So I'm only able to concentrate on the important chapters." And yet such students are likely to be passed on to the next grade, which only compounds their future problems.

Theoretically, the *projet d'établissement* is intended to address the concerns that this teacher raises. That is, this intervention responds to problems that educators at the school identify as responsible for student underachievement. At Henri III, the focus is language, especially written French, believed by teachers to be students' most fundamental problem. As the assistant principal explained it,

> This project is something we've been working on every year, and what we do is put all our emphasis on French, particularly for the students in tenth grade. Why? It speaks for itself, language, whether it's written or spoken. It's an indispensable element because if you can't express yourself correctly, whatever the subject, you're going to be handicapped. So what we ask of all our teachers, from the first trimester and in every subject, is to be very vigilant in correcting their French, misspelled words, etc., and to highlight this in all their work. Everything is very much centered on French, which, for us, puts everyone on the same page.

These efforts were reinforced by in-class work in small groups and by unstructured tutoring sessions provided by aides (*surveillants*) working at the school who were former or current university students, or young men doing their required military service. However, as the assistant principal confessed, this measure, instituted several years ago at Henri III, did not always produce the desired results, especially when teachers disagreed about the causes of students' academic difficulties, or simply refused to participate in the effort altogether:

> Making students work in small groups according to their needs is part of our *projet d'établissement*. It's not revolutionary, but with that said, there is also some important unfinished work to be done because, well, some teachers are reticent, and there are other colleagues who are in full support of our project. But I think that there's still some work remaining on the small group sessions . . . where a teacher can really observe each student's difficulties. It's very important, especially in our district where we have a considerable number of at-risk students. Our goal is to try to address this problem. We try.

This effort is contentious among teachers for a host of reasons having to do with the system of education in France itself. That is, this type of intervention requires a considerable amount of additional work and effort from teachers accustomed to teacher-response-dictation format, a style of pedagogy that they experienced themselves. Moreover, teachers have limited time in which to effectively structure this type of assistance, since their course schedules are already overloaded, and they are under pressure to complete the national curriculum and prepare students for their exams. And while unstructured tutoring was provided in math and French by aides at the school, such people often lack the necessary training to serve students whose difficulties are not rooted in poor test-taking skills or poor study techniques. Rather, the problem is poor prior preparation, itself rooted in social structures of inequality.

Again, students like Fatou speak to this issue, and I saw her face a range of educational difficulties throughout her schooling. When I asked her why she did not seek extra help from tutors more often, she said that they concentrated too much on correcting her verb conjugations, adding, "that's not my problem."[7] As another teacher interviewed at Henri III explained it, the tutoring is not well structured, nor is it mandatory:

> It's a catastrophe. There's help in math and French, but it's voluntary. Teachers propose this option to certain students who meet in small groups of ten or fifteen, maximum. It's not all year, and if their level rises, they can quit. It's all voluntary. But we're not going to impose this on students, either, because if they don't want to do it, then it's not interesting for anyone.

Given that these are high school students who need guidance and who do not always act in their own best interest, it would not be a terrible idea to require and enforce this sort of assistance. The steady failure rates and low student achievement (measured by tests) make it seem unlikely that the current efforts are addressing the difficulties confronting at-risk students. More to the point, the host of issues that these young people come to exemplify reminds us that France has not escaped Bourdieu's and Passeron's verdict—the school remains at the center of social and cultural reproduction despite efforts to disrupt educational inequality and its effects beyond the schools. In many ways, the schools are placed in the impossible position of being expected to solve problems that exceed their capacities. That is, schools in France are expected by the public to correct social issues that a retreating providential state has been equally incapable of addressing. How do schools battle the ideological dimensions of an educational system in which the continued tracking and social segregation of children in schools and neighborhoods persist, indeed are internalized by some as normal, perhaps even acceptable? This, too, is symbolic and material violence. Similarly, the increasing perception that quality schools, jobs, housing, and even "Frenchness" are scarce creates the conditions that expose the virulence and violence of racism, an unpopular topic that some simply disavow altogether. Moreover, the violence of miseducating children is permitted in a national system of learning that turns children into French citizens, even when they are not recognized as such and may not even want to be such. All the same, these youths resist the forces of cultural and social reproduction, but they are also sometimes complicit with them.

Acts of Conflict, Resistance, and Conformity

Often, without being conscious of the impulses guiding her actions, a Muslim girl can experience challenging situations at school in which she is constantly reminded that in order to integrate into French society, she must discard, along with her "veil," any ostentatious symbol or cultural practice that works against her cultural adaptation. That is,

> she finds herself [on the one hand] in a society that requires that she emancipate herself . . . and on the other hand, in a neighborhood where a large part of her life takes place and where her parents and her circle of friends and family demand that she behave chastely, thus preserving the lack of symmetry between women and men in the name of the sacred logic of modesty and of female decency. (Khosrokhavar 1997, 127)

The franco-conformity of these girls may well indeed militate against their upbringing in their home and their self-understanding as Muslims, which, in turn, can be in opposition to the assimilative forces in the school making them French. In many respects, to be Muslim in France and in secular institutions can be a difficult obligation to fulfill, especially when attempting to maintain a cultural equilibrium between expected behavior (e.g., fasting, praying, dressing modestly) and the realities of work and school in which such practices are deemed disruptive or unacceptable in secular public space. This is especially true for those girls who practice or want to publicly display their understanding of Islam. It is they who are placed in an often unfathomable position of sifting through course content, adhering to tasks, or being exposed to information that conflicts with or invites confusion about what they believe is expected of them as both Muslims and French teenage girls in secular schools and societies. In their quest for some common ground between their schools, their neighborhoods, and their homes, these girls can encounter terrific sources of contradictory information, especially since they often turn to their peers for clarity. In schools where trained personnel are lacking to address these issues, the task often, unfairly, falls on teachers, who are equally caught in this stressful situation because they, as representatives of the school's authority, are also expected to enforce the social conformity of all their students, including Muslim girls.

Teachers are, reluctantly, the first people to whom these girls' problems are revealed, because they are the very people whom they see during the majority of their day. Theirs can be an extremely difficult relationship, particularly when their students seek recourse to the Koran, religious authorities, or their parents' teachings to justify their resistance to mandates issued by national education, which, again, the teachers are expected to enforce. The expulsion of headscarf-wearing Muslim girls from the schools (a topic addressed in chapter 5) is a prime example of these tensions. Another is course content that is considered taboo in some of these girls' homes, which prompts them to develop strategies to resist what they are learning or conceal it from their parents and other authority figures in the household, such as their brothers. One example is natural sciences and physical education, required courses in French national education. Keep in mind that these girls do not attend schools segregated by gender, as might have been the case for their parents' generation. Not just the information conveyed in their classes, then, but the co-ed nature of the classes themselves can prove culturally problematic for certain Muslim girls, especially those who desire the knowledge and are expected to be chaste and irreproachable in their deportment around young men and in public places. Natural sciences were controversial because of the topics covered, such as human reproduction and anatomy, and physical education because of the obligation to participate in swimming class.

However, natural science courses were coveted by some girls who hoped to strike a balance between maintaining their customs and understanding their bodies, particularly those who had been taught little to nothing about these subjects, or how to protect themselves if they were sexually active. Students shared, for example, that they had been informed by teachers that the type of fasting expected during Ramadan was detrimental to their health and depleted their energy, thereby jeopardizing their grades. The mere idea that fasting could adversely impact their studies and ultimately their exams frightened some students who struggled with the desire to fast and the need to pass classes in order to obtain their *bac*. Interestingly, officials of the secular school have been forced to recognize this conflict of interests where Muslim students predominate. Some teachers (including at Henri III) have felt compelled to reschedule tests or reduce the intensity and number of assignments during Ramadan and other religious holidays. And while such allowances are the norm in Muslim countries, and in workplaces owned and run by Muslims in France, this cohabitation remains difficult in other public places. These difficulties serve as a constant reminder to the public that Muslims are different, somehow less capable of being integrated into a secular French society. Habiba discussed the differences between France and Algeria, a country that she has only visited during school vacation:

> Well, take Ramadan, for instance: there's no break. We have to work the same as the day before. In Algeria, things slow down. They work less because everyone does Ramadan there and the kids have three days off from school. Three days! And us, we have to go to school. We have to do the same thing as before; it's tiring. Sometimes, though, the teachers don't understand; they give us tests and stuff. And even during the Aïd we have to go to school. There's no break, but we take one anyway. That's the difference.

And take one they do, which forces educators at their schools to take seriously the differences of their Muslim students, differences that never seemed to be an issue prior to their increased presence in the educational system. Teachers have also noted how the contents of their courses affected their Muslim students, especially when they countered popular understandings and myths. For example, one natural sciences teacher related that Muslim girls expressed disbelief upon learning that a woman could be born without her hymen: "They asked questions about the hymen because I really shocked them when I told them that the hymen is not always present, even in a virgin." In traditions that construct systems of honor based on the virginity of women, such information can indeed be troubling. No less disconcerting was the national educational policy instituted in November 1999 that allowed school nurses to dispense the "morning-after pill" to secondary school students on request. Critics contend that this policy undermines existing educational efforts aimed at promoting traditional contraception, arguing further that making emergency contraception available will encourage sexual irresponsibility among adolescents, who might use it as their only means of birth control. Advocates contend that the measure responded to the realities of the more than 10,000 unwanted pregnancies among adolescents each year, of which more than 6,500 end in abortion.[8] These facts make the issue of teen pregnancy an educational one, argued proponents.

Contraception has been available free and without the need for parental consent at family planning centers in France since 1975. Also, the "morning-after pill" is available without a prescription at most pharmacies for a little more than seven euros. It was made available in schools because, as school health counselors pointed out, girls frequently requested information about terminating pregnancies, requests that the schools were ill-equipped to handle. Some Muslim girls and their parents were immediately at odds with this policy, as were a number of Catholic parents. In fact, parents continue to express outrage at the government's policy, which has been interpreted as undermining parental authority and ignoring the family's preferences concerning sex education. Nonetheless, the public school system is a national school system, so those parents and students who are unable to accept its policies are left with few alternatives beyond private or parochial schools. Students both covet and reject this aspect of the "common culture," according to a guidance counselor I interviewed, who told me that they will readily seek information about contraception provided that their request for information remains in strict confidence.

Curricular content is a volatile issue, particularly in the national program, where certain Muslim students find the critical topics of sex education and reproduction difficult to digest in mixed-gender classrooms. Teachers and students alike discussed discomfort experienced by students in viewing videos on human anatomy, learning about contraception, having it readily dispensed in school, or even discussing the importance of women's health. For teens who are not often exposed to this information at home, such lessons can be disarming, if not alarming, as Aïcha explained in her journal:

> The only course that seems to bother me is natural sciences because in this course they teach us how to have sexual relations without having children . . . but I have the impression that I'm different from others. I have the impression that everyone goes to the gynecologist except me. Also, my teacher told us to go regularly to a gynecologist, but my mother is never going to let me. Things like that are for women, not for girls. Sexual relations are forbidden in my family before marriage.

This was no less true for Assia, who considered herself very modest. As with many of the girls, the contradictions in Aïcha's and Assia's opinions about and reactions to the curriculum find their outward expression in their protean self-representations and the ways they seek to reconcile delicate, often loaded, course content with lessons learned outside school. Assia may have a practical outlook on this subject, but her rejection of how it is taught reflects a concern echoed by other Muslim girls interviewed. The issue is not mere embarrassment, but the idea that certain information, especially relating to a girl's sexuality, is outside the school's purview, as she wrote in her journal:

> In my natural sciences class on reproduction, we talked about contraceptive methods, the pill, condoms, etc. It's science, so we should study it. I'm not ashamed of that, but when we have to test the condoms, I think that that's exaggerating things. It's not our teachers who should be teaching that. It will come when it should come.

Assia's parents have had more formal schooling than those of many of my other focal participants, and she also expressed beliefs that women are equal to men intellectually, but not emotionally or physically. She was quick to point out the dissonance between home and school during an interview: "Everything is different here [compared to her parents' upbringing], like the fact that you can go out with a boy and it's accepted here, no problem . . . for a Muslim girl, I've noticed that, that everything is upside down. Everything that we're taught not to do, we do; it's what we're taught, and I'm not sure I like it."

For girls like Aïcha, Khadija, and Assia, the natural sciences class is something they accept and suffer through when tensions emerge between their desire to know the information in their courses and their feelings that such knowledge is tainted, if not strictly taboo. More often than not, such girls develop coping devices or strategies to attenuate the intensity associated with a difficult or uncomfortable situation. As psychologists Carmel Camilleri and Hanna Malewska-Peyre argue, these girls attempt "to consciously separate or suppress painful information or experiences [or] unconsciously repress or suppress the source of [their] anguish" (1990, 123), anguish over, in this case, sexually oriented information.

These girls may use such strategies as not watching certain school films or not challenging the content of their courses to harmonize the conflicting messages they receive from home and school. In the home, such strategies can take on another dimension. That is, for certain Muslim girls even the simple act of doing homework becomes a lesson in skilled negotiation when their families find the content of their courses unacceptable. Such was the case for a teenager that I met early in my fieldwork who came from a very strict home that was made more "unbearable," to use her term, by the abrupt departure of her older sister, who had run away to be with her non-Muslim boyfriend. She also shared with me that even her younger brother began to interfere increasingly in her private life, demanding more frequently to know where and with whom she had been when she did not return directly home from school. In this climate, the seemingly innocuous act of doing her homework only made matters worse:

One time, I had this big problem. I was doing homework from my natural sciences class, it was about sex education, and I had left my work on the table in the dining room. My father saw it and was really upset. [He said,] "But you know all of that!" I didn't know what to say. Now, I hide my work . . . He screamed that we're supposed to learn all of that when we grow up.

When I asked one of the science teachers whether Muslim girls were disturbed by the material in her class or if they ever protested it, she stated that some girls were disturbed by the nudity in a film on human anatomy. Though the film was provided by a gynecologist and is often used in the classroom, it was considered controversial, and some girls and boys found it quite disturbing:

A gynecologist gave it to me. It's a film that he shows himself because he teaches in the schools. He shows it to the students. And it's true, there's a nude man, but it's very short. And yes, you can see his genitals, but it's obscured; it's his anatomy. It's true that they [the Muslim students] talk about it quite a lot.

When I queried students about their reaction to the film to learn if they ever contested the use of such material or made their feelings known to the teacher, they acknowledged that they did not. One student offered a common response: "I never contested it, but when there are scenes like that, I lower my head anyway . . . I was raised like that." It should be mentioned that not all girls interviewed felt this way, and some students found such information both necessary and important because of the simple fact that they do not discuss these issues at home. Clearly, this is true of more than just Muslim girls. One Muslim student even went as far as to give a presentation on her first visit to the gynecologist in order to dispel fears and myths about women's health among her classmates. Yet when parents disapprove of course content or dismiss schooling itself, the entire experience becomes punitive, structured by competing obligations or dueling belief systems. Amina, a teen who enjoyed all forms of science and who had the potential to pursue higher education, personifies this tension. She is also continually placed in the unenviable position of explaining to teachers, peers, and then me why her father throws away her books or prevents her from going to school on occasion:

Since my father didn't go to school, he just doesn't know that what they teach us isn't bad; if it's about the human body and how it functions, it's science. I don't think that God ever said that we shouldn't know that. He's not against it; the proof is that it's He who created us!

Amina's response and experiences typify how these young people have become masters of contradiction and why they must learn
to strike a delicate, often subtle balance between school, society, and
home. Their self-representations and self-understandings are products of this balance. This fact is revealed even in the seemingly banal
act of watching television, which shows that these girls do, in fact,
consciously detach from that which seems to them to be culturally
incompatible, as Camilleri and Malewska-Peyre argue and one of
Aïcha's friends explained:

> We were doing homework from our natural sciences class. It was during
> Ramadan, and on TV there was a boy and girl completely naked. And since
> we were observing Ramadan, well, I didn't want to watch that. I would be
> breaking my Ramadan if I watch those kinds of things; I have to keep my
> thoughts pure.

To contextualize this passage a bit further, it is important to keep in
mind that nudity is permitted on television in France, unlike in the
United States. As I often witnessed, while in the homes of my participants and from my own experiences, watching television in some
Muslim homes in a non-Muslim country carries channel surfing to
new levels, since someone will change the channel at the slightest
hint or anticipation of nudity, or, as my focal participant Rima confessed, "even if there's a little kiss." So normalized has this act become that even girls whose parents are not in the room or even at
home will change the channel at the approach of sexually oriented
scenes. As an older sister of one student stated, "Sometimes you
never see an entire film; you always wonder what happened in certain parts." To lessen the discomfort or embarrassment felt by family
members on such occasions, some families, including those of some
of the students I surveyed, have more than one television in the
home.

If the natural sciences course is the bane of some girls' existence,
the same is also true of physical education, in which certain girls
have developed strategies to avoid participating in gym class when
the required activities conflict with their ways of being. This was especially clear in the case of co-ed swimming classes. Assia wrote in
her journal,

> As far as my gym class is concerned, I do all the sports except swimming
> because I can't show myself in a swimsuit in front of my teacher [who was
> a man]. But that does not prevent me from wearing a swimsuit and shorts
> when I go to the beach in Egypt.

When I asked the school's only woman gym teacher to explain to me the nature of Muslim girls' problem attending swim class, she stated that the heart of the issue is the fact that classes are co-ed:

> The problem with swimming class is, well, the first thing they say is, "Madame, we do *what* with the boys?" That's the first question and then, "Are there going to be boys at the swimming pool?" As I understand it, showing oneself is not permitted for Muslim girls, so the first shock that they have to overcome is hearing, "*Oui*, there will be boys at the swimming pool!"

But these girls are not without recourse where this problem is concerned. As teachers have explained, either the girls do not show up for class or, more often, they obtain medical excuses, exempting them from swimming class altogether. In the classes that I observed, only one Muslim girl actually attended swimming class. Moreover, when I reviewed the stack of medical excuses shown to me by a teacher, they came predominantly from three doctors located in the girls' neighborhood. Many of the students unhesitatingly told me that they would seek this option rather than attend co-ed classes. Although the school did not investigate or challenge these medical excuses, not all teachers agreed with this *de facto* tolerance. In fact, one of the male teachers saw it as an affront to national education:

> In our secular, Republican system, swimming class is expected. The problem, if you will, was not resolved. Not for me. We only sidestepped it. These girls get out of going to PE class, but the issue has not been resolved.

And while this issue has not been resolved, neither has the very delicate problem some girls face in taking showers following gym, when doing so challenges their principles of modesty. Some students noted that the solution was, again, to obtain a medically excused absence. Another was to make it back to the locker room before the teacher, so that "you take a quick wash-up or spray a bit of perfume on yourself," as one student confessed doing. Again, this problem is not unique to Muslim girls, but it, like the others, have been constituted or cast as a "Muslim problem," one specific to Muslim girls in French schools. Unlike the medical excuses, students' avoidance of showers was made a real issue at Henri III, so much so that administrators at the school issued a formal policy requiring students to take showers. Gym teachers were expected to enforce this policy and keep a written record of the students' "shower-participation" in their grade books, as I was shown. Students' refusal to shower thus affects one form of educational capital that they care about a great deal: their grades.

Teachers also mentioned Muslim girls' difficulty participating in gym class when they had their period. The solution to this problem for teachers and school officials was simple: a tampon. This conflicted, however, with the commonly held belief that a tampon "devirginizes" a girl. So firm was this belief among those I spoke with that none of the girls would use them, fearing that the consequences would be too great if they were not virgins on their wedding night. Interestingly, each one could recount tragic stories concerning girls who lost their virginity before marriage and the consequences they suffered, which included everything from beatings to their complete disappearance. For them, the risk of using a tampon was too great, as a teacher explained: "For some, they reject it totally. They say, 'I can't' or 'My parents won't allow it' or 'I couldn't stand it.' It's really a total rejection." Swim class thus became a dramatic issue for some girls who rejected tampons or refused to participate because of their periods. However, for certain girls supported by their families, the solution to such a dilemma was, again, simple: obtain a medically excused absence. The importance of these examples lies in what they reveal about national education and French society's structuring impact on the practices and self-perceptions of these young people. Though they may reject or resist aspects of their schooling and of French society, they equally resist aspects of their home teachings that countervail the "common culture," such as dating and other examples cited in chapter 5. In many ways, their self-representations and self-understandings are catching up to what they already are but are not yet perceived to be: French youth of "x" origin.

If such courses render schooling difficult for certain Muslim girls, they find solace in another, their Arabic class. There, students are not merely learning language, they are being exposed to cultural frames beyond the dry dates and facts typically given (or omitted) in their history course. In this class, the majority of the students excelled academically, having grades well above twelve on a twenty-point scale. In this class, they had that "x" in their self-representations validated in ways that they did not experience either in their other courses or outside of school. However, Arabic is not among the living languages valued in the selection process for higher education in France. Rather, this role is reserved for German and English. But given the high rates of academic failure among these students, this point becomes nearly moot. Language learning is required in French national education and is a highly respected accomplishment in French society. And while the Arabic course is a positive aspect of my participants' schooling and resonates with Muslim students, the forces of national education have yet to offer courses in the languages of its former, non-Arabic-speaking colonies in Africa. It is important to note, however, that Hebrew is among the non-European languages taught in these schools. There are, however, students in French outer-city schools whose home languages are Wolof or Soninké, languages not unknown in France. Validating such languages through national education could have a spill-over effect in the greater society where, for the moment, only European languages have cultural currency in higher education.

Despite these myriad issues faced by these girls, they are expected to conform to what is presented to them as French culture in the schools or risk expulsion, as headscarf-wearing Muslim girls have painfully found out. And while France produces some of the greatest minds in the world from this very educational system, it is clear that others are being thrashed in national education for whom gross inequities persist. The schools attended by outer-city youths are representative of the uglier, less successful face of national education. Nevertheless, some Muslim girls see their schooling in positive terms, especially when they compare their experiences to those of their counterparts in their parents' home countries. Schooling and France itself provide, then, the means for circumventing gendered expectations or opening avenues to possibilities that their mothers may not have known. A non-focal student, quoted below, captured this idea, which was echoed by Habiba during my last visit to Paris:

> Me, I like Morocco, but life over there is a bit like a prison. You know, I see my cousins over there and how they are. I mean, they don't have the right to go out by themselves because that's how it is . . . Here, if you're a girl, you're free, but over there, my cousins tell me it's not like that. I mean they can go out, but only in a group with other cousins because over there, the routine is school, directly home, housework, and when they're fifteen, they start thinking about marriage. Then they're in a hurry to have babies, like my mother. When she was fourteen, she got married, and by the time she was sixteen, she already had a baby, my sister. I don't want to live like that . . . And the girls over there don't like the girls here. They say, "yeah, the girls over there are just like the French . . . they do what they want; they become just like them."

Some teenagers, however, pay a price for being "just like them," or even being perceived as such. On the last leg of this journey, I turn to the more personal worlds of my participants and the issues they face both in and outside the schools, schools in which those who wear the "veil" have been warned to leave it at home.

5

Beyond Identity:

Muslim Girls and the Politics of Their Existence

To be a Muslim girl, for me, only means having a different religion. Otherwise, I'm not any more different than a Christian or a Jewish girl. But it's true that at the family level, and especially at the father level, I can't do the same things as any other girl. For a Muslim girl the only way to get ahead, to show her true worth, is through her studies!
—**High school participant**

I want to be like a French girl—not exactly like a French girl, but I want to be free to do what I want.
—**High school participant**

Female, even feminist, who wants to wear a skirt without being seen as a slut!
—**Louisa, a hip-hop artist from Marseille**[1]

Often I am asked by friends and colleagues how it is that I, someone born and raised in northern Ohio and the granddaughter and daughter of southern Baptists from Tennessee, became involved in a world that seems so far removed from my background. The long answer has much to do with my desire to join what anthropologist Obiagele Lake (1995) refers to as "diaspora Africans." In my case, this meant becoming a part of the mythical Paris of Black American expatriation, a place seemingly far removed from U.S. racism. For the shorter answer, I must take you back toward the future, back that is, to Greece in the early 1990s, where my foray into the world of Muslim girls began with the lived tragedy of a former in-law. I open this chapter with her story because she embodies the very real violence experienced by *certain* Muslim girls who violate gendered expectations in their home.

Her story also provides insights into the strategies these girls use to circumvent and often defy those very expectations. Unlike many of their parents, these teenage girls neither envision nor desire an eventual return *au bled* (to the "old country") beyond short holidays or visits. Certainly my cousin-in-law, whom I call Jamila, did not, nor did the other Muslim girls whom I have subsequently met. Like them, Jamila had expectations of her own, and her self-understanding, like those of the girls I met in France, had been shaped by living in her diaspora and attending schools within a society that challenged the education she was receiving in her home. Indeed, my participants, like Jamila, saw their futures in their Western country, a place they equated with a type of independence and freedom unavailable to their mothers and elder sisters. The politics of their existence derive from a number of opposing forces and interests, and these girls have learned—because of those forces—to manage shrewdly the internal and external constraints imposed by their families, national education, and their communities.

In their attempts to create a zone of comfort and security amidst cultural dissonance and violence, these youths have set their sights on schooling as the surest path to a lifestyle free from gendered constraints, or at least one in which they are attenuated. However, the school also challenges the ways of being and knowing taught to them as Muslims. This chapter examines some of the internal and external constraints operating in their worlds that affect their self-understandings. As I argue, these constraints and expectations are predicated not on religion but rather on patriarchy and hegemonic masculinity expressed as forms of authority, constraints that can degrade into a gendered violence directed at women and girls. These lived realities are forces pushing these youths toward an idealized "national identity" that they rearticulate. Jamila was the first one to invite me into a more private space, so it feels only appropriate to begin this final section with her narrative, which is neither unique nor the worst-case scenario.

Jamila: The Stuff Nightmares Are Made Of

When I first met Jamila, a study of Muslim girls was the farthest thing from my mind. And yet this teenager would come to symbolize and embody every issue confronted by my participants in Paris. Like them, she is Muslim of African origin and was born and raised outside her parents' countries of origin—in her case, in Athens, Greece. And like many of them, she was attempting to live up to competing cultural demands without a great deal of understanding from her family and educators of the difficulty that this requires. Indeed, Jamila seemed to personify all the pains of being a teenage girl whose youth, intelligence, and beauty proved to be more handicaps than assets in a life that seemed to hold little promise for a happy ending. In the early 1990s I was invited into her life, and since then I have been searching for a way to keep a promise to this enlightened Muslim girl of Egyptian-Sudanese origin, who began our first private conversation one evening with the pointed question, "Trica, do they cut girls in your country?"

In giving form to these words, I hear her mirthless voice, and I see her brown face, dwarfed by the thick pearl-rimmed glasses that she used to wear. These glasses tended to give her eyes a Bambi-in-the-headlights look whenever she was surprised or afraid, or even when she smiled. On that night in Athens she was not smiling, nor did she believe me when I ignorantly responded "no" to her perceptive question. Only later would I learn just how many girls in the U.S. suffer excision or infibulation, commonly referred to in the West as "genital mutilation" or "female circumcision," a practice banned in a number of countries.[2] However, this bodily violation was not the most pressing of Jamila's concerns. Simple survival coupled with her expressed desire to finish her studies preoccupied this multilingual and multilayered young woman who wanted nothing more than to be whisked away, far away, from her abusive brother and what had become a life of domestic servitude in her home. Looming over her was an inevitable return to Egypt, where she feared that a marriage had been arranged for her with a man she did not know. She also dreaded returning to a country that was a sad reminder of her deceased mother, whom she described as a friend, a best friend, to whom she had confided her most personal and secret thoughts.

Jamila's life had changed drastically following the mysterious death of her mother a year prior to my arrival on the scene. This vibrant and extremely beautiful woman, whose portrait adorned a wall of the main living room, had died from what everyone commonly referred to as a fatal "microbe" while still in her summer years. Jamila believed, however, that the "microbe" was somehow her father's hand, though she had no evidence to support her claim other than the domestic violence that she witnessed and suffered in silence.

When I first met Jamila, she was only sixteen years old, though of marriageable age, as her father was known to say. At that time, I had just returned from a two-month stay in the Greek islands with my then husband, a man whom Jamila seemed to adore and around whom she displayed a certain lightness and affection. This happy mood, however, would quickly evaporate around her eldest brother, the only son of her father's first wife, a Sudanese woman who lived in Egypt. Mehdi was in his twenties, and was as somber as he was circumspect. And for reasons that only he knew, he wore a constant, intimidating scowl on his face, which was matched in its intensity by a stern, even voice that would issue orders to a frightened Jamila, who jumped to attention when he entered the room. Their father, incapacitated by alcoholism and dismissed from his prestigious job, no longer dominated the household. That role had been taken over by Mehdi, who kept close rein on the other four children and laid down strict rules of conduct for them. Yet one evening Jamila and I were left alone, and little did her family know that she was waiting for that moment to share her story, which began with the question about excision and infibulation and ended with further violence.

Jamila had been beaten, severely beaten, by her brother Mehdi not long before my arrival, and with a surprising detachment she recounted how between blows Mehdi had cut her long black tresses with a knife. She described how he accused her of all manner of immorality that only a woman or girl is presumed to commit. When he left her room, Jamila believed that the beating was over, but the abuse did not end there, and worse was yet to come. That brief respite turned out to be nothing more than the time Mehdi needed to fire up the stove's burners, on which he placed a knife. When it was searing hot he returned with it to Jamila's room, held her down, and, amidst her screams, proceeded to burn her with the blade up and down her legs. She showed me the blackened, angular scars that marred what had been the flawless limbs of a sixteen-year-old girl, legs that conveyed a clear message to anyone who saw them. Like a neon sign flashing out a warning, those marks, even hidden by her long skirts, signaled that this girl had transgressed the rules and been dealt with. After calmly describing what had happened to her, Jamila then explained why she cared so deeply for my then husband. It was he who had pulled Mehdi off of her, perhaps preventing him from going still further, taking some incomprehensible extra step. What was her crime? What awful violation had Jamila committed to provoke such rage? She had been accused of sitting in a café in the company of a boy one day after school.

After telling me this story, Jamila added later that she was going to be sent back to Egypt, and feared that this meant an arranged marriage. She also spoke of her fears concerning "the wedding night" and told me that she and other friends were worried about a girl in their entourage who was to be married that summer. As a child, their friend had apparently undergone a pharaonic infibulation, a painful procedure that entails removing the clitoris along with much of the inner labia. The outer labia are sewn nearly shut, leaving only a small opening for menses and urine. It was the pain that she and her friends dreaded on "the wedding night," having heard that "it" hurts a great deal and that there would be a lot of blood. Her descriptions were so detailed that it seemed that the friend about whom she was speaking was actually she, but I had no tangible proof to confirm this suspicion. Ultimately, Jamila wanted me to clarify these facts; sadly, at the time, I could not.

Jamila's story eventually led me to the Somalian filmmaker Soraya Mire, who vividly depicts this reality in her acclaimed film *Fire Eyes,* a documentary about infibulation. Soraya described herself as a survivor of genital mutilation, having experienced it firsthand without anesthetic, its aftereffects, and the consequences of having this procedure reversed. When I interviewed her at her California home in 1994, she described in sharp and accurate detail why women who have been infibulated fear and loathe their wedding night, or often sex in general. She also explained why she entitled her documentary *Fire Eyes:*

> It's like fire coming out through her eyes. You just want to kill him if you can. A lot of women are hitting or refusing him or running away from him . . . You're happy if your husband doesn't ask you to sleep with him, even if you've been opened and you have a child. You just pray he won't come for you. You don't want it. It's always painful.

I am continually reminded of just how far removed I am from what Jamila and Soraya had to undergo. I had nothing to equate with Jamila's (or her friend's) experience, and no words of solace to offer this woman-child who seemed to have seen more in her life than I, though I was older. Jamila explained that hers was a life of seclusion and fear, and her only moments of liberty and freedom were at school. At school, she could lose herself in her studies, pretend that she was one of the characters in her books, embarking on journeys and adventures. But after her beating, even this pleasure was taken away, since she was forbidden to show her face in the community because of the shame she had brought to the family. Only after some time was she allowed to resume her studies, and then she learned that arrangements had been made to send her and her brothers back to Egypt.

Upon hearing this story, I wanted to immediately confirm it with my husband, though the scars on her legs already bespoke volumes. Her brother, who had always treated me with respect and kindness, became a sort of twisted monster in my eyes, and whatever family feeling I might have had for him was extinguished with each word from Jamila's mouth. More than anything, after hearing her story, I wanted to confront Mehdi and demand an explanation for what can only be described as a vicious, brutal act designed to rob this young girl of her dignity and humanity. The legitimacy of the act derives from expectations subjectively interpreted through a faulty lens, as Nawal El Saadawi, an Egyptian scholar and human rights advocate, has demonstrated in her writings over the years.

While I was prepared to go to battle in Jamila's defense, she reminded me that she, not I, would pay the price for such defiance. For me to confront her brother, or any man in her family, could expose her to further physical abuse, and though they might pretend to agree with whatever points I could make in Jamila's favor, the truth of the matter was that she had violated a code of secrecy by revealing the family's private affairs to an outsider. The expectation of silence and secrecy is tremendously powerful, as was illustrated by the case of Hawa Gréou, a Malian woman living in France who in 1999 was sentenced to eight years in prison for excising forty-eight girls between 1983 and 1994. The girls' parents received three-to-five-year suspended sentences. Like Jamila, these girls were bound to secrecy by their families, not solely because the act is illegal, but additionally because they consider it a practice internal to their ways of being, that outsiders do not understand. The plaintiff was one of the excised girls who broke the vow of silence by publicly denouncing her parents and Madame Gréou. In their defense, the parents and Madame Gréou argued that excision is a common practice in their traditions, not a criminal one. The court did not agree, and the severity of the penalty sent a shock wave through immigrant communities.[3]

As I would later learn from my participants, by keeping Jamila's secret, I demonstrated that I could be trusted. But earning this trust and keeping that secret weighed heavily upon my sense of justice. For months I kept silent, not mentioning what had happened to her to anyone, including my then husband. And eventually she opened more widely the door to the most private spaces of her life. The most astounding revelation, and the most dangerous, was that she had

On October 4, 2003, a plaque was placed on the tomb of Simone de
Beauvoir and Jean-Paul Sartre in memory of the slain teenager
Sohane Benziane. It reads, "In memory of Sohane, burnt to death,
so that boys and girls may live together in equality and [mutual]
respect. Sohane Benziane, 1984–2002." Photograph by Trica Keaton.

met a boy at school, someone for whom she had great affection, and
about whom she talked in the romantic ways that teenage girls often
do when smitten by a boy's smile. She went on to confess that she
had gone as far as to allow him to surreptitiously slip love letters and
candies through her bedroom window, thanks to a code the two had
developed to signal when the coast was clear, that is, when Jamila's
brothers were not at home. I often wondered if this boy knew that
he was jeopardizing her life with these gestures. The consequences
could have been terrible, given what she had already experienced.

Ultimately, Jamila was returned to Egypt, but by a stroke of luck,
she was sent to her mother's family rather than to some unknown
prospective husband, as had been threatened. And for my sake,
Jamila released me from my vow of silence, asking only that I wait
until she was in Egypt before confronting everyone with what she
had shared. Once she was back with her grandmother and aunts,
who apparently had no love for Jamila's father, I would have the lib-

erty to divulge all. When I learned that Jamila and her brothers had arrived there safely, I felt a strange mixture of relief, freedom, and loss. Her telephone call was my cue that the burden of silence that had been laid on me was lifted, that I could demand answers, which is exactly what I did. Everyone confirmed her story, but Mehdi vehemently insisted that his actions were unremarkable, that he had been carrying out his responsibility to "set her on the good path." He tried to convince me that the beating was justified and had not been as bad as Jamila had described it. In his defense, he argued that he could have done much worse, and told me stories of women and girls who had received even more severe treatment from their brothers, fathers, or husbands for similar or lesser "crimes." That is, being forced to marry a stranger old enough to be her father, or continued and random beatings for transgressing the slightest rule, could be worse. Not being allowed to study, being placed in forced seclusion, or having one's comings and goings monitored by everyone could be worse. Indeed, death could be worse.

While this was not Jamila's fate, the proliferation of cases of Muslim girls and women killed for violating codes of honor or for challenging masculinity seems almost surreal. In France, this is clearly illustrated by the cases of Nazmiyé, a fifteen-year-old girl of Turkish origin, and Sohane, an eighteen-year-old of Algerian origin who grew up in the outer cities. Their stories, indeed their murders, serve as constant reminders of just how tragic life can be for some Muslim girls.

Nazmiyé, like some of my participants and Jamila, wanted to resemble the young French girls around whom she had grown up. And she was expected to display modest behavior in public. Her friends described her as a modern girl, one who "refused to wear the veil . . . [and,] like many of the girls her age, forever wore blue jeans and tennis shoes . . . [she] had the allure of a young girl 'integrated' into French society" (Hermet 1997, 22). (In this, she was like Fatima, described in chapter 1.) However, on the night of August 14, 1994, she paid the ultimate price for her modernity, which included dating a boy and running away from home. On that night, Nazmiyé was strangled to death by her brother with the consent of her parents and her cousin, who all watched and did nothing to interfere. Her life was taken because she "had transgressed against the community's prohibitions [and] ridiculed her family's honor" (Khosrokhavar 1997, 119). This view was shared by Nazmiyé's best friend's father, whose daughter described him as "cool." Yet, during a controversial televised interview, he expressed what most people would find unthinkable: "In the name of honor, everyone would have done the same thing . . . since it was a question of honor, it's normal that they would kill their daughter" (Hermet 1997, 22). According to the Muslim women's advocacy association *Les nanas beurs,* many young women in France face this threat, but as these acts of violence often occur clandestinely, they go undocumented outside the community.

Then there is the case of Sohane, which has become emblematic of violence directed at Muslim girls from the outer cities identified as *putes* (whores or sluts) by teenage boys in their neighborhoods. On October 4, 2002, one such young man dragged Sohane to a refuse depot, doused her with gasoline, and set her ablaze for shunning his advances. Sohane was noted for her beauty and her tenacious defiance of machoism, and her rebuff, in this young man's mind, translated into a right to murder her, this young woman who was left rolling in agony while he and his friend watched. Spurred by Sohane's death and grisly tales of gang rapes of other young women in the "other France," Fadela Amara and Sohane's sister founded the association Ni putes ni soumises (Neither Whores nor Submissive), which staged massive marches across France to bring greater light to these neglected problems in the outer cities (Amara 2003).

Historian Nikki Keddie offers some insight into these acts of violence against Muslim girls and women. It is important to emphasize that Keddie is referring to historical Muslim societies "and their reliance on family regulation to maintain social control."

> The Quran gives men control of their wives, which extends to beatings for disobedience, and adulterers of both sexes are to be punished by lashing when there is either confession or four eyewitnesses to the act. Islamic law and tradition changed this to the far more severe punishment of stoning to death, but in practice women were often killed by their brothers and many escaped punishment. Islamic practices about women are often said to be resistant to change because of their Quranic sanction, believed to be the word of God. This has some truth, but there has been much breaking and bending of Quranic admonitions throughout Muslim history. The Quran has been interpreted, against the meaning of its text. (Keddie and Baron 1991, 5)

However, Keddie's perspective cannot be generalized, nor can it fully explain the forces driving men—fathers, husbands, brothers, uncles, cousins, and neighbors—to such acts, particularly if they do not strictly follow the teachings of the holy books or have never even read them. The impulses behind the actions of men such as Mehdi remain a conundrum and a source of controversy. Indeed, much more research needs to be done on gender issues pertaining to men who commit these reprehensible acts, rather than on the consequences of their behavior: emotionally and physically scarred women and girls. Despite Mehdi's brutality, the question to ask is what makes "a Mehdi," which means not simply condemning him for behavior and beliefs whose structuring source lies in the people and institutions that contribute to shaping his person, if not personality. To attempt to understand him or what motivates him is not to endorse his acts or an ideology, rather it is an important first step in disrupting a patterned, violent response reserved for women and girls who suffer the pains of their conceived status, often in utter silence.

However, in sharing Jamila's story and those of other young women, I cannot caution readers enough not to overgeneralize and attribute such abuse to all Muslims, as the media so often do. Admittedly, both academic studies and popular literature do tend to focus on the sensational and grotesque, including violence and discrimination experienced by Muslim women and girls, as in Afghanistan. But it is equally critical to examine all forms of male domination, which Nawal El Saadawi has battled throughout her career. "The oppression of women is not essentially due to particular religious ideologies," writes El Saadawi; rather it is the "patriarchal cataract and class optics" that underpin the violence directed at girls and women across countries and cultures. The optic is reinforced by *le regard des autres*, the eye of the community, which weighs heavily upon girls' and women's actions when their behavior carries moral implications (El Saadawi 1982, 201). This observation is widely documented in the literature on Muslims across disciplines. More importantly, the Jamilas, Nazmiyés, and Sohanes of the world rely on others to give voice to their existence and their experiences. A variety of advocacy associations for Muslim girls and women of all origins take on this role, as well as offering them much-needed resources and relief. It is equally important to share these stories because the complexities interwoven in their cultural calculus may not be understood or even known by those outside their communities, and this is particularly true in places like France, where there is an established and accepted line between public and private spheres of life. And for that reason, the schools know even less.

Negotiating and Resisting "Mistakes"

The crux of these problems emerges at the point where cultures and expectations collide. Habiba articulates this difficulty as Arabs face it, but the concerns she raises are not specific to any group.

We are educated like an Arab in a place where the culture is French. Sometimes it's very hard to live like this because if we do something normal in the French world it can be considered a mistake in the Arab world.

A mistake can include sitting or just being accused of sitting in a café with a boy, as Jamila sorely discovered, or simply, and with consequences, being the multicultural teenagers that their society has shaped. Though Jamila's case may seem extreme, it is similar to that of my focal participant Anita, who experienced domestic servitude in her aunt and uncle's home, which drove her to attempt suicide on more than one occasion. She had also suffered genital mutilation, an experience she described in these terms: "you never forget that pain." In listening to Anita recount her lived realities, I was reminded of Jamila's narrative. For example, I asked all students interviewed to describe a typical day from start to finish. In doing so, Anita expressed a mixture of pride and shame in being able to carry out a number of domestic duties, knowing that this was not how her friends lived, though she was aware of others who shared her plight.

Beginning at 5:00 A.M., Anita was expected to clean house and cook breakfast, and then ready her younger cousins for school. She was also expected to do any early-morning errands, such as fetching bread from the bakery. The evening similarly involved cooking, laundry, and cleaning for the entire family, as well as baby-sitting. When I asked her how she found time to study, she confessed that she tried to do a bit around 3:00 A.M., before beginning her day, but added that it was nearly impossible because she shared a bedroom with three of her cousins. She also said that she tried to go to school early to use the library facilities, if she could finish her morning chores in time. As I learned from her student files, Anita was failing many of her classes; it would be difficult to imagine otherwise, given her daily routine. To guarantee that Anita would remain silent about her treatment, her aunt and uncle threatened to send her back to Côte d'Ivoire, where a husband had already been selected for her. Reconciling herself to her plight, Anita remained silent until her aunt threatened to cut off her one avenue of freedom—going to school—because it increasingly interfered with the duties expected of her at home. For Anita, that was the last straw, and she sought assistance from the one place where it was available, again the school.

Similar cases have been documented by the French human rights group Le comité contre l'esclavage moderne (the Committee against Modern Slavery). This organization has documented numerous cases similar to Anita's, but it primarily handles the cases of migrant women and girls brought to France by employers who eventually enslave them. In an interview, the director of the Paris office explained that young women, brought to foreign countries as contract labor, are often left with few or no options when they find themselves in abusive settings. Many find themselves trapped in domestic servitude by employers who use tactics of intimidation such as taking their passports, not renewing their visas, and threatening them with the prospect of jail if they divulge their situation to anyone. As foreigners, they are largely unaware of their rights and resources. More sadly, they have come to places like France with the hope and expectation of providing for impoverished families in their home countries. They endure inhuman treatment because so much is riding on their employment.

The issue of domestic slavery has received greater attention in France, especially following high-profile cases such as that of Henriette Akofa, a young Togolese woman who documented her experiences in her book *Une esclave moderne* (Michel Lafon, 2000). Brought to France as a teenager, Henriette was held in servitude for several years by two separate families, during which time she was beaten, undernourished, forced to sleep on the floor, forbidden to leave those residences or use the telephone, and subjected to other horrible treatment. In a moment of bravery, she accepted an offer of help from a neighbor, but only after reassurances that she would not be arrested or deported for reporting her "employers" to the authorities. The Committee estimates that more than two thousand women are living a life of domestic slavery in France, 98 percent of them young African and Asian women.

Young people like Anita initially accept their servitude for much the same reasons that women like Henriette do. Both groups also have often internalized the idealistic image they are fed of France and the West, as compared to their or their parents' home countries. Anita described it in near euphoric terms: "It's a dream country; we all dream of coming to France, either France or the United States, because life there is, well, it seems like a dream. There's television, lots of channels, all kinds of different things. And there's lots of food, lots! I was so happy to come here . . ." When I asked her why she had waited so long before seeking help from school officials, she stated that she had believed no one would care, or even believe her, and added, "my aunt and uncle didn't beat me, starve me, or rape me," meaning that her mistreatment had left no physical, visible scars, only psychological and emotional ones. And because the boundaries between private and public life are firmly respected by the schools, it is perhaps not surprising that Anita endured this misery in silence for so long. Her resistance came at a price. It cost her all contact with her mother, whom she had hoped to "rescue one day" from what Anita described as an unhappy polygamous marriage and poverty.

Then there was Amina, whose situation worsened throughout my fieldwork. She was a bright science major, and her father had repeatedly thrown her books and notes into the garbage, and on occasion prevented her from going to school at all. School officials said that they were finally forced to take official action against him. Sadly, as members of the Nanas beurs and the Comité contre l'esclavage moderne pointed out, such intervention can backfire, sometimes resulting in the disappearance of the person it was intended to help. Moreover, one must not forget Fatou. She described a state of tension and competition in her home between her co-mothers and their respective children for the father's favor. This situation created a climate of hostility in their home that was exacerbated by cramped living conditions. There was Naïma, who, though fearing her parents' reprisals, risked having a boyfriend, whom she secretly saw with the help of friends.

Most telling, however, is the case of Fatima, who, with her five sisters, brother, and mother, maneuvered around a violent father who used to secretly follow his daughters to school to see if they talked to boys. His extreme acts of domestic violence toward the girls and his wife—including throwing her down a flight of stairs, causing her to miscarry—has prompted three of his daughters to pursue law degrees. In fact, in an interview the eldest told me of confronting her father about his cruelty toward everyone in the family. This act of defiance might have triggered an all-out brawl, if not for her younger brother, who interceded on his sister's behalf. As I heard on several occasions, the brother has taken on the role of protector in the family. This time he blocked his father's hand, which was headed toward his sister's face after she threatened to use her knowledge of the law against him should he continue to treat his children with such malice. Prevented from hitting her, her father looked at her in disbelief and screamed, "I can't believe it! You would use your studies against me?" In his own account of these events, her brother especially noted the flush of joyful and frightened agitation on his sister's face, which suddenly turned into a deathly chill stare when she coldly responded, "yes." The father had not hit any of the children since, but he still forbade the girls from leaving the house after 6:00 P.M., even the ones attending the university.

What is startling about this family's case, as I mentioned in chapter 1, is that these girls' teachers considered this family to be a shining example of successful integration into France. And while Fatima and her sisters all self-identified as French or French of Algerian descent, their self-understandings seem to be due as much to their schooling as to the pernicious atmosphere of their home. As French youth, they have been taught to see the value of relying on French institutions, including the schools, which encourage them to resist practices and teachings in their home that appear antithetical to the national culture taught to them as their own. Their high academic achievement signified full assimilation, especially because the girls seemed independent and expressed strong feminist views, which themselves are not disconnected from their home life. In fact, one of the few criticisms teachers had about Fatima's coursework was that it seemed to overemphasize a feminist perspective. In concealing the trauma unfolding in their home from school officials, they, like others, became masters of secrecy, and the societal structures unknowingly support them in this since it remains taboo to transgress the line between private and public life in France.

Although I had varied experiences with my participants, it was clear that those who had suffered greatly suffered in almost debilitating silence, often believing that their experiences were unique, thus their fault. This is why I share their narratives, which contain important lessons for us all. However, these glaring cases of abuse make it all the more imperative to acknowledge the abundant counterexamples. Indeed, there were some extremely supportive male figures in my participants' families, fathers and brothers who had positive, nurturing relationships with their daughters and sisters. Habiba and Su'ad's father, for instance, was extremely attentive to his daughters and allowed them considerable freedom in their comings and goings (as did the fathers of several other girls I knew), though they did, understandably, have curfews. He encouraged them to show me around their neighborhood and to speak candidly about it, and they were allowed to visit my home unchaperoned, which was not the case for Fatima. Teachers also noted, as I witnessed myself, that he always attended teacher-parent conferences and strongly supported his daughters' schooling. Their brother also appeared to have an open, carefree relationship with his sisters, as Leïla's elder brother did with her, although a great deal of responsibility had fallen on his shoulders following the death of their father. While both attended Henri III, Leïla noted that her brother never interfered with her socializing with other students or sought to reprimand her if she was speaking with a boy. When I observed them together from a distance, I saw that they were playful with each other in the ways typical of brothers and sisters. Further, Leïla, who had adopted a retro Sixties look, often commented on her brother's positive influence on her tastes in clothes and music, noting that it was he who introduced her to her favorite musicians, Madonna and George Michael.

Perhaps the most telling aspect of male character that I encountered throughout this journey is this: In France, where divorce rates are extremely high and absentee fathers a problem, the vast majority of the fathers that I have met worked—sometimes in degrading, awful jobs—supported their families, and were present in the home. They provided for their children, despite poverty and social rejection, and contributed to a nurturing family structure. This speaks volumes, as does the care provided for elders within the extended family—they are not sent off to nursing homes—and the importance of family itself within their communities. However, for those young women whose family dynamics are difficult and who must negotiate gendered tensions, schooling can be a liberating weapon in their hands. For some, the school is a refuge from strict expectations and rules that dictate their behavior and restrict their movement within the communities and countries that have become their own. The school, unlike the home, readily becomes the place where they can demonstrate their value, both economic and social, in the face of perceptions and beliefs that they have none. It is the place that teaches them that they are French, and thus capable of assuming any number of roles beyond wife and mother. This point was acknowledged by a male Muslim teacher at Henri III during an interview, parts of which I used as stimulus with participants so that they might comment on its veracity. Further, in using the following passage with my participants, it opened a door for them to speak more candidly about their private lives. As the passage illustrates, someone else already revealed that which they may not wish initially to share. To bring a more nuanced understanding to their complexities, I offer a the perspective of a male teacher who confessed to having struggled with the issues that he describes:

> They are students whose parents are relatively young, in their forties or fifties for the most part. Some of these parents already had the opportunity to have an education or pursue their studies, more or less. However, their mentality, in general, remains more or less traditional with regard to the education of their girls. That is, a girl of Arabian descent does not have the same rights as her brother, her own brother who has the right to go out, the right to not take part in the housework. It's a perspective, a relative perspective because no one experiences the same situation, but in general,

it's the tendency, a general tendency. In fact, a young girl, in general, must negotiate several things at the same time—her relationship with her own family, which is a relationship based on complicity or conflict, conflict with the father, sometimes with the brother, because the father doesn't always want the emancipation of his girls. That is, according to Arabian cultural traditions, a girl, like a boy, represents the family, but the girl represents the family's honor. Therefore, girls must negotiate their internal relations within the family and their relations with the outside world, because most of the girls' relations with the outside are not the same. They are sometimes diametrically opposed to those at the heart of the family. At home she has clearly integrated the interdictions and the place that one wants to assign to her . . . but that doesn't mean that the situation is as clear-cut as that. Many girls refuse this situation and sometimes succeed in finding a compromise with their parents . . . School is, therefore, a way to show what she's capable of, and a means for social advancement. The school is also a place of emancipation.

Although the teacher mentions Arabs, his description applies to Muslims of non-Arab decent as well. Catherine Quiminal, Babacar Diouf, and their colleagues note that girls of sub-Saharan African origin faced similar constraints. Marriage, going out at night, and sexuality are the subjects that cause the most conflict in intergenerational relations, since any misconduct in these areas may undermine the family's values. As these scholars argue, "Girls can accept or refuse these norms, or attempt to attenuate them; nonetheless, in case after case, they are aware of them because these norms are first and foremost in the family, irrespective of its social status and irrespective of how these norms are inculcated" (Quiminal et al. 1997, 18).

When I showed this teacher's comments to my focal participants, all but one agreed that he had accurately captured, in part or in whole, aspects of their lived conditions; they could identify with what he described. More importantly, it is those dimensions of their lives that push them toward an idealized "national identity" presented in their schooling and in French media (especially popular television) that seems more appealing than the family dynamics in their homes. Aïcha's reaction to his comments was particularly insightful, appearing to be shaped by a combination of factors that have convinced her to view her life in clear and practical terms:

Me, all I want is to have my apartment, my car, and my job. If I think that way it's because I see how society is made. I don't want to depend on a man. No way, I want my independence. Maybe this comes from hearing people say all the time [*here her voice became mocking*] "Yeah, women are submissive to men" . . . or when I used to go to my aunt's, I always saw women bringing the meals, the tea, always women; I never saw a man do the dishes. That always bothered me. And so it's probably for that reason that I think like that.

The exception was Sylvie, my Jewish participant who had converted to Islam. While she agreed that extra expectations could be placed on Muslim girls in French society, she recognized, too, that she had certain freedoms that the other girls did not enjoy, especially the right to go out as she pleased, even at night and unsupervised. During an interview, she told me one reason why the rules are so strict, rules that she did not observe since, as she had often said, "I'm Muslim, but I'm also French":

> I'm free, it's true. I have my freedom. And it's true, I never really thought about it: their fathers believe that they are protecting their daughters. It's so clear; it's the truth. I even spoke about it with my friend's father [someone instrumental to her conversion]; it's really a total fear of everything and it's true that sometimes it's excessive, but remember the only reason they do these things is to protect their daughters.

The teacher's observations and Sylvie's understanding are extended by Naïma's mother, who stressed that the weight of honor is directly tied to how girls are sometimes treated because of a critical, additional element: *le regard des autres,* the community's surveillance of everyone's actions. Again, it is these constraints that girls resist, constraints measured against the images of a perceived freedom they see in their schools, in their communities, and among their peers. Naïma's mother elaborated on a point that applies to both child and parent:

> We live as a community, and for Muslims, the woman is the family's honor! If the girl is good, the family is good; if the girl is bad, the parents are no good. It's really hard for a girl. It's not because the dad and mom aren't cool. They can't be! For example, I'm very cool with my daughters. I'm their mother, their sister, and their friend. Everything! I know when they go out, when they go to the cinema, and that they have friends who are boys. I know their friends, all of them. And I know that I could never let them do this in Algeria or Egypt.

It is not only in Algeria or Egypt that the symbolic violence of *le regard* is inflicted. For those living in France, the U.S., and any other country that is part of the Muslim diaspora, it is difficult to escape the weight of the community's eye. I recall the experience of a woman from North Africa who spent a year at my university as a visiting scholar and became a dear friend. Among her multitude of talents, she was a highly accomplished singer and was often invited to share her exquisite voice at various academic functions. While dining one night at a local Middle Eastern restaurant known for its live music and traditional belly dancers, she and her sister, who also sings professionally, were invited to perform. They gave an awe-inspiring performance that left everyone wanting more. However, the next day, my friend informed me that the news of their performance had made it back to her home department, and she and her sister had been reprimanded by one of the senior faculty. They were summarily informed that their performance reflected badly on the department. Both women were more than thirty years old and were university professors—*le regard des autres* in operation.

The importance accorded to the twin issues of honor and shame, particularly in relation to marriage, defines the limits of acceptable behavior for those girls and women, whose entire group membership is balanced on this teetering scale. This, among other reasons, is why school can become the site where "the visible signs of bad behavior" are displayed, such as smoking in public, wearing one's hair down, using make-up, wearing tight or revealing clothing, and flirting with boys (Lacoste-Dujardin 1992, 49). However, as liberating as the school can be, it can be just as punitive for certain Muslim girls whose ways have no place in the secular, Republican school. It is this tension between school expectations and home expectations that often encourages these young people to seek refuge in their religion or cultivate the "x" in their self-representation as "French of 'x' origin," against rejection and exclusion (Khosrokhavar 1997; Venel 1999). If Muslim girls are the "suitable enemy" because of the "veil," as I have argued, national education can be the ultimate enemy for certain Muslims, when the school's customs and course content undermine the lessons taught and internalized in the home. As Naïma's mother insisted, "For us Muslims, we say that the first school is the mother!" And therein lies another dimension to the complexity of issues facing certain Muslims attending the public schools. My study participants indicated that schooling and diplomas are important to them because they had no intention of repeating their mothers' educational and social trajectories. Even if they do not consider themselves French, many reject the lifestyle and roles to which the women in their families and communities have been relegated, because those roles are seen as deleterious. Fatima's eldest sister, who, as recounted earlier, defied her father, articulated this point. She is a self-proclaimed feminist and self-understands as French:

A girl has twice as much to prove as a boy. They want to make it because, first, they see their mothers, who are dependent on their fathers because their mothers don't work. And then, too, their mothers put up with a lot because they have five or six kids. So they put up with their husbands' bad moods and temper because they know what it means for them to be divorced. Also, their mothers don't know how to work because all of their lives they have been dependent on someone—a father, a brother, an uncle, etc.—so these girls see all of this at home, and it motivates them to go to school and to find a job because they will never let themselves be treated the way their mothers have been treated. And I agree totally with them. This is exactly what they feel . . . Really, it's a running theme everywhere . . . It's true that I have a father who's really abusive, and to be honest with you, for him, a girl will never be like a boy. Although she does all that she can to show her worth, a boy, because he is *male,* will always be better than a girl.

Indeed, her statements are echoed by her mother:

I am very unhappy because I have to depend on someone, and I never wanted to depend on a man. Staying at home all day means working too—cleaning the house, ironing, washing clothes—all that's work too. But I want to work outside, have a little pocket money for my personal needs, but my husband doesn't want me to. He never wanted me to work! Later I understood why—because then I wouldn't be dependent on him—and couldn't do anything about it.

The feeling of helplessness, of being locked in, or of fulfilling a prescribed role driven by self-perpetuating ideologies carries with it an image and lived reality that these girls resist each time they see their mothers' missed opportunities and their happiness dwindling into despair. In a survey, I asked the girls, "Would you like to have the same job as your mother? Why or why not?" Almost all responded "no" to that question, and several added that their mothers were *femmes au foyer,* housewives. One student clarified her statement further, writing, "She doesn't work, and I think that the only way to be independent is to study and work." And another declared, "No, because my mother never went to school and so she's a housewife. I can attend school, and I want to work and not end up being a housewife." These responses were typical, although some students, such as Rima, indicated that they would prefer to have the best of both worlds: "My mother doesn't have a job. I would like to have a profession and also be able to take care of my home." And then there are responses like those of Habiba and her classmates, to whom I put the question during a discussion of women's roles in their Arabic class, a class made up primarily of girls. Although the students insisted that there was nothing wrong with being a housewife, when I pressed them a bit more, asking them to raise their hands if they were willing to be just housewives, not one girl in the class of twenty raised her hand. Habiba explained, "It's not well remunerated."

Given the range of issues that these girls confront, it is no wonder that they have become ardent strategists in negotiating all that is expected of them by home, neighborhood, and school. The most common strategy is simply to lie, sometimes with the help of friends and siblings; lying serves as protection and as resistance to the rigid constraints that they encounter. As most of the girls in the study did not have the right to go out at night, or to parties, and certainly not to clubs, lying became a way to avoid embarrassing questions from friends who simply did not comprehend what was expected of these girls. This is especially true when the friends enjoy typical teen activities that these girls are denied. When I asked one student how she deals with these tensions, she responded,

> I lie. I lie! I have become a specialist in lying. It's true. For example, when there's some holiday, and I want to go hang out with friends—girl friends! Just so that you know—well, I lie. I say something like "I'm going to the national library" because I know my father will never put a foot in such a place, and if he did, it's so big that he would never find me.

In interviews with other girls, I used this passage to encourage them to speak openly about this highly sensitive topic, and to illustrate that someone else already had discussed this issue. It proved quite useful; many girls confessed to having resorted to lying. For some, it was a way to stay after school to study, pass a bit of time with friends, or simply avoid trouble at home for having made some "mistake." And while lying is certainly not unique to Muslim girls, it is one of their strategies for coping with the myriad tensions that they face in highly volatile social contexts. They are continuously maneuvering around competing expectations. For example, Amina admitted that she often had to make up excuses to her father in order to explain why she had stayed after school, which she had had to do because he had again thrown her books in the trash, and she had to copy notes and assignments provided by classmates and teachers. Interestingly, new technologies have helped such strategies. Cell phones have given girls a freedom that they did not know prior to their arrival. Initially, they were relatively affordable in France, thanks to the multitude of options available to consumers following the decentralization of France Telecom, the national telephone company; they have since become more expensive. But the cell phone has allowed, for example, male friends or boyfriends to reach them discreetly without running the risk of having a call intercepted by a parent or troublesome sibling. It also allows quick communication with an ally who can run interference for a girl who, for example, anticipates arriving home late. Often, a simple call makes a world of difference.

As girls attempt to negotiate the external and internal constraints operating in their lives, school can be both a slice of heaven and a bit of hell, as shown in chapter 4. Some have a tenuous, often violent relationship with the school and with the traditions, ideologies, and policies that educators are expected to enforce. Nowhere is this better illustrated than in the emotionally charged issue of French secularism, its application and interpretations in relation to headscarf-wearing Muslim girls in the Republican school.

La laïcité—French Secularism

La laïcité (secularism), France's highly specific response to religion, presupposes a firm and unambiguous separation between statist institutions and the religious sector. As a historically entrenched ideology born of religious wars and honed with the forging of the nation-state, French secularism is a culturally charged issue subject to diverse interpretations, often far removed from its original intent (Poulat 2003). The 1905 law separating church and state could not have been passed in the absence of other pivotal legislation in France, beginning with article 10 of the 1789 Declaration of the Rights of Man and of the Citizen, which allowed freedom of religious expression. This article was later reinforced by the 1958 constitution, which reiterated that France was an indivisible, secular (*laïque*), democratic, and social republic (Gaillard 1989; Barbier 1995). *La laïcité* was intended to establish equal protection for all people under a "neutral," non–religiously influenced state, while allowing freedom of religious expression and free thinking within state institutions. And herein lies the problem faced by the public school: neutralizing religious influence in the schools means denying freedom of religious expression. This contradiction derives from two opposing logics through which French secularism continues to be understood. "The debate," argues Étienne Balibar, is "between those who support an interpretation of *la laïcité* as the school's *neutrality toward* religious beliefs (therefore its equal respect for their expression), and those who insist on the idea that religious beliefs must be *suspended* within the walls of the school. They both are right and wrong" (2004, 19).

How did France arrive at such a contradiction? While Jules Ferry was the main architect of French secularism, historians argue that he was not anti-religious, but rather anti-clerical. The primary objective of French statesmen in the nineteenth century was to break the Catholic Church's long-standing power and influence over such critical areas as the educational system, which was seen as the path to modernity, cultural assimilation, and national unity. However, religion and religious tolerance are violent, contentious issues, as both French history and present world events illustrate. And while the 1789 Declaration allowed religious freedom, this freedom was limited by an implicit understanding of secularism, according to which liberty of religious expression was a right. With the law of 1905 separating church from state, French secularism became the state's response to the enduring power and influence of the Catholic Church, particularly in the area of education. Politicians like Jules Ferry believed that the church's influence over the educational system interfered with the government's goal of imposing a new morality via the schools. These men sought to replace religious doctrine in schools with statist doctrine against the Catholic Church. That is, the state's function would include integrating a culturally, linguistically, and religiously diverse people into a unified modern nation, that is, into a nation of French citizens, through secular, national education.

Nonetheless, the Catholic Church still wields some power over national education in France. This is most clearly shown in its success in blocking the government's attempts to change the school week. A law of 1882 stipulates that one day a week, excluding Sunday, must be set aside for religious instruction outside the school. In the early 1970s, Wednesdays were designated for this purpose. To compensate for the loss of instruction time, Saturday mornings were added to the school schedule. When the government tried to transfer Saturday classes to Wednesday, the bishops managed to preserve half the day for religious instruction, so that today students attend school for only a half day on Wednesday and on Saturday mornings. And because the schools are under the state's control, meaning that they are secular, religion can be taught only in a historical context.

Coming as I do from a country that has been characterized as semi-secular, I was surprised by the passion and fury that this subject continues to ignite in France. At times, I felt as though I had stepped back into the nineteenth century and were walking among the statesmen of the Third Republic as they drastically changed how religion would be understood in French society, and especially within that society's cherished public institution—national education. French secularism is often interpreted literally, in a way that appears wholly abstracted from the challenges of a multidenominational France, which become ever more complicated as non-Christian religions become more visible. It has been suggested that *la laïcité* involves more than a separation of church and state because it refers to that which is neither ecclesiastic nor religious, but rather political in application. As Maurice Barbier concludes,

> In the strict sense, *la laïcité* refers to the separation between the state and religion, which comprises two complementary components. On the one hand, the state is entirely independent of all religions and all churches. On the other, religions are equally free with respect to the state. (1995, 7–9)

However, Barbier admits that this analysis is an idealization, one that is rarely manifested for two basic reasons: (1) the state cannot be entirely disinterested in or disconnected from any social entity that could challenge its authority, and (2) the state and religion share potentially confrontational and imbricate domains: education and ethics.

In attempting to sensitize the U.S. public to the French perspective on secularism, Guy Coq, author of numerous writings on *la laïcité*, expressed the following in a January 30, 2004, op-ed piece in the New York Times:

> Our uneasiness about head scarves and other religious symbols in schools is a result of our long, often painful history. If we bow to demands to allow the practice of religion in state institutions, we will put France's identity in peril . . . Laïcité includes, foremost, tolerance . . . Prime Minister Jules Ferry founded the public school system, which barred priests as teachers and took over the job of transmitting common values and the sense of social unity—in short, forming the citizens of the republic—without reference to religion.

Coq's views clearly reflect a number of my arguments. However, is wearing religious symbols the same as practicing or advocating religion? The imposition and tenacious defense of an ideology of secularism whose definition is neither clearly understood nor clearly conveyed in public institutions risks subverting the very thing that it seeks to promote—tolerance within the schools and society. Enter legislation banning religious symbols.

The events leading up to the 2004 law banning "the wearing of signs and dress manifesting a religious affiliation in the elementary, middle, and high schools"[4] began at least two decades ago, when

France's Muslim communities started to organize politically. As French citizens, they made various demands, ranging from permission to build more mosques to better government documentation of acts of racialized discrimination against them. In fact, in response to increased reports of such violence, the government created a national telephone hotline in May 2000 for reporting such acts. According to media reports and one of the co-directors of the Paris office of SOS-Racisme, whom I interviewed, the hotline was overwhelmed the first day. She stressed that racialized discrimination is often politicized as an immigration problem, but the calls that her office received were not coming from immigrants, but rather from people who self-identified as French.[5] Nor has the significance of France's growing and visible Muslim populations been entirely lost on career politicians such as Alain Juppé, Jean-Pierre Chevènement, and Nicolas Sarkozy, who have been characterized as no friends to "immigrants." Indeed, they have made some symbolic gestures of inclusion toward Muslims in France. For example, in a move that was later deemed politically motivated, Chevènement organized a major event billed as "Islam in France," which was attended by thousands of people in May 2000. According to Chevènement, the event was designed to "definitively integrate the Muslims into a secular framework."[6] The stage had already been set by Alain Juppé, the mayor of Bordeaux, who in the 1990s, as prime minister, had been in the forefront of campaigns against immigrants, leading to their expulsion from France. But in 1999, in a *mea culpa* that stunned the nation, Juppé publicly acknowledged Muslims as a community that must be "accepted and respected in France."[7] (However, this was before his 2004 conviction for political corruption.) In 2002–2003, Interior Minister Nicolas Sarkozy spearheaded the formation of the French Council of the Muslim Religion. Like the Catholic and Jewish Councils that predated it, the Muslim Council was created to incorporate Muslims into a broader political body. However, when a Muslim organization identified as extremist by the state unexpectedly won a large number of seats in the first elections to select representatives for the Council, the elections were invalidated amid protests. Sarkozy threatened to deport any religious leader considered a fundamentalist, and an official from the organization supported by Sarkozy was made head of the Council, despite this group's weak showing at the polls. The Council is also viewed as a self-interested means for controlling France's growing Muslim population rather than a mechanism for inclusion. This is the same Sarkozy who, in the spring of 2003, steadfastly supported a contentious initiative that requires Muslim women to remove their headscarves in photographs for national identification cards. This is the same Sarkozy who supported his party in wooing Muslim politicians from Socialist strongholds, only to marginalize them when they attempted to run in the 2004 regional elections. Ironically, those elections resulted in Sarkozy's losing his position as interior minister, a position he regained following the defeat of France's referendum on the European constitution. He is now positioning himself for the presidency as the crimebuster candidate and exponent of "zero tolerance" directed at the outer cities.

The "integration" of Muslims in the national education system takes on new dimensions when headscarf-wearing girls are singled out as proof that Islamic fundamentalism has escalated in France, and French secularism is used as a weapon against such girls. Such an escalation has yet to be clearly documented and differentiated from a return to religion as a cultural reference and a way of coping with exclusion. Nonetheless, what spurred educational policy and present legislation was the infamous 1989 "veil affair" (*l'affaire du foulard*), in which a middle school principal expelled three girls who refused to remove their head coverings on school grounds. His act triggered a media frenzy that sent a clear message to the public: "the Republican school was in danger" from the reported ten to fifteen thousand "veiled" Muslims within its walls (Venel 1999, 21). Though the Ministry of Education documented only two thousand such girls in 1994 (a figure reduced to 1,256 at the beginning of the 2003 academic year),[8] the message did not change: "France's identity was in peril" because of a scarf worn by certain Muslim girls (Venel 1999). Even more striking are the results of a survey reported by the newspaper *Le monde,* which showed that 91 percent of teachers that they polled had never been confronted by a "veiled" student in the schools where they teach, while a reported 65 percent had never seen a "veiled" girl in their class in their career. And yet 76 percent of teachers polled favored the law banning "ostensible" religious symbols.[9]

The so-called Islamic "veil" is considered a proselytizing symbol of religious affiliation, anti-secular, and thereby anti-French. Since 1989, the issue of its being worn in schools has engendered heated, often violent debates involving all sectors of French society, and before the passage of the current legislation, the judicial high court—*le Conseil d'état*—was called upon to determine whether a headscarf worn by Muslim girls was religious provocation or free expression. In keeping with preexisting legislation concerning the principle of neutrality associated with the freedom of religious expression in public schools, the courts determined in 1992 that

> The wearing of symbols by students manifesting their religious affiliation is not in itself incompatible with the principle of *la laïcité* insofar as it constitutes their freedom of expression and a manifestation of their religious beliefs. However, this liberty does not permit students to display symbols of religious affiliation which, by their nature or by the conditions in which they might be worn collectively or individually, or by their ostentation, could constitute an act of cohesion, provocation, proselytism, or propaganda. (Kessler 1993, 114)[10]

   The court further ruled that the headscarf itself is prohibited if it meets the last four conditions mentioned above, and if it disrupts the normal operation of the school. Additionally, if the wearing of the "veil" represented a "breach in the dignity, freedom, health, or the security of a student," then students could be prohibited from wearing such a headscarf on school grounds. Cultural gatekeepers of the French school earnestly seized this latter point, arguing that the "veil" endangered students in physical education classes and those doing laboratory work involving chemicals or burners in science classes. Feminists seized on the "dignity" clause, arguing that the "veil" was a sign of gender oppression that denied women and girls their most basic right, that is, equality in public space, as guaranteed by the constitution. So although the court had sought to resolve this highly volatile issue in keeping with the established principles of religious freedom, the ambiguous phrasing of its ruling made it subject to multiple partisan interpretations that led to the same end: the expulsion of girls from schools whose sole crime is to be Muslim and to wish (or be forced) to cover their hair as part of their cultural or religious practices.

   The 2004 law, informed by this decision, is equally ambiguous in its application and borders on absurdity. Though much of the wording and spirit of the court's decision underpins it, it forbids automatic expulsion. Rather, students are to be counseled to determine why they "veil." If they refuse to remove their head covering, however, they can be expelled. And while yarmulkes and large crosses are included in the ban, when it came to the turbans worn by Sikh males, who are also a significant population in the schools, enforcement was not so rigid. The Sikh turban was initially determined to be cultural, not religious, unlike the headscarf. This has changed, and Sikh students are now subject to expulsion too for their head covering.

But it is ultimately up to the principal of a school to interpret the cultural or religious significance of a piece of clothing.

Muslim girls have been granted a concession; they may wear bandanas, provided they have no "religious connotation," cover only the hair and not the neck, and do not touch any other part of the student's clothing. The effect, however, is the same; these girls are penalized for the politics of others, people who would sacrifice the girls' education to their own beliefs, thereby reducing the girls' life chances in a credential-driven society. Already, those in the outer cities receive a woefully inadequate education, and it is only further compromised by this law. Moreover, the law contributes to their stigmatization and social exclusion. Considering that the school is the only site where teachers and school officials exercise clear authority over the development, both ideological and emotional, of children, it would seem a better idea to keep these girls in school in the hope of influencing their self-understandings than to expel them and take away the one place where they could learn to address this issue.

This law has been described as racist, and some of my participants called it an example of "French intolerance," arguing that it was being used to deflect attention away from other pressing issues, such as high unemployment, the crisis in national education, conditions in the outer cities, and the prospect of social change that French youth of color and immigration represent. As Habiba put it,

> Me, I personally think that this whole debate is about hiding our problems. There have always been girls wearing veils in the schools. [*Which problems?*] Fundamentalism, exclusion. But this law isn't necessary. Even those bandanas that everyone's wearing now, I don't see why that bothers them so much. They have to be either fashion or cultural, but not religious. It's crazy! They're not criminals; they're just trying to go to school!

These views and the charge of racism have merit. After all, this legislation targets members of a specific group constituted as "other," who are classified according to their visible features, names, and religion, all of which are stigmatized and have been given social meanings. These meanings are used to explain and justify discriminatory treatment and existing social arrangements that serve to exclude them at all levels of French society, and they themselves are then blamed for their exclusion. This is racism. On another level, this law, and the resistance to it, perfectly illustrate how the workings of symbolic power and violence are intertwined in these circumstances.

That is, proponents and opponents alike of the "veil" have used its loaded symbolism to achieve their ends. In so doing, they reinforce the very social divisions they claim to oppose. The state reasserted its authority on this issue during a period when its policies and its ideals have come under attack, a period that also saw heightened anti-Muslim sentiment. With the state unprepared to take on these problems, soft issues become the order of the day, and the "veil" has been a convenient issue during periods of heightened tensions, precisely because of its amplified visibility. The "veil" is also associated with both old wounds and current fears. On the other end of the spectrum, headscarf-wearing girls challenged state authority, although they did so by means of a symbol of patriarchal domination, in Western imaginings, something that sets them apart from the "national identity." In other words, a form of authority is being used to challenge authority, both subtly and overtly, and authority is thus legitimized through those very challenges. However, the state holds the trump card, despite resistance to this law. Its power to expel protestors from the schools and even the country for any act it considers a threat to its values, representations, and myth is an expression of the state's monopoly of the means of violence, following Weber's concept. It sustains a status quo. Nonetheless, as Dounia Bouzar (2004) argues, "veiled" cleaning women working in public space, including the schools, never posed a threat to French secularism. Rather, it was those seeking inclusion on equal terms as "veiled" girls who became a menace.

La laïcité in Practice

It is important to note that Muslim women and girls wear different types of "veils," often reflecting the customs of their particular people. Head coverings can range from a simple wrap covering only the hair, to a long, iridescent scarf that envelopes the woman, to black flowing robes. Interestingly, scarves with West African motifs were very much in fashion during my fieldwork, but also were a type of "veil." When I asked school counselors and administrators why they allowed certain headscarves and not others, they were unaware of the differences. In fact, one counselor became so enraged that girls might be "getting away" with wearing a "veil" at school that she wanted me to identify the ones who fell into that category. When I explained that a head covering could simply be a matter of fashion, not unlike the one I was wearing at that moment, she sank back in her seat and said, "It's so complicated." Although girls can wear bandanas, as fashion or a cultural reference, things are more complicated for girls like Khadija, the only one of my participants who wanted to wear a headscarf in school. Being a science major ultimately worked against her since her scarf could block her view or catch fire during labs, as indicated by the courts. Khadija's science teacher, while sympathetic to her plight, viewed the headscarf as a sign of intolerance and oppression. She communicated the spectrum of her feelings to me in an e-mail message:

> Khadija is very intelligent, animated, and lively in class (sometimes too much). She's very likable. We have had long conversations about religion, her country, and wearing the veil. One time, Fatima [Khadija's friend] saw her trying to sneak and wear the veil in the bathroom at school before leaving to go out on the street, and that really hurt her [Fatima] because she thinks that Khadija is looking for her identity in her religion. When I spoke to her about it, Khadija told me that it's her decision and that her parents have nothing to do with it (I find that hard to believe. I believe, all the same, that she is unconsciously influenced by her upbringing). She says that she wears it in order to protect herself from men looking at her aggressively. (She didn't know how to answer me when I asked her if the solution was to lock women up or to change men's behavior.) I also understood this attitude when I witnessed the lack of respect toward women dressed in European fashion in the south of Tunisia, this disrespectful attitude that men have vis-à-vis women. It's true; it can push you to cover yourself up. But the problem is that she pushes her classmates, to the point of persecuting them, about the Muslim religion. I told her that it was intolerance to force others who have chosen another religion to convert with such vigor. However, I believe that if she wears the veil, it's her decision even if she's not mature enough to understand the reason that she wears it.

After several conversations with Khadija and observing her in and outside of class, as well as attending conferences organized by her mosque, it appears that she is part of the new generation of Muslim girls who, as sociologist Farhad Khosrokhavar describes them, "are not looking to break with a French identity, but wish to assume it differently" (1997, 117). That is, they wish to integrate themselves into French society without being assimilated or absorbed completely by the dominant culture. And, as I have argued, it is this kind of tension, along with the need to bring into consonance all aspects of their "selves," which almost forces them to self-understand as French. Khosrokhavar argues further that their expression of Islam is a "neo-communitarian" reaction honed in the "other France" by the social and economic exclusion, and sometimes outright rejection, that they experience in multiple ways. As Khosrokhavar (1997) and Venel (1999) argue, some youths seek refuge in religion and practices that they interpret as "Islamic" in response to such exclusion. This was particularly true of a student aide at Henri III, a young man who openly discussed his belief that women must wear the "veil." And, as a student aide, he was sought out by boys seeking advice about cultural conflicts that they experienced within the secular school (e.g., having their modesty challenged by co-ed swimming classes). When I interviewed him on the topic of compulsory "veiling" for women and not men, he explained that the Koran requires women to "veil," adding, "It's God who says it. It's because of man's weakness, which means that even if someone tries to be serious in their religion, God made us weak . . . If a man sees a woman pass by, he'll have bad thoughts about her." He concluded by saying that a woman must cover herself to avoid triggering those "bad thoughts." When I countered that women can also have the same kinds of thoughts when looking at a man, he responded that in such cases, men should not look a woman in the eye or catch her glance. That is, "a man need only lower his eyes," while the woman "has two things to do, first she must wear the veil, and she must lower her eyes."

Like this twenty-one-year-old man, Khadija and others read the Koran and cited it in defense of their actions. Scholars have noted that some young people are confused about their religion, which they conflate with customs that are not necessarily grounded in doctrine. Khadija and this aide attended mosque and participated in the conferences and discussion held there. There is great controversy over the interpretation of the Koranic passages on wearing the "veil," as Nikki Keddie explains:

> Although Islamic traditions say veiling and seclusion for all Muslim women are in the Quran, this is a tendentious reading. One verse tells women to veil their bosoms and hide their ornaments, later taken to mean all except the hands, feet, and perhaps the face. This interpretation makes no sense, because if everything were to be veiled, there would be no point in ordering bosoms to be veiled separately. Another verse tells women to draw their cloaks tightly around them so they may be recognized and not annoyed. These are the only words generally taken to refer to veiling. (Keddie and Baron 1991, 4–5)

As Fatima Mernissi (1992) and Amina Wadud (1992) further show, the text is intended to be universal, dynamic and flexible enough to support varying cultural contexts, but all too frequently a narrow perspective or interpretation is enforced, severely circumscribing its application and its universality. Singular interpretations become lived reality for certain Muslims who, like Khadija and the aide, acccpt and attempt to adhere to beliefs that clearly conflict with the secularism of French public schools. Nonetheless, Khadija and other girls who believe that the "veil" should be allowed assert that wearing it need not conflict with being French and functioning in French society. Khadija explained her perspective this way in her journal:

> Personally, I want to wear the veil because I'm Muslim and the Koran requires women to dress this way. But understand that it is forbidden for fathers to force their daughters to wear the veil, as well as their wives. If a woman wears the veil, she has to do it because she wants to, herself . . . In fact, we can practice our religion while being totally integrated in France: adhere to the styles of dress, wear jeans (large ones with a long shirt), do sports, work and become doctors, lawyers, schoolteachers in private schools (because the veil is prohibited in public schools) etc. . . . The Islamic woman is . . . , on the contrary, greatly valued, and it's for this reason that she must be protected. A woman is so beautiful, fragile. How do we protect her? Response: the veil, the *foulard*, the *hijab*.

On the surface, these beliefs may appear to reflect the romantic notions of a teenager, but they also illustrate a number of social contradictions faced by such young women, which the recourse to a religious text appears to harmonize. Khadija is now married, and regularly wears an "Islamic veil." Habiba and her sister, who live in the same building, described her as very pious. Fatou now wears a headscarf as well, a bandana that covers only her hair.

Few among those I encountered seemed to understand or agree upon what is meant by *la laïcité*, the principle underpinning the law that determines how religious expression is interpreted in the schools. Such an understanding seems particularly critical for those individuals most directly affected by its application, the teachers and the students, who often gauge it according to their own belief systems rather than how the law is intended to work. In my quest, both personal and academic, to grasp individuals' understanding of this concept, I asked the same question of all participants: "What is *la laïcité*?" The following are some representative responses, taken from interviews and journals. They reflect popular understandings of the term more than they do the meaning it is intended to have. These understandings are often formed in the process of schooling, the very process that transforms a Muslim girl into a French Muslim girl, that is, a young woman who is expected to satisfy everyone's competing expectations of who and what she must be in French society.

Teacher

> La laïcité means taking students from all origins and seeing them as being the same. Period. Taking them as they are, putting them all together, having them pass through the same grades, the same teachers, with the same quality of instruction . . . But there's no laïcité in France, not totally, because we know very well that these kids are tracked. It happens in terms of where they live, how they're segregated, and the way that they're placed together. It's true.

Teacher

> La laïcité for me is to try to erase the maximum number of differences within the school, always, because it ultimately just creates problems for everyone.

Anita

> Above everything else, religion doesn't exist within the school. You can be Muslim and also be comfortable in a secular school . . . You're just like the others.

Naïma

> It's being cosmopolitan, do you see what I mean? It's completely cutting out religion. That's for you, in your heart. It's having open relationships with everyone. You can be Jewish, Buddhist, Christian, Muslim, and nothing prevents you from being friends.

Teacher

> You see, for me, la laïcité, above everything else, is citizenship, the public and political sector that is separated very clearly from, well, religious beliefs that are private, personal. Well, I'm strongly attached to la laïcité because I think it's the only opportunity, initially, for all students to live together and to forget what could separate them.

School aide

> One is given two completely different definitions of la laïcité. Either la laïcité is a place in which people put aside everything that has some religious connotation, or it's a place where everything having some religious connotation is found, along with the different religions. Me, I'm for the second definition. I can't imagine going to a place and saying, "this is the cloakroom where I hang my religion, and over there is where I pick it up again when I leave." It's part of me.

Fatou

> Whatever it is, it's not very clear. It should mean letting people live their lives as they wish. But we have to accept it; and to totally force people to take off their veils, I don't understand it. It seems like a lack of tolerance to me.

Teacher

> La laïcité is respecting others, ultimately, right. Yes, it's respecting opinions from every arena provided that they do not intrude into the freedom of others.

Sylvie

> No religious stuff. Everything that's tied to religion, we don't have the right to wear it in school.

Teacher
> The law of the Republic which must apply to everyone, with the understanding that there are no personal laws.

Rima
> It means that I feel okay here. I'm in a secular school, so I respect the things we have to do here.

Aïcha
> *La laïcité* is a way to battle segregation, racism, and intolerance. In secular schools, the teachers are more tolerant than somewhere else. I think it's a good thing. Now and then, we think that we are excluded from society, but when we go to school, we feel very close to one another.

Indeed, Habiba and her sister Su'ad noted this lack of clarity in the meaning óf *la laïcité* when I first met them, the year I began my research. Even as little girls in middle school they had troubles digesting the cohabitation imposed on them. During an interview at that time, we were talking about the difference between their parents' education and their own schooling when an interesting exchange took place between Habiba and her sister, which highlights some of the tensions and incomprehension that result from the way French secularism is put into practice:

> Su'ad: Madame, what I don't like about our school is that they say it's a secular school, but they only have vacation for Christmas, not the Aïd.
>
> Habiba: Well, you don't understand. We're in France. When I go to Algeria, there's no vacation during Christmas.
>
> Su'ad [*agitated*]: What is the use, then, if they say it's a secular school, if there're only French holidays? It's not a secular school, is it, except that they accept everybody!
>
> Habiba: But when the French go to Algeria, they're not going to ask why there isn't Christmas vacation.
>
> Su'ad: It's not secular there. Everything's Muslim there.

This exchange demonstrates that these girls, while having to adopt *la laïcité,* have some objections to the way it is imposed. Moreover, they recognize certain contradictions between the law and its application within the schools. Interestingly, when they were older, many of these girls seemed to conceptualize secularism more positively, as an asset that allows them, as Muslim girls, to have equal access to formal education: "*La laïcité* has allowed me to be in school today. I think that religion must be kept separate from education. More often than not it is taught subjectively," noted Fatima. During our last conversation, in 2004, Su'ad described *la laïcité* this way: "It's allowing people to freely assume their religion as they choose. As long as what we wear is discreet. Those girls who wear the veil are not trying to convert their friends; it's just clothing, and they should have the right to wear it if they choose."

It is relevant to also note that French history is filled with antagonisms connecting France to the Muslim world, and that history plays an integral role in how French secularism and Muslims are viewed in the country. Further, that history helps to explain current antagonisms and poor social relations between French Muslims and French people of European heritage. This history goes back to the early eighth century and the Muslim conquests in Europe, especially the invasions of southern France by the Saracens. The Saracens were defeated in 732, a date known by "all French people," according to one of my former professors. Then there is colonialism, underlain by slavery, whose hegemonic "civilizing missions" in Africa during the nineteenth century led to the imposition of French language and culture in the north, west, and central regions of the continent, regions having significant Muslim populations. Algeria, for example, was occupied from the 1830s until the end of its war of liberation in 1962. During that war both sides committed atrocities, including the massacres of Algerians in Paris in 1961 and the execution of thousands of French (*pieds-noirs*) and Algerians who supported France (Harkis) in Oran in 1962. Similarly, Côte d'Ivoire and Senegal only achieved their independence in 1960, having been under colonial rule since the mid-nineteenth century. And with migration from Africa to France during the 1960s and 1970s, these entrenched hostilities were only amplified in the country, antagonisms now unleashed on and by the offspring of this history in French schools and society.

As it was in Ferry's day, the secular school remains the most efficient instrument for integrating a diverse populace into a unified nation. And in the words of a former assistant principal at Henri III, whom I interviewed early in my fieldwork, this continues to be the school's essential function:

> We have to make them understand something: what we mean by *la laïcité*, how it was constructed in our tradition, and why it was constructed. And from the moment that these girls enter a secular school, they, too, must respect this *laïcité* because one can't have everything, right? One cannot come to France, become French, and choose what pleases us and reject what doesn't. When one marries a country, one marries it, right? One adapts. That is called integration here. We care about it a great deal.

Indeed, the circumstances accounting for the presence of diverse Muslims of color in France are complex and inseparable from the country's colonial past, which engenders its own symbolic violence, as when Africans such as the Senegalese *tirailleurs* have been forced to defend France in ways that locked them further into their conditions of misery (see chapter 3). No less problematic is France's failure to recognize the Harkis, the Algerians who defended French interests with their lives and reputations during the Algerian War. Not only were they never officially welcomed in France, as had been promised, but when they immigrated, they were so heavily stigmatized that their children have inherited that stigma, being called "children of traitors" by other Maghrebins. And while many Harkis expected to be integrated into French society, they were, instead, relegated to the French outer cities where they, and especially their children, are excluded and rejected from all sectors of French society. To illustrate this sentiment felt by certain youth, during one Ramadan I volunteered in a soup kitchen along with students from Henri III. After we had served everyone one evening, the young man who organized it and I sat together and informally conversed about Muslims in France. During that conversation, he readily identified as French, but whispered also that he was the son of a Harki. When I asked him why he whispered this information, he simply stated that it was something of which he was not proud.

Clearly, the historical context that has given rise to the presence of Muslims in France is contentious, and the tensions it engenders intensify with the growing realization that these young people expect equal treatment as the French citizens that so many already are. Muslim families have settled in France, and although some maintain that they intend to return *au bled* (to their native countries), they are entrenched in the French context. This fact becomes more and more true with each generation of children who pass through the doors of a French school. Perhaps Gilles Kepel sums it up best:

> The assimilationist culture of the French Republic, "One and Indivisible," has been sufficiently stable to suffer no losses due to demands for social inclusion made by its immigrant populations. It is not certain if this will always be the case. (1991, 384)

Clearly, this will no longer be the case once these "suitable enemies" organize politically across national origins and assert with conviction the self-understandings that they are claiming. Already, those whom I surveyed indicated that they intend to do just that, in response to a survey question regarding how they intend to improve their lot in France. And once they organize in this way, politicians will be forced to court the Muslim vote, as some have already begun to do. Nonetheless, this has yet to materialize in French society beyond a veneer of support that harbors manipulation. And some sectors of French society still hope that they will simply disappear, or "go home." The reality, however, is that these youths who declare that they are "French of 'x' origin" are already home, and it is in France, not *au bled*, that they plan to stay.

Epilogue

And So It Goes . . .

Muslim youths of African origins have been made into "suitable enemies" of a socioeconomically troubled France that is resisting the unmixing of its "national identity," which these youths come to represent. In actuality, this unmixing has already occurred. In this France, they are, for the most part, neither immigrants nor foreigners, despite public opinion to the contrary. Nor are they at risk of deportation, as their parents and some who share their origins may be or have been. However, in this France, these young people, and other stigmatized groups in outer cities, have been convenient scapegoats for many social ills. Increased violence, high unemployment, low-performing schools, and a perceived loss of the "national identity" are but a few of the problems attributed to these young people and their families. Unwilling or unable to identify the root causes of France's troubles, public officials have played on public insecurity in a period of heightened anti-Muslim sentiment and made false issues national concerns. In so doing, they have deflected attention away from root causes toward absurd responses to those issues. So a law targeting and expelling girls wearing the so-called "Islamic veil" from school becomes a necessity, because the veil is made a menace to French values, indeed culture. However, effective responses to an educational system in utter crisis take a back seat, which is a true menace to French society. More importantly, what does the need for such a law say about French values and French "identity" in the first place? If a veil can derail them, then maybe it is time for a change. Cartoonists in *Le monde* have sharply criticized those absurdities. The most telling image shows a teenager wearing hip-hugging jeans, a headscarf, and a cropped shirt that exposes her midriff; she is explaining to an Imam that because she is showing her navel, no one will notice her veil.

The discourse of urban violence intensifies these tensions when a supposedly unsuspecting public is told that, ultimately, they will be the victims of outer-city youths, if they are not controlled and confined. Enter, then, lived realities approaching U.S.-style ghettos and ghettoized schooling, with prisons not far behind. However, the degraded conditions typical of outer-city public housing and schools in the "other France" are not understood as a form of violence. They are, nonetheless, a reality that has persisted for generations, despite French affirmative action and the convenient explanations that are always ready at hand. That is, the low academic achievement and downward mobility of disadvantaged young people are attributed to their supposed cultural deficiencies. They are often misdiagnosed as intellectually incapable, yet suitable for dead-end vocational studies, if they remain in the educational system at all.

These places, with all their degradation and neglect, are not invisible or hidden, though these conditions remain largely unknown to or ignored by people seduced by France's illusions of inclusion. And, for those of us who seek global cities like Paris in order to escape racialized antagonisms in the U.S. or elsewhere, it is important to remember that the same dangers, violence, terror, and mistreatment that drive us to this City of Light are also present there (in living color). These young people are more than willing to show this truth to anyone who cares to know, and so am I. More importantly, the glaring and dismissed reality that they represent is this: no people will ever truly be safe, comfortable, or economically stable in their homeland while vulnerable peoples in that land are made into "suitable enemies" and denied the same comfort and security. Clearly, it is in our interest to recognize the unexamined assumptions that render places like the "other France" typical, acceptable instances of poor urbanization. And, most certainly, we must not ignore neighborhoods like the Courtillières, because *human beings* (lest we forget) live there. They are people struggling to have better lives, people stigmatized by every negative category imaginable, and people battling against racialized barriers not easily documented in France. And some of them are succeeding, despite these obstacles. However, many more are not, and they are blamed for social problems of which they are not the architects. Certainly some have become hardened, often very early in life, and respond in ways that ultimately work against them.

Certain Muslim girls must navigate an additional layer of gendered constraints attached to competing home, neighborhood, and school expectations. They must also develop strategies to cope and exist within those often incompatible arenas, sometimes to their own peril. These circumstances make the politics of their existence highly complex and in some ways unique. Their assertions of being French, at some level in these identity politics, foreground rights that they have yet to actualize fully as French citizens, or even, at times, to comprehend. Politicians, on the other hand, are grasping the significance of that claim and thus courting the Muslim vote. Moreover, as France has already adopted some of the worst aspects of U.S. society, it will be interesting to see who will eventually be made its "model minorities," targeted for sociopolitical incorporation. Will they also be used as weapons against demonized groups viewed as more recalcitrant in French society? In this context it is powerful and empowering for socially rejected young people to declare with conviction that they are French. However, as "beings perceived," they are never totally reducible to that.

[Handwritten annotations:]

danger (above "peril")

Preguntas futuro inmononía? imninonía? acceptadas

Francia: resiste "un-mixing" — national identity
outer-city youth

Main discourse: (Muslims) are a problem
  - Housing problems, poor school system → no se un como violencia
if they don't do "good" → due to their "cultural deficiencies"

* Estos problemas no son tan conocidos
  - Francia acepta exiliados (victimas de racismo U.S)
    pero no acepta a la juventud de descendía North Africana
  - mientras esto exista there will be no seguridad
    for the rest of the people.

* It should be recognized that Human beings lived
  in this "ghettos". Despite all struggles some succeed, but many don't.

* Must know that this is far worst for girls, home,
  school & neighborhood expectations — disagree among them.

  - They assert to be French → rights

closing France adopt worst of U.S society
  - ¿Qué hará con sus minorias?
  - ¿A quién aceptará / incorporara sociopolitically?
  - ¿Which group will be used to demonized against another group?

* Es importante q' los chicos declare con convicción
  q' son "franceses", pero q' no se los puede
  reducir como se les percibe.

Notes

1. Except where indicated, all interview and journal data were generated from my fieldwork. All participants' names have been changed. Translations are my own, in addition to those of scholars and professional translators.

2. In the spring of 2004, thousands marched in Paris (and London) to protest the bill banning all conspicuous religious symbols, such as headscarves, in the schools. This bill was overwhelmingly passed by the French government and strongly supported by the French public, which feared increases in Islamic fundamentalism in France.

3. "Racialized" in this text refers to the process of categorization in which meaning (objective and subjective) is assigned to groups' observable differences and cultural practices in a dialectic of signification. See Omi and Winant 1994; Wieviorka 2002; Small 2002; and Miles and Brown 2003.

4. As Loïc Wacquant explains, "Ceaselessly blacklisted, suspected in advance if not in principle, driven back to the margins of society and hounded by the authorities with unmatched zeal, the (non-European) foreigner mutates into a 'suitable enemy'—to use the expression of the Norwegian criminologist Nils Christie—at once symbol of and target for all social anxieties, as are poor African Americans in the major cities of their society" (Wacquant 1999b, 219).

5. France is considered to have the largest Muslim population in Western Europe.

6. Since July 2003, twelve Imams, some of whom were long-term residents of France, have been detained or deported for preaching views "contrary to Republican values . . . that constitute a danger to the public" (Landrin 2004).

7. Rogers Brubaker (2001, 531) has argued that arrogant assimilationism or franco-conformity—turning immigrants into Frenchmen—is both "analytically discredited and politically disreputable." Indeed, contemporary writers share this critique of the canonical formulations of assimilation, which are most closely associated with W. Lloyd Warner and Leo Srole (1945) and Milton Gordon (1964). However, as a social fact and as the historical and expressed objective of French national education, arrogant assimilationism, buttressed by an ideology of a "common culture," inheres nonetheless in French society and schooling. It is, therefore, a phenomenon to be explored and explained, not something that explains social phenomena. For reconceptualizations of assimilation see Zhou 1997; Portes and Rumbaut 2001; and Alba and Nee 2003.

8. Nancy Venel's *Musulmanes françaises* (1999) warrants particular attention, within the context of this study, because of its provocative title, which highlights and supports the self-understandings that I examine. However, her target population and research questions differ significantly from mine. Venel focuses only on advanced university students of North African origin who choose to "veil" and who live in Lille (one of three cities featured in the media at the start of the "veil controversy"). Her goal is not to analyze their self-understandings within existing social structures, but to "understand the logic pushing them to veil" (29) in terms of religion, wherein their self-understandings seem inscribed. Interestingly, we were conducting research during the same period.

9. For instance, the television program *La voile de la République* (aired on France 2, February 12, 2004), in discussing the headscarf ban, highlighted non-Arab Muslim girls of African origin.

10. I use the word "participant" to refer to those young people who pursued this work with me. Since this is an interdisciplinary study, the term also reflects my desire to

use one that is not perceived as limited to a specific discipline, as "informant," "subject," and "social agent" often are. Also, although I often refer to my participants as "girls," the word does not always adequately capture all the manifestations of their gendered experiences. It is sometimes unsuitable but also indicative of existing discourse pertaining to these youths.

11. In this analysis, "black," in lower case, refers to the social category and the notions of biological "race" that it harbors, while "Black," capitalized, is used in its most inclusive sense to refer to a group designation that often implies ethnicity. I recognize its limitations as a classification and category operating within a larger dialectic of identification.

12. See *The Souls of Black Folk* (1903), in which Du Bois argues that Black Americans possess a double consciousness split between their self-understandings and an identification refracted through white supremacist structures.

13. The most prominent anti-racist groups include Mouvement contre le racisme et pour l'amitié entre les peuples (MRAP), SOS Racisme, La ligue des droits de l'homme (LDH), and Group d'études et de lutte contre les discriminations (GELD). Under President Chirac's administration, a new "High Authority" has been developed to centralize national anti-discrimination efforts. GELD representatives expressed grave concern that "racial discrimination" would not be given adequate attention. See Sylvia Zappi, "Vers une haute autorité unique contre toutes les discriminations," *Le monde*, February 17, 2004, p. 10.

14. In November 2002, Alec Hargreaves hosted an international conference titled "French and U.S. Anti-discrimination Policy: Making a Difference," through the Winthrop-King Institute for Contemporary French and Francophone Studies and the Department of Sociology at Florida State University, where he is a professor. The ethnic identification of the French was one of several key topics discussed. See also Simon and Stavo-Debauge 2002.

15. For example, the Commission nationale consultative des droits de l'homme (CNCDH) publishes an annual report on the state of racism and xenophobia in France, and is composed of representatives from various prominent anti-racist associations, such as SOS Racisme. See chapter 1.

16. See J. Montvalon, "L'UDF reste trés réservée sur le droit de vote des étrangers aux élections locales," *Le monde*, November 30, 1999; and J. Montvalon and Sylvia Zappi, "Détente sur l'immigration," *Le monde*, August 1, 2000.

17. Currently, all children born in France whose parents are foreigners can obtain French nationality upon reaching the age of majority, but naturalization is contingent upon proof of continued residency in the country and other juridical restrictions. See "La nationalité française," at http://www.france.diplomatie.fr/etrangers/vivre/nationalite/, accessed March 30, 2005.

18. While the French national educational system has decentralized with regard to school choice, political scientist Erik Bleich rightly observes that the structure of the French educational system remains highly centralized, with fewer decision-makers than exist in the English or U.S. system (1998, 81–100).

19. The dates of these bombings are relevant since these events effectively set the stage for my entry into the field. During this time all Muslims in France were considered suspects by virtue of their religious and cultural affiliation. The 1995 bombings, like those of 1986, occurred in tourist areas and in metros heavily used by Parisian commuters, such as the metro station at St. Michel. From July to October 1995, France was confronted with the worst urban violence in ten years. I began my fieldwork in France on August 16, 1995.

20. In April 1996, three hundred undocumented Africans, forty of whom were less than one year old, were forcibly expelled from the Saint Ambroise cathedral in Paris, where they had taken refuge as a political move to force the French immigration services to reexamine their status in the country and to protest the increased restrictions on immi-

gration imposed by the Pasqua laws. Those whose status was deemed "irregular" were expelled from France. The French press covered the story extensively in March and April; in particular, see *Le monde,* March 25 and April 17.

21. My thanks to Stéphane Beaud, formally of the École normale supérieure and now professor of sociology at the Université de Nantes, for providing the model for my survey, which derives from his study of the socioeducational conditions of youths whose parents work in factories in Sochaux-Montbéliard, France.

1. Unmixing French "National Identity"

1. Once it became clear that Fatou was receiving little help with or advice about her academic difficulties, I attempted to learn how she came to be in a general studies track. The person charged with advising students about their options had not spoken with Fatou by late April in an academic year that ended in June. During an interview with me, she stated that she has a hands-off policy concerning outreach to students, preferring that they seek her out. Fatou did not, since this person is also responsible for recommending placement in vocational studies, which she was attempting to avoid. Some of Fatou's teachers told me that they were instructed "not to push her too much," given her academic record. Others thought she might be dyslexic. This information was not in her student file, though a doctor recommended that she wear glasses. She did not own a pair, and when I tried to find out why, she became angry and refused to discuss the matter further, informing me that the matter was personal. Her French teacher told me that she had strongly urged a different track for Fatou following her first year in high school, and her academic record confirmed this. Her parents were noted as having contested her placement in vocational studies.

2. In a phone conversation in February 2004, a statistician with INSEE confirmed that "French by acquisition" remains a subcategory under "immigrant," but added that this may change in the next census.

3. Benjamin Barthe, "Objectif bac pour Fatoumata," *L'humanité,* July 19, 2000, http://www.humanite.presse.fr/journal/2000-07-19/2000-07-19-228692, accessed April 8, 2005.

4. "Connubial Wrongs," *Economist,* November 2001, p. 10. Also see the *British Muslims Monthly Survey* 6 (June 2001): 5.

5. Tony Clark, "Polygamy or Abuse? Utah Case Stirs Controversy," CNN, August 8, 1998; also at http://www.cnn.com/US/9808/08/polygamy/, accessed April 8, 2005.

2. Structured Exclusion

1. See A. Campana and Jean-Charles Eleb, "Un vote contre l'immigration . . . et l'injustice: Statistique sur les raisons pour lesquelles des habitants de Seine-Saint-Denis votent Front National," *Le monde diplomatique,* March 1998, p. 10, for the results of their study of the National Front's (i.e., the extreme right's) success in recruiting under- and unemployed French of European origin who reside in Seine-Saint-Denis. Such people insisted that they were not, to use their term, "racists" for joining the Front. Nonetheless, Campana and Eleb argue that people do have "a general feeling of being invaded by foreigners, resulting in a loss of the national identity." The Front heightens such feeling by attributing all social ills to "immigrants" and those perceived as immigrants, specifically to this generation of young people from economically disadvantaged areas. See also Taguieff and Tribalat 1998.

2. The statistical data cited derive primarily from the Institut national de la statistique et des études économiques (INSEE) and the archives of the city of Pantin, unless otherwise noted.

3. See the local press: Laurent Dilbos, "L'histoire du Serpentin," *Canal, le magazine de Pantin*, November 1999; and Manuel Delluc, "Pantin retour à l'ordre urbain aux Courtillières," *Le moniteur*, November 3, 2000.

4. *Le monde*, October 1, 1999, p. 6; see also Stovall 1996.

5. On African conscripts, see Dewitte 1985; White 1979; Echenberg 1991; and Stovall 1996.

6. The lessor of the Courtillières, and of several other developments in the area, was the Société d'économie mixte immobilière interdépartementale de la région parisienne (the Semidep), overseen by the city of Paris. On January 1, 2000, public housing authorities in Pantin became the new lessor. Their first order of business entailed assessing the neglected repairs to the buildings controlled by the Semidep. These matters received extensive coverage in the local press, such as *Canal, le magazine de Pantin* (November 1999–January 2000) and the *Moniteur* (November 3, 2000), and in the *Parisian* (June 6, 2001).

7. See Massey and Denton 1993. For a comparative analysis of the American and French contexts, see Wacquant 1992.

8. SOS Racisme 2000. Also see Olivier Noël, "La face cachée de l'intégration: Les discriminations institutionnelles à l'embauche," *Ville-École-Intégration enjeux*, no. 121 (June 2000): 106–116.

9. William Julius Wilson offers great insights into the consequences of, and viable solutions to, sustained social exclusion in the U.S. and beyond (1999). Also see Loïc Wacquant, "How Penal Common Sense Comes to Europeans," *European Societies* 1 (1999): 319–352, on how the rhetoric of "individual responsibility" has been imported from the U.S. to Europe through the politics of "zero tolerance."

10. The best information on the poor management of public housing in this area comes from the local press. See *Canal, le magazine de Pantin* between November 1999 and January 2000, in addition to the minutes of public meetings, which are available at the city archives in Pantin.

11. Ghislaine Bouskela, *Canal, le magazine de Pantin*, December 2000–January 2001; and April 1997, p. 38.

12. For interesting analyses of French bureaucracy, see Crozier 1970, 1979.

3. Transmitting a "Common Culture"

1. Here I am drawing on Richard Alba and Victor Nee's (2003) reanalysis of Milton Gordon's (1964) model of assimilation. The emphasis they place on Gordon's distinction between cultural assimilation and structural assimilation (inclusion in a society's institutions) is particularly important in this context. What they reject is the deterministic aspect of Gordon's formulation, that is, the idea of an inevitable and absolute march toward a "mainstream" culture, uninfluenced by other sectors of the society, such as the inner or outer city. In the French context, the social expectation of cultural assimilation and the realities of social exclusion illustrate the usefulness of Gordon's distinction.

2. These strikes had some serious political consequences. For example, in March 2000, Claude Allègre was dismissed as minister of education after a brief tenure of two years. From its inception, Allègre's ministry was marked by conflicts with educators who rejected his ill-fated reforms, aimed at streamlining secondary education (described as creating a "*lycée*-light"). Allègre's parting words included, "Too many teachers live in fear: fear of their students, of new technologies, fear of the ever-increasing advances in education. In essence, they understand all of this rather poorly" (*Le monde*, April 8, 2000). Allègre was replaced by Socialist Jack Lang, who had held the post in 1992–1993. In 2004, during regional elections, voters expressed overwhelming displeasure with the Chirac government, resulting in several dismissals, including that of the man who had replaced Lang as minister of education, Luc Ferry, who is indirectly a descendant of Jules Ferry.

3. In the United States, the issue of establishing curricula on the basis of a "common culture" continues to incite passionate debates, largely because of disagreements over what constitutes such an entity. In France, the issue of a "common culture" is only beginning to emerge in schools as a curricular and cultural question, owing to greater and more visible ethnic diversity.

4. Another example concerns the meals served in the cafeteria. School administrators receive increasing numbers of complaints that meals are not *halel*. In my observations, I saw that many students did not eat cafeteria food, but either brought food to school, went home for lunch, or ate in fast-food restaurants near the school (many of which serve *halel* food), or did not eat lunch at all. See "L'école fait face à une montée des revendications identitaires des élèves," *Le monde,* April 15, 2000.

5. Ferry was minister of foreign affairs during France's occupation of several countries, most notably the Congo, in the nineteenth century. See Gaillard 1989.

6. Teachers have criticized the IUFM for placing too much emphasis on preparation for the certification exams, which are given at the end of the two-year program. Teachers and IUFM administrators have additionally identified other problems that are poorly addressed in teacher preparation, such as the gap between educational theory and practical strategies useful in real-world teaching situations. They also found that practicums did not prepare teachers for the challenges they would face from students with multiple needs, not all of them academic. In other words, the IUFM has been described as "a world far removed from the realities of teaching in an actual classroom." J. Four, "Les ratés de la machine à former," *Le monde de l'éducation,* September 1998, p. 49.

7. For more on "ebonics," see Rickford 2000; Delpit 1995.

8. This language is typical of educational discourse in official bulletins issued by the Ministry of Education, available on its website (http://www.education.gouv.fr/index.php). The quotation is from a section of the 1999 official program entitled "Choix des textes."

9. See Huot 1989 for a lively historical perspective on the politics of textbook selection in France, particularly with regard to the practice of selecting textbooks authored by district inspectors. Also see Alain Auffray and Paul Quinio, "Devoir de rentrée: Êtes-vous pour ou contre les manuels scolaires?" *Libération,* September 9, 1998.

10. Also see Jeanne Fouet's analysis of the Coordination internationale des chercheurs sur les littératures du maghreb: "Juin 2001: État des lieux: La présence de la littérature francophone maghrébine dans les nouveaux programmes des classes de premières de lycée," http://www.limag.refer.org/Textes/Fouet/Etatdeslieux.htm, accessed April 15, 2005.

11. *Histoire-Géographie,* official bulletin from the Ministry of Education, August 2000, 88.

12. The historian Alain Choppin has been in the forefront of textbook research in France. In his online database Emanuelle (created in conjunction with the Institut national de recherche pédagogique), he attempts to categorize and quantify the breadth of French studies in this field. While he documents works exploring issues pertaining to women and Africans under colonization, more critiques are needed of how slavery, colonization, decolonization, and the Algerian War are represented in French history textbooks and in the official curriculum. See *Histoire de l'éducation* 58 (May 1993), a special issue edited by Choppin. On the Algerian war in history textbooks, see Laamirie and Le Dain 1992.

13. Maschino 2001; SOS Racisme 1999; Human Rights Watch 2001; and Suzanne Citron, *Le mythe national: L'histoire de la France en question,* 2nd ed. (Paris: Éditions ouvrières, 1991).

14. On November 12, 2003, European Deputy François Zimeray wrote a scathing letter to President Chirac demanding that the Delagrave textbook be withdrawn because of its anti-Semitic rhetoric and depictions. Similarly on another front, groups based in Marseille led a letter-writing campaign against Hatier and Hachette for demonizing Arabs and Muslims.

15. See http://www.assemblee-nationale.fr/12/dossiers/rapatries.asp, accessed June 25, 2005.

16. Specifically, I am referring to the textbooks published by Belin, Hatier, and Nathan in 1998.

17. As reported on the French radio station *RTL* in May 2001.

18. See Stora 1999; and Human Rights Watch 2001.

19. Also see Dewitte 1985, 1996; and Valensky 1995.

4. Counterforces

Educational statistics cited in this chapter were generated by the school district (the Académie de Créteil) and the Direction de l'évaluation et de la prospective (DEP; the statistical division of the Ministry of Education). Statistics referring to "ethnicity" were generated by that school. District statisticians readily admit that figures produced prior to 1992 are not always reliable, as data were manually generated until that date.

1. Only 0.8 percent of French high schools were recipients of ZEP subventions during the initiative's early phases. See Catherine Moisan, "Les ZEP: Bientôt vingt ans," *Éducation & Formations* 61 (October–December 2001), http://www.education.gouv.fr/stateval/revue/revue61/resuef.htm, accessed April 2004.

2. Alain Savary, bulletin of July 1, 1981, *Bulletins Officiels* (Paris: Ministry of Education).

3. Richard Descoings, administrator of the Fondation nationale des sciences politiques and a member of the Council of State, clearly expresses this distinction in his communiqué "Conventions ZEP: L'excellence dans la diversité," dated February 26, 2001. For a parallel argument in the U.S. context, see Wilson 1999.

4. E-mail from the DEP, March 16, 2004.

5. See "Trois indicateurs de resultats de lycées: Dossier d'information," published by the Ministry of Education and available on its website (http://indicateurs.education.gouv.fr/brochure.html, accessed April 25, 2005), and DEP 2003.

6. E-mail from the DEP, February 4, 2004.

7. This point is well illustrated by Fatou's third-trimester grades in French from middle through high school. Keep in mind that French is a core subject in national education, and third-trimester grades are used to gauge academic performance in addition to influencing strongly how students will be tracked. Grading is based on a twenty-point scale. In the sixth grade (*6e*) Fatou's mark in French was a 9 out of 20, while in seventh grade (*5e*) it was 11. In eighth grade (*4e*) it was 6, and in her last year of middle school, the ninth grade (*3e*), it was 7.5. However, in her first year of high school, tenth grade (*2de*), her grade in French was only a 1, and after she had repeated this level, her grade was only 2.5, still out of 20. Fatou's case is still more tragic because, given her age, she should have already completed her high school studies.

8. The availability of the morning-after pill was debated for weeks in the media, particularly in the press; see *Libération*, November 30, 1999, which also carries comparative information about teen pregnancy in Britain.

5. Beyond Identity

1. In *Ni putes ni soumises*, Fadela Amara (2003, 8) praises the defiance expressed by this artist, whose lyrics speak to violence committed against outer-city Muslim girls who, in asserting their femininity or rejecting submissiveness, are labeled *putes* (whores) or *salopes* (bitches).

2. According to reports issued during the U.N.'s National Assembly for Human Rights, women and girls, predominantly from Africa, the Middle East, and Asia, continue

to be subjected to genital mutilation, of which excision is the most common form. Indeed, in 2000 alone 85–114 million cases were reported. Though banned in the United States and many European countries, the practice continues among migrants to these areas. Contrary to popular belief, female circumcision is not mandated in the Koran. For interesting perspectives on this issue, see Shell-Duncan and Hernlund 2000.

3. For media coverage of this case, see *Le monde* between February 4 and February 18, 1999.

4. The quotation is from the preamble to the law, which is law 2004-228, of March 15, 2004. Its full text is available at http://www.legifrance.gouv.fr/WAspad/UnTexteDe-Jorf?numjo=MENX0400001L, and the Ministry of Education has a website explaining the principle and application of *la laïcité* at http://www.education.gouv.fr/dossier/laicite/default.htm.

5. See SOS Racisme 2000.

6. See "La consultation Chevènement en débat au rassemblement musulman du Bourget," *Le monde,* May 3, 2000.

7. P. Bernard, "Alain Juppé veut sortir du 'conflit idéologique' sur l'immigration," *Le monde,* October 1, 1999.

8. "Foulard à l'école: La réalité cachée derrière les chiffres officials," *Le monde,* December 10, 2003.

9. Phillippe Bernard, "Trois enseignants sur quatre veulent l'interdiction des signes religieux," *Le monde,* February 5, 2004. The survey was carried out by L'institut CSA for *Le monde.*

10. See also M. Kheroua and Mme. Kachour, M. Balo and Mme. Kizic, *Arrêt du Conseil d'état,* November 2, 1992.

Bibliography

Abu-Lughod, Lila. 1991. "Writing against Culture." In *Recapturing Anthropology: Working in the Present*, edited by R. G. Fox, 137–162. Santa Fe, N.M.: School of American Research Press.

———. 2002. "Do Muslim Women Really Need Saving? Anthropological Reflections on Cultural Relativism and Its Others." *American Anthropologist* 104(3): 783–790.

al-Hibri, Azizah, ed. 1982. *Women and Islam*. Special issue of *Women's Studies International Forum* 5(2). Oxford: Pergamon.

Alba, Richard, and Victor Nee. 2003. *Remaking the American Mainstream: Assimilation and Contemporary Immigration*. Cambridge, Mass.: Harvard University Press.

Altschull, Elizabeth. 1995. *Le voile contre l'école*. Paris: Éditions du Seuil.

Amara, Fadela, with Sylvia Zappi. 2003. *Ni putes ni soumises*. Paris: La Découverte.

Amougou, Emmanuel. 1998. *Afro-métropolitaines: Emancipation ou domination masculine?* Paris: L'Harmattan.

Amselle, Jean-Loup. 1998. *Mestizo Logics: Anthropology of Identity in Africa and Elsewhere*. Translated by Claudia Royal. Stanford, Calif.: Stanford University Press.

Andersen, Margaret L., and Patricia Hill Collins. 1995. *Race, Class, and Gender: An Anthology*. 2nd ed. Belmont, Calif.: Wadsworth.

Archer-Straw, Petrine. 2000. *Negrophilia: Avant-Garde Paris and Black Culture in the 20s*. New York: Thames & Hudson.

Bâ, Mariama. 1979. *Une si longue lettre*. Dakar: Nouvelles Éditions Africaines.

Balibar, Étienne. 2004. "Dissonances dans la laïcité." In *Le foulard islamique en questions*, edited by Charlotte Nordmann, 15–28. Paris: Éditions Amsterdam.

Balibar, Étienne, and Immanuel Wallerstein. 1991. *Race, Nation, Class: Ambiguous Identities*. New York: Verso.

Banton, Michael. 1977. *The Idea of Race*. London: Tavistock.

———. 2002. *The International Politics of Race*. Oxford: Polity.

Barbier, Maurice. 1995. *La laïcité*. Paris: L'Harmattan.

Beaud, Stéphane, and Michel Pialoux. 2001. "Révolte dans les quartiers: Emeutes urbaines, violence sociale." *Le monde diplomatique* (July): 18–19.

Ben Jelloun, Tahar. 1984. *Hospitalité française: Racisme et immigration maghrébine*. Paris: Éditions du Seuil.

Benguigui, Yamina. 1997. *Mémoires d'immigrés: L'héritage maghrébin*. Paris: Canal + Éditions.

Benoist, Jean-Marie. 1977. "Facettes de l'identité." In *L'identité: Séminaire interdisciplinaire dirigé par Claude Lévi-Strauss, 1974–1975*, edited by J.-M. Benoist and Claude Lévi-Strauss, 13–24. Paris: Bernard Grasset.

Bernasconi, Robert, and Tommy L. Lott. 2000. *The Idea of Race*. Indianapolis: Hackett.

Beyala, Calixthe. 1995. *Lettre d'une africaine à ses soeurs occidentales*. Paris: Éditions Spengler.

———. 1996. *Les honneurs perdus*. Paris: Albin Michel.

Bhabha, Homi. 1994. *The Location of Culture*. New York: Routledge.

Bleich, Erik. 1998. "From International Ideas to Domestic Policies: Educational Multiculturalism in England and France." *Comparative Politics* 31(1): 81–100.

———. 2003. *Race Politics in Britain and France: Ideas and Policymaking since the 1960s*. Cambridge: Cambridge University Press.

Bodman, Herbert, and Nayereh Tohidi. 1998. *Women in Muslim Societies: Diversity within Unity*. Boulder, Colo.: Lynne Rienner.

Bonelli, Laurent. 2001. "Renseignements généraux et violences urbaines." *Actes de la recherche en sciences sociales* 136–137: 95–103.

Boudimbou, Guy. 1991. *Habitat et modes de vie des immigrés africains en France.* Paris: L'Harmattan.

Bourdieu, Pierre. 1984. *Distinction: A Social Critique of the Judgment of Taste.* Translated by Richard Nice. Cambridge, Mass.: Harvard University Press.

———. 1990a. *In Other Words: Essays towards a Reflexive Sociology.* Translated by Matthew Adamson. Stanford, Calif.: Stanford University Press.

———. 1990b. *The Logic of Practice.* Translated by Richard Nice. Stanford, Calif.: Stanford University Press.

———. 1991. *Language and Symbolic Power.* Edited by John B. Thompson. Translated by Goni Raymond and Matthew Adamson. Cambridge, Mass.: Harvard University Press.

———. 1994. "Rethinking the State: Genesis and Structure of the Bureaucratic Field." *Sociological Theory* 12(1): 1–18.

———. 1996. *The State Nobility: Elite Schools in the Field of Power.* Translated by Lauretta C. Clough. Stanford, Calif.: Stanford University Press.

———. 1996. *Sur la télévision, suivi de L'emprise du journalisme.* Paris: Raisons d'agir.

———. 1998. *La domination masculine.* Paris: Éditions du Seuil.

Bourdieu, Pierre, and A. Accardo, eds. 1993. *La misère du monde.* Paris: Éditions du Seuil.

Bourdieu, Pierre, and Jean Claude Passeron. 1979. *The Inheritors: French Students and Their Relation to Culture.* Translated by Richard Nice. Chicago: University of Chicago Press.

———. 1977. *Reproduction in Education, Society, and Culture.* Translated by Richard Nice. London: Sage.

Bourdieu, Pierre, and Loïc J. D. Wacquant. 1992. *An Invitation to Reflexive Sociology.* Chicago: University of Chicago Press.

———. 1999. "On the Cunning of Imperialist Reason." *Theory, Culture & Society* 16(1): 41–58.

Bouzar, Dounia. 2004. "Françaises et musulmanes, entre réappropriation et remise en question des normes." In *Le foulard islamique en questions,* edited by Charlotte Nordmann, 54–64. Paris: Éditions Amsterdam.

Broccolichi, Sylvain. 1995. "Orientations et ségrégations nouvelles dans l'enseignement secondaire." *Sociétés contemporaines* 21:15–27.

Broccolichi, Sylvain, and Françoise Oeuvrard. 1993. "L'engrenage." In *La misère du monde,* edited by Pierre Bourdieu and A. Accardo, 639–648. Paris: Éditions du Seuil.

Broccolichi, Sylvain, and Agnès Van Zanten. 1997. "Espaces de concurrences et circuits de scolarisation. L'évitement des collèges publics dans un district de la banlieue parisienne." *Annales de la recherche urbaine* 75:103–123.

Brubaker, Rogers. 1996. "Aftermaths of Empire and the Unmixing of Peoples: Historical and Comparative Perspectives." In *Nationalism Reframed: Nationhood and the National Question in the New Europe,* 148–178. Cambridge: Cambridge University Press.

———. 2001. "The Return of Assimilation? Changing Perspectives on Immigration and Its Sequels in France, Germany, and the United States." *Ethnic and Racial Studies* 24(4): 531–548.

Brubaker, Rogers, and Frederick Cooper. 2000. "Beyond 'Identity.'" *Theory and Society* 29(1): 1–47.

Cacouault, Marlaine, and Françoise Oeuvrard. 1995. *Sociologie de l'éducation.* Paris: La Découverte.

Cahm, Eric. 1996. *The Dreyfus Affair in French Society and Politics.* London: Longman.

Caillaud, Pascal. 2002. "Le diplôme professionnel: Quelle valeur juridique sur le marché du travail?" In *Les patrons: L'état et la formation des jeunes,* edited by Gilles Moreau, 179–190. Paris: La Dispute.

Calhoun, Craig. 1994. *Social Theory and the Politics of Identity.* Cambridge, Mass.: Blackwell.

Camilleri, Carmel, and Hanna Malewska-Peyre. 1990. *Identité et question de la disparité culturelle: Essai d'un typologie.* Paris: Presses Universitaires de France.

Cesari, Jocelyne. 1994. *Être musulman en France.* Paris: Karthala.

————. 1998. *Musulmans et républicains: Les jeunes, l'Islam, et la France*. Bruxelles: Éditions Complexe.

Charlot, Bernard, Elisabeth Bautier, and Jean-Yves Rochex. 1992. *École et savoir dans les banlieues et ailleurs*. Paris: Armand Colin.

Choppin, Alain. 1992. *Les manuels scolaires: Histoire et actualité*. Paris: Hachette.

Choppin, Alain, and Martine Clinkspoor. 1993. *Les manuels scolaires en France de 1789 à nos jours*. Paris: Publications de la Sorbonne.

Clark, Kenneth B. 1965. *Dark Ghetto: Dilemmas of Social Power*. New York: Harper and Row.

Clark, VèVè A. 1991. "Developing Diaspora Literacy and Marasa Consciousness." In *Comparative American Identities: Race, Sex, and Nationality in the Modern Text*, edited by Hortense J. Spillers, 40–61. New York: Routledge.

CNCDH (Commission nationale consultative des droits de l'homme). 2000. *La lutte contre le racisme et la xénophobie: 1999*. Paris: La Documentation française.

————. 2001. *La lutte contre le racisme et la xénophobie: Rapport d'activité 2000*. Paris: La Documentation française.

————. 2002. *La lutte contre le racisme et la xénophobie: Rapport d'activité 2001*. Paris: La Documentation française.

————. 2003. *La lutte contre le négationnisme: Bilan et perspectives de la loi du 13 juillet 1990 tendant à réprimer tout acte raciste, antisémite, ou xénophobe*. Paris: La Documentation française.

————. 2004. *La lutte contre le racisme et la xénophobie: Rapport d'activité 2003*. Paris: La Documentation française.

Collins, Patricia Hill. 2000. *Black Feminist Thought: Knowledge, Consciousness, and the Politics of Empowerment*. New York: Routledge.

Comité d'organisation. 1999. "Quels savoirs enseigner dans les lycées?" Paris: Ministry of Education.

Condé, Maryse. 1974. "Négritude césairienne, négritude senghorienne." *Revue de littérature comparée* 48: 409–419.

————. 1999–2000. "Les 'Black British' donnent l'exemple?" *Black Renaissance/Renaissance Noire* 2(3): 108–121.

————. 1996. *Laïcité et république: Le lien nécessaire*. Paris: Éditions du Félin.

Coq, Guy. 1999. "La laïcité, la république et les religions." In *La laïcité*, edited by Sophie Ernst, 1–20. Paris: Institut national de recherche pédagogique.

Costa-Lascoux, Jacqueline. 1994. "La nationalité par la naissance et par le choix." *Hommes et migrations* 1178 (July): 18–22.

Crozier, Michel. 1970. *La société bloquée*. Paris: Éditions du Seuil.

————. 1979. *On ne change pas la société par décret*. Paris: Bernard Grasset.

De Jesus Vaz, Celine. 2002. "De la crise du logement au grand ensemble: Le quartier des Courtillières à Pantin-Bobigny, 1954–1966." Dissertation, Université de Paris, Nanterre.

de Rudder, Véronique, Christian Poiret, and François Vourc'h. 2000. *L'inégalité raciste: L'universalité républicaine à l'épreuve*. Paris: Presses Universitaires de France.

Delpit, Lisa. 1995. *Other People's Children*. New York: New Press.

DEP (Direction de l'évaluation et de la prospective). 2003. "Repères et références statistiques sur l'enseignement, la formation et la recherché." Paris: Direction de l'évaluation et de la prospective.

Dewitte, Philippe. 1985. *Les mouvements nègres en France, 1919–1939*. Paris: L'Harmattan.

————. *Les musulmans algériens dans l'armée française, 1919–1945*. Paris: Harmattan, 1996.

Diallo, Kadiatou, and Craig Wolff. 2003. *My Heart Will Cross This Ocean: My Story, My Son Amadou*. New York: One World/Ballantine.

Diawara, Manthia. 1998. *In Search of Africa*. Cambridge, Mass.: Harvard University Press.

————. 2003. *We Won't Budge: A Malaria Memoir*. New York: Basic Civitas.

Diop, Cheikh Anta. 1954. *Nations nègres et culture*. Paris: Présence Africaine.

Diop, Moustapha, and Laurence Michalak. 1996. "'Refuge' and 'Prison': Islam, Ethnicity, and the Adaptation of Space in Workers' Housing in France." In *Making Muslim Space in North America and Europe,* edited by Barbara Daly Metcalf, 74–91. Berkeley: University of California Press.

Djité, Pauline. 1992. "The French Revolution and the French Language: A Paradox?" *Language Problems and Language Planning* 16(2): 162–174.

Drake, St. Clair. 1982. "Diaspora Studies and Pan-Africanism." In *Global Dimensions of the African Diaspora,* edited by Joseph E. Harris, 451–514. Washington, D.C.: Howard University Press.

Dubet, François. 1987. *La galère: Jeunes en survie.* Paris: Fayard.

———. 1997. *École, familles: Le malentendu.* Paris: Éditions Textuel.

Du Bois, William Edward Burghardt (W. E. B.). 1903. *The Souls of Black Folk.* Chicago: A. C. McClurg.

———. 1935. *Black Reconstruction in America.* New York: Harcourt, Brace.

Durkheim, Emile. 1938/1977. *The Evolution of Educational Thought: Lectures on the Formation and Development of Secondary Education in France.* Translated by Peter Collins. London: Routledge and Kegan Paul.

———. 1956. *Education and Sociology.* Glencoe, Ill.: Free Press.

———. 1993. *Les règles de la méthode sociologique.* Paris: Alcan and Presses Universitaires de France.

Dyson, Anne Haas. 1992. "The Case of the Singing Scientist: A Performance Perspective on the Stages of School Literacy." *Written Communication* 19:3–47.

———. 1997. *Writing Superheroes: Contemporary Childhood, Popular Culture, and Classroom Literacy.* New York: Teachers College Press.

Echenberg, Myron. 1991. *Colonial Conscripts: The Tirailleurs Sénégalais in French West Africa, 1857–1960.* Portsmouth, N.H.: Heinemann.

Edwards, Brent Hayes. 2003. *The Practice of Diaspora: Literature, Translation, and the Rise of Black Internationalism.* Cambridge, Mass.: Harvard University Press.

El Saadawi, Nawal. 1982. "Women and Islam." In *Women and Islam,* special issue of *Women's Studies International Forum* 5(2), edited by Azizah al-Hibri, 193–206.

Elias, Norbert. 1965. *Established and Outsiders.* London: Sage.

Erikson, Erik H. 1968. *Identity, Youth, and Crisis.* New York: W. W. Norton.

Etienne, Bruno. 1989. *La France et l'Islam.* Paris: Hachette.

Eze, Emmanuel Chukwudi. 1997. *Race and the Enlightenment: A Reader.* Malden, Mass.: Blackwell.

Fabre, Michel. 1993. *From Harlem to Paris: Black American Writers in France, 1840–1980.* Urbana: University of Illinois Press.

Fanon, Frantz. 1952. *Peau noire, masques blancs.* Paris: Éditions du Seuil.

———. 1961. *Les damnées de la terre.* With a preface by Jean-Paul Sartre. Paris: François Maspero.

Faure, M. 1999. "Des immigrés, bannis de la 'double peine.'" *Le monde diplomatique* (November): 24–25.

Favell, Adrian. 2001. *Philosophies of Integration: Immigration and the Idea of Citizenship in France and Britain.* New York: Palgrave.

Feraoun, Mouloud. 2000. *Journal, 1955–1962: Reflections on the French-Algerian War.* Translated by Mary Ellen Wolf and Claude Fouillade. Lincoln: University of Nebraska Press.

Fosset, R. 1991. *L'espace social en contraste.* Paris: Éditions Autrement.

Foucault, Michel. 1971. *L'ordre du discours.* Paris: Éditions Gallimard.

———. 1991. "Faire vivre et laisser mourir: La naissance du racisme." *Les temps modernes* (February): 37–61.

Fouet, Jeanne. 1998. "Connaissance et diffusion de la littérature francophone maghrébine dans les manuels scolaires à l'usage des lycées." *Études littérature maghrébines* 16:36–41.

Gaillard, Jean-Michel. 1989. *Jules Ferry.* Paris: Fayard.

Garcia, Sandrine, Franck Poupeau, and Laurence Proteau. 1998. "Dans la Seine-Saint-Denis, le refus." *Le monde diplomatique* (June): 15–16.

Gaspard, Françoise. 2004. "Femmes, foulards et République." In *Le foulard islamique en questions*, edited by Charlotte. Nordmann, 72–80. Paris: Éditions Amsterdam.

Gaspard, Françoise, and Farhad Khosrokhavar. 1995. *Le foulard et la République*. Paris: La Découverte.

Geertz, Clifford. 1973. *The Interpretation of Culture*. New York: Basic Books.

Geisser, Vincent. 2003. *La nouvelle islamophobie*. Paris: La Découverte.

Gibson, Margaret A. 1988. *Accommodation without Assimilation: Sikh Immigrants in an American High School*. Ithaca, N.Y.: Cornell University Press.

Gilroy, Paul. 1993. *The Black Atlantic: Modernity and Double Consciousness*. Cambridge, Mass.: Harvard University Press.

Girault, Jacques. 1998. *Seine-Saint-Denis: Chantiers et mémoires*. Paris: Éditions Autrement.

Giroux, Henry A. 2001. *Theory and Resistance in Education: Towards a Pedagogy for the Opposition*. Westport, Conn.: Bergin & Garvey.

Gondola, Ch. Didier. 2004. "'But I Ain't African, I'm American!' Black American Exiles and the Construction of Racial Identities in Twentieth-Century France." In *Blackening Europe: The African American Presence*, edited by Heike Raphael-Hernandez, 201–215. New York: Routledge.

Gordon, Milton. 1964. *Assimilation in American Life: The Role of Race, Religion, and National Origins*. New York: Oxford University Press.

Gossett, Thomas F. 1963/1997. *Race: The History of an Idea in America*. New York: Oxford University Press.

Guichard, Éric, and Gérard Noiriel, dir. 1997. *Construction des nationalités et immigration dans la France contemporaine*. Paris: Presses de l'École normale supérieure.

Guilhaume, Philippe. 1980. *Jules Ferry*. Paris: Albin Michel.

Haddad, Yvonne. 1991. *The Muslims of America*. New York: Oxford University Press.

Hall, Stuart. 1990. "Cultural Identity and Diaspora." In *Identity: Community, Culture, Difference*, edited by Jonathan Rutherford, 222–237. London: Lawrence and Wishart.

———. 1996. "Race, Articulation, and Societies Structured in Dominance." In *Black British Cultural Studies: A Reader*, edited by Houston A. Baker, Manthia Diawara, and Ruth H. Lindeborg, 33–52. Chicago: University of Chicago Press.

Hargreaves, Alec G. 1993. *French and Algerian Identities from Colonial Times to the Present: A Century of Interaction*. Lewiston: E. Mellen.

———. 1997. *Immigration and Identity in Beur Fiction: Voices from the North African Immigrant Community in France*. Oxford: Berg.

Haute conseil de l'intégration. 1993. *L'intégration à la française*. Paris: La Documentation française.

Hermet, Annick. 1997. "Au nom de l'honneur, l'affaire Nazmiyé." *Le monde diplomatique* (June): 22–23.

Hochschild, Jennifer. 1996. *Facing Up to the American Dream*. Princeton, N.J.: Princeton University Press.

hooks, bell. 1994. *Teaching to Transgress: Education as the Practice of Freedom*. New York: Routledge.

Howe, Kenneth R., and Michele S. Moses. 1999. "Ethics in Educational Research." *Review of Research in Education* 24:21–61.

Human Rights Watch. 2001. "France Must Investigate Alleged War Crimes." Press release. http://hrw.org/english/docs/2001/05/16/france117.htm, accessed July 4, 2005.

Huot, Hélène. 1989. *Dans la jungle des manuels scolaires*. Paris: Éditions du Seuil.

INRP (Institut national de recherche pédagogique). 1998. *Lycées, lycéens, savoirs*. Paris: Institut national de recherche pédagogique.

INSEE (Institut national de la statistique et des études économiques). 1999. *Recensement de la population: Population immigrée, population étrangère*. Paris: Institut national de la statistique et des études économiques.

———. 2000. *Données sociales: La société française*. Paris: Institut national de la statistique et des études économiques.

———. 2004. "Chômage et emploi." Paris: Institut national de la statistique et des études économiques.

Irele, Abiola. 1981/1991. *The African Experience in Literature and Ideology*. Bloomington: Indiana University Press.

Joubert, Jean-Louis. 2000. "Francophonies et enseignement du français." In *Actes du séminaire national: Perspectives actuelles de l'enseignement du français*. http://www.eduscol.education.fr/D0033/actfran_joubert.pdf, accessed March 29, 2005.

Jules-Rosette, Bennetta. 1998. *Black Paris: The African Writers' Landscape*. Urbana: University of Illinois Press.

Julien, Eileen. 2000. "Terrains de Rencontre: Césaire, Fanon, and Wright on Culture and Decolonization." In *The French Fifties*, edited by Susan Weiner, 149–167. New Haven, Conn.: Yale University Press.

Keddie, Nikki R., and Beth Baron, eds. 1991. *Women in Middle Eastern History: Shifting Boundaries in Sex and Gender*. New Haven, Conn.: Yale University Press.

Kelman, Gaston. 2003. *Je suis noir et je n'aime pas le manioc*. Paris: Mad Max Milo Éditions.

Kepel, Gilles. 1988. *Les musulmanes dans la société française*. Paris: Presses de la Fondation nationale des sciences politiques.

———. 1991. *Les banlieues de l'Islam*. Paris: Ponts Actuels.

Kessler, David. 1993. "Neutralité de l'enseignement public et liberté d'opinion des élèves." *Revue française de droit administratif* 9(1): 112–119.

Khosrokhavar, Farhad. 1997. *L'Islam des jeunes*. Paris: Flammarion.

Laamirie, Abdeljalil, Jean-Michel Le Dain, Gilles Manceron, et al. 1992. *La guerre d'Algérie dans l'enseignement en France et en Algérie*. Paris: Centre national de documentation pédagogique.

Lacoste-Dujardin, Camille. 1992. *Yasmina et les autres de Nanterre et d'ailleurs: Filles de parents maghrébins en France*. Paris: La Découverte.

Lake, Obiagele. 1995. "Toward a Pan-African Identity: Diaspora African Repatriates in Ghana." *Anthropological Quarterly* 68(1): 21–36.

Landrin, Sophie. 2004. "L'imam salafiste de Vénissieux, favorable à la lapidation, a été expulsé pour 'atteinte à l'ordre public.'" *Le monde*, April 22, p. 11.

Lefeuvre, Daniel. 1997. *Chere Algérie: Comptes et mécomptes de la tutelle coloniale, 1930–1962*. Saint-Denis: Société française d'histoire d'outre-mer.

Lenoir, Remi. 2003. *Généalogie de la morale familiale*. Paris: Éditions du Seuil.

Leveau, Rémy. 1986. *Présence musulmane en France*. Paris: Assas Éditions.

Leveau, Rémy, and Gilles Kepel. 1988. *Les musulmans dans la société française*. Paris: Presses de la Fondation nationale des sciences politiques.

Lévi-Strauss, Claude. 1977. "Avant-propos." In *L'identité: Séminaire interdisciplinaire dirigé par Claude Lévi-Strauss, 1974–1975*, edited by J.-M. Benoist, 9–11. Paris: Bernard Grasset.

Lévy, Catherine. 2003. *Vivre au minimum*. Paris: La Dispute.

Loewen, James. 1995. *Lies My Teacher Told Me: Everything Your American History Book Got Wrong*. New York: New Press.

Lorcerie, Françoise. 2003. *L'école et le défi ethnique: Education et intégration*. Paris: ESF/Institut national de recherche pédagogique.

Macgaffey, Janet, and Rémy Bazenguissa-Ganga. 2000. *Congo-Paris: Transnational Traders on the Margins of the Law*. Bloomington: Indiana University Press.

Maffesoli, Michel. 1988. *Le temps des tribus: Le déclin de l'individualism dans les sociétés de masse*. Paris: Librairie des Méndiens Klincksieck.

Manesse, Danièle, and Isabelle Grellet. 1994. *La littérature du collège*. Paris: Institut national de recherche pédagogique.

Maschino, Maurice. 2001. "La colonisation, telle qu'on l'enseigne, l'histoire expurgée de la guerre d'Algérie." *Le monde diplomatique* (February): 8–9.

Massey, Douglas S., and Nancy A. Denton. 1993. *American Apartheid: Segregation and the Making of the Underclass.* Cambridge, Mass.: Harvard University Press.

Memmi, Albert. 1965. *The Colonizer and the Colonized.* Boston: Beacon.

Mernissi, Fatima. 1987. *Beyond the Veil: Male-Female Dynamics in a Modern Muslim Society.* Bloomington: Indiana University Press.

———. 1992. *The Veil and the Male Elite: A Feminist Interpretation of Women's Rights in Islam.* New York: Perseus.

Miles, Robert. 1982. *Racism and Migrant Labour.* Boston: Routledge & Kegan Paul.

Miles, Robert, and Malcolm Brown. 2003. *Racism.* 2nd ed. London: Routledge.

Mire, Soraya. 1995. Interview by Trica Keaton, Los Angeles, Calif.

Moreau, Gilles. 2003. *Le monde apprenti.* Paris: La Dispute.

Morin, Edgar. 1998. "Pourquoi et comment articuler les savoirs." Paris: Ministère d'éducation nationale.

Morin, Gilles. 1992. "L'enseignement de la guerre d'Algérie en classe de troisième: Instructions officielles et sujets au brevet des collèges en France." In *La guerre d'Algérie dans l'enseignement en France et en Algérie,* edited by Abdeljalil Laamirie and Jean-Michel Le Dain, 109–135. Paris: Centre national de documentation pédagogique.

Mucchielli, Laurent. 2000. "L'expertise policière de la 'violence urbaine': Sa construction intellectuelle et ses usages dans le débat public français." *Déviance et société* 24(4): 351–376.

Mudimbe, V. Y. 1988. *The Invention of Africa: Gnosis, Philosophy, and the Order of Knowledge.* Bloomington: Indiana University Press.

Muel-Dreyfus, Francine. 1993. "La messagère." In *La misère du monde,* edited by Pierre Bourdieu and A. Accardo, 1301–1322. Paris: Éditions du Seuil.

Münch, Richard, and Neil Smelser, eds. 1992. *Theory of Culture.* Berkeley: University of California Press.

Myrdal, Gunnar. 1944/1975. *An American Dilemma; The Negro Problem and Modern Democracy.* 2 vols. With the assistance of Richard Sterner and Arnold Rose. New York: Pantheon.

Ngugi wa Thiong'o. 1986. *Decolonising the Mind: The Politics of Language in African Literature.* Portsmouth, N.H.: Heinemann.

Nöel, Olivier. 2000. "La face cachée de l'intégration: Les discriminations institutionnelles à l'embauche des jeunes issus de familles immigrées." *VEI enjeux,* no. 121 (June): 106–116.

Noguera, Pedro. 2003. *City Schools and the American Dream: Reclaiming the Promise of Public Education.* New York: Teachers College Press.

Noguera, Pedro, and Antwi Akom. 2000. "Disparities Demystified." *Nation* 270(22): 29–32.

Noiriel, Gérard. 1988. *Le creuset français: Histoire de l'immigration, XIXe–XXe siècle.* Paris: Éditions du Seuil.

———. 1992. *Population, immigration, et identité nationale en France, XIXe–XXe siècle.* Paris: Hachette.

Olsen, Laurie. 1997. *Made in America: Immigrant Students in Our Public Schools.* New York: New Press.

Omi, Michael, and Howard Winant. 1994. *Racial Formation in the United States: From the 1960s to the 1990s.* 2nd ed. New York: Routledge.

Pasqua, Charles. 1992. *Que demande le peuple.* Paris: Albin Michel.

Payet, J. P. 1995. *Collège de banlieue: Ethnographie d'un mode scolaire.* Paris: Méridiens.

Poiret, Christian. 1996. *Familles africaines en France: Ethnicisation, ségrégation et communalisation.* Paris: L'Harmattan.

Portes, Alejandro, and Rubén Rumbaut. 2001. *Legacies: The Story of the Immigrant Second Generation.* Berkeley: University of California Press.

Poulat, Emile. 2003. *Notre laïcité publique: La France est une république laïque.* Paris: Berg International.

Poupeau, Franck. 2001. "Professeurs en grève: Les conditions sociales d'un mouvement de contestation enseignant." *Actes de la recherche en sciences sociales* 136–137:83–95.

———. 2003. *Une sociologie d'état*. Paris: Raisons d'agir.

———. 2004. *Contestations scolaires et ordre social: Les enseignants de Seine-Saint-Denis en grève*. Paris: Éditions Syllepse.

Prost, Antoine. 1992. *Education, société, et politique: Une histoire de l'enseignement en France de 1945 à nos jours*. Paris: Éditions du Seuil.

Quiminal, Catherine, Mahamet Timéra, Babacar Fall, Babacar Diouf, and Hamédy Diarra. 1997. *Les jeunes filles d'origine africaine en France: Parcours scolaires, accès au travaille et destin social*. Paris: Association pour la promotion de la langue et de la culture soninke.

Rabinow, Paul. 1987. *Reflections on Field Work in Morocco*. Berkeley: University of California Press.

Raissiguier, Catherine. 1994. *Becoming Women, Becoming Workers: Identity Formation in a French Vocational School*. Albany: State University of New York Press.

Recham, Belkacem. 1996. *Les musulmans algériens dans l'armée française, 1919–1945*. Paris: L'Harmattan.

Reed, Adolph L., Jr. 1997. *W. E. B. Du Bois and American Political Thought: Fabianism and the Color Line*. New York: Oxford University Press.

René, Maran. 1938. *Batouala: Veritable roman nègre*. Paris: Albin Michel.

Rhein, Catherine. 1998a. "Globalisation, Social Change, and Minorities in Metropolitan Paris: The Emergence of New Class Patterns." *Urban Studies* 35(3): 429–447.

———. 1998b. "The Working Class, Minorities, and Housing in Paris: The Rise of Fragmentations." *Geojournal* 46(1): 51–62.

Rickford, John. 2000. *Spoken Soul: The Story of Black English*. New York: Wiley.

Rignault, Simone, and Philippe Richert. 1997. *La représentation des hommes et des femmes dans les livres scolaires: Rapport au Premier ministre*. Paris: La documentation française.

Robeson, Eslanda Goode. 1936. "Black Paris." Parts 1 and 2. *Challenge* (January): 12–18; (June): 9–12.

Robiquet, Paul, ed. 1893–1898. *Discours et opinions de Jules Ferry*. 7 vols. Paris: Armand Colin.

Said, Edward. 1979. *Orientalism*. New York: Vintage.

Sayad, Abdelmalek. 1991. *L'immigration, ou les paradoxes de l'altérité*. Brussels: De Boeck & Larcier.

Seguin, Boris, and Frédéric Teillard. 1996. *Les Céfrans parlent aux Français: Chronique de la langue des cités*. Paris: Calmann-Lévy.

Shell-Duncan, Bettina, and Ylva Hernlund. 2000. *Female "Circumcision" in Africa: Culture, Controversy, and Change*. Boulder, Colo.: Lynne Rienner.

Silverman, Max. 1992. *Deconstructing the Nation*. London: Routledge.

Simon, Patrick. 2001. "Les discriminations raciales et ethniques dans l'accès au logement social." Paris: GELD. http://www.le114.com, accessed April 10, 2005.

———. unpublished. The Measuring and Mismeasuring of Populations: The Statistical Use of Ethnic and Racial Categories in Multicultural Societies.

Simon, Patrick, and Joan Stavo-Debauge. 2002. "Lutte contre les discriminations et statistiques: La recherche d'une cohérence." Paris: GELD. http://www.le114.com, accessed April 10, 2005.

Small, Stephen. 1994. *Racialised Barriers: The Black Experience in the United States and England in the 1980s*. London: Routledge.

———. 2002. "Racisms and Racialized Hostility at the Start of the New Millennium." In *A Companion to Racial and Ethnic Studies*, edited by David Theo Goldberg and John Solomos, 259–281. Malden, Mass.: Blackwell.

Smith, M. G. 1998. *The Study of Social Structure*. New York: Research Institute for the Study of Man.

Smith, William Gardner. 1975. *The Stone Face*. Chatham, N.J.: Chatham Bookseller.

SOS Racisme. 1999. *Colonisation et racisme dans les nouveaux manuels scolaires de troisième.* http://www.sosracismereims.org/txt/manuels3e.htm, accessed April 20, 2005.

———. 2000. *Études de SOS Racisme sur les discriminations.* Annual report.

———. 2002. *L'esclavage et ses abolitions dans les manuels scolaires français de quatrième.* http://perso.wanadoo.fr/yekrik.yekrak/manuels4.htm, accessed April 20, 2005.

Stora, Benjamin. 1991. *La gangrène et l'oubli: La mémoire de la guerre d'Algérie.* Paris: La Découverte.

———. 1999. *Le transfert d'une mémoire: De l'Algérie française au racisme anti-arabe.* Paris: La Découverte.

Stovall, Tyler. 1990. *The Rise of the Paris Red Belt.* Berkeley: University of California Press.

———. 1996. *Paris Noir: African Americans in the City of Light.* Boston: Houghton Mifflin.

Suárez-Orozco, Carola, and Marcelo Suárez-Orozco. 2001. *The Children of Immigration.* Cambridge, Mass.: Harvard University Press.

Suárez-Orozco, Marcelo. 1987. "Becoming Somebody: Central American Immigrants in U.S. Inner-City Schools." *Anthropology and Education Quarterly* 18: 287–299.

———. 1989. *Central American Refugees and U.S. High Schools: A Psychosocial Study of Special Education.* London: Rutledge & Kegan Paul.

Taguieff, Pierre-André. 1987. *La force du préjugé: Essai sur la racisme et ses doubles.* Paris: La Découverte.

Taguieff, Pierre-André, and Michèle Tribalat. 1998. *Face au Front national: Arguments pour une contre-offensive.* Paris: La Découverte.

Talbott, John. 1969. *The Politics of Educational Reform in France, 1918–1940.* Princeton, N.J.: Princeton University Press.

Thiesse, Anne-Marie. 1999. *La création des identités nationales: Europe, XVIIe–XXe siècle.* Paris: Éditions du Seuil.

Thual, François. 1995. *Les conflits identitaires.* Paris: Ellipses.

Trancart, Danièle. 2000. "L'évolution des disparités entre collèges." in *Données sociales: La société française.* Paris: Institut national de la statistique et des études économiques.

Tribalat, Michèle. 1995. *Faire France: Une grande enquête sur les immigrés et leurs enfants.* Paris: La Découverte.

Tyack, David B. 1974. *The One Best System: A History of American Urban Education.* Cambridge, Mass.: Harvard University Press.

Valensky, Chantal. 1995. *Le soldat occulté: Les malgaches de l'armée française, 1884–1920.* Paris: L'Harmattan.

Van Zanten, Agnès. 2001. *L'école de la périphérie: Scolarité et ségrégation en banlieue.* Paris: Presses Universitaires de France.

Varro, Gabrielle. 1992. "Les 'langues immigrées' face à l'école française." *Language Problems and Language Planning* 16(2): 137–162.

Vasconcellos, Maria. 1993. *Le système éducatif.* Paris: La Découverte.

Venel, Nancy. 1999. *Musulmanes françaises: Des pratiquantes voilées à l'université.* Paris: L'Harmattan.

Viard, J. 1997. *En marge de la ville, au coeur de la société: Ces quartiers dont on parle.* Paris: Éditions de l'Aube.

Wacquant, Loïc. 1992. "Banlieues françaises et ghetto noir américain: De l'amalgame à la comparison." *French Politics and Society* 10(4): 81–103.

———. 1999a. *Les prisons de la misère.* Paris: Raisons d'agir.

———. 1999b. "Suitable Enemies: Foreigners and Immigrants in the Prisons of Europe." *Punishment and Society* 1(2): 215–222.

———. Forthcoming. *Deadly Symbiosis: Race and the Rise of Neo-liberal Penality (Themes for the 21st Century).* Cambridge: Polity.

Wadud, Amina. 1992. *Quran and Woman: Rereading the Sacred Text from a Woman's Perspective.* New York: Oxford University Press.

Warner, W. Lloyd, and Leo Srole. 1945. *The Social Systems of American Ethnic Groups.* New Haven, Conn.: Yale University Press.

Weil, Patrick. 1996. "Nationalities and Citizenships: The Lessons of the French Experience for Germany and Europe." In *Citizenship, Nationality, and Migration in Europe,* edited by David Cesarani and Mary Fulbrook, 74–87. London: Routledge.

———. 1997. *Mission d'étude des législations de la nationalité et de l'immigration.* Paris: La documentation française.

Weis, Lois, and Michelle Fine. 1993. *Beyond Silenced Voices: Class, Race, and Gender in United States Schools.* Albany: State University of New York.

White, Dorothy Shipley. 1979. *Black Africa and De Gaulle: From the French Empire to Independence.* University Park: Pennsylvania State University Press.

Wieviorka, Michel. 1993. "Tendencies to Racism in Europe: Does France Represent a Unique Case, or Is It Representative of a Trend?" In *Racism and Migration in Western Europe,* edited by John Wrench and John Solomos, 55–66. Oxford: Berg.

———. 1995. *The Arena of Racism.* Translated by Chris Turner. London: Sage.

———. 2002. "The Development of Racism in Europe." In *A Companion to Racial and Ethnic Studies,* edited by David Theo Goldberg and John Solomos, 460–474. Malden, Mass.: Blackwell.

Wihtol de Wenden, Catherine. 1999. *L'immigration en Europe.* Paris: La documentation française.

Wihtol de Wenden, Catherine, and Rémy Leveau. 2001. *La beurgeoisie: Les trois ages de la vie associative issue de l'immigration.* Paris: CNRS.

Wikan, Unni. 2000. "Citizenship on Trial: Nadia's Case." *Daedalus* 129(4): 55–76. http://www.findarticles.com/p/articles/mi_qa3671/is_200010/ai_n8928238/pg_2, accessed April 8, 2005.

Willis, Paul E. 1977. *Learning to Labor: How Working Class Kids Get Working Class Jobs.* New York: Columbia University Press.

Wilson, William J. 1999. *The Bridge over the Racial Divide: Rising Inequality and Coalition Politics.* Berkeley: University of California Press.

Wong Fillmore, Lilly. 1991. "When Learning a Second Language Means Losing the First." *Early Child Research Quarterly* 6(3): 323–347.

———. 2000. "Loss of Family Languages: Should Educators Be Concerned?" *Theory into Practice* 39(4): 203–210.

Woodson, Carter G. 1933. *The Miseducation of the Negro.* Washington, D.C.: Associated Publishers.

Wrench, John, and John Solomos, eds. 1993. *Racism and Migration in Western Europe.* Oxford: Berg.

Wright, Gordon. 1987. *France in Modern Times: From the Enlightenment to the Present.* 4th ed. New York: Norton.

Wright, Richard. 2003. "I Choose Exile." In *Writer's Presence: A Pool of Readings,* edited by D. McQuade and Robert Atwan, 289–295. Boston: Bedford.

Zhou, Min. 1997. "Segmented Assimilation: Issues, Controversies, and Recent Research on the New Second Generation." *International Migration Review* 31(4): 975–1008.

Index

Page numbers in italics indicate photographs and tables.

abductions, 53
abortion, 148–149
abuse. *See* violence and abuse
Académie française, 108
achievement scores, *93, 94,* 145
affirmative action, 6, 17, 127, 129–133, 142, 194
Afghanistan, 28, 166
Africa, 100–101, 117, 125. *See also specific countries*
African Diaspora, 4, 17, 21, 60–61, 157. *See also specific countries*
Aïcha (subject): on assimilation, 96; background, 33–35; on independence, 172–173; on integration, 73; introduced, 25; on *la laïcité,* 189; on national identity, 41; on school curriculum, 149, 152; on school environment, 136; school performance of, 137; on workplace discrimination, 141
Aillaud, Emile, 59, 82
Akofa, Henriette, 168
Algeria and Algerian immigrants: "Algerian exceptionalism," 3; and class divisions, 88; France and Algeria compared, 148; massacres in, 29; occupation of Algeria, 190–191; perception of assimilation, 11; and *le regard des autres,* 173; Rima on, 42–44
Algerian War, 110, 117–118, 121–124, 191
Allègre, Claude, 111
Amara, Fadela, 164
Amina, 43, 151–152, 168–169
Amnesty International, 57
Amselle, Jean-Loup, 46, 48
Anita (subject), 26, 44, 167, 168–169, 188
anti-immigrant legislation, 11–12
anti-racism groups, 117
anti-Semitism, 49–50, 96, 118
Arabic language, 45, 154
Arabs, 9, 32. *See also specific nationalities*
Assia (subject), 45, 143, 149–150, 152–153

assimilation: and academic achievement, 170; and colonialism, 101; and education, 10, 92, 94, 96–97, 99–100, 124, 146; and franco-conformity, 100–110; versus integration, 185; and language, 103–104; and national identity, 3, 9, 32–33, 47; and political organization, 191–192; resistance to, 127; and sexuality, 52; and social exclusion, 4; and symbolic struggles, 11; and textbook selection, 112, 123
assistance, 143–145

baccalauréat tests, 114–116, *138,* 138–142
Baccardi, Pit, 58
Bacon, Francis, 37
Balibar, Étienne, 112, 177
Banton, Michael, 8
Barbier, Maurice, 179
Beaud, Stéphane, 69–70
beauty standards, 52. *See also* fashion/dress
Beauvoir, Simone de, *163*
Ben Jelloun, Tahar, 11, 12, 113
Bendo, Marie-Clémentine, 73–74
Benguigui, Yamina, 58, 63
Benziane, Sohane, 5, *163,* 164
Berbers, 44
Beyala, Calixthe, 68
bidonvilles, 63
biological race, 101
Bobigny borough, 73–75, 140
bombings, 19–20, 33
Bourdieu, Pierre: on class divisions, 132; on functions of education, 96–97; on perceptions of groups, 1; and social reproduction theory, 17–18, 145; on symbolic struggles, 10, 13, 97–100
Bouzar, Dounia, 184
Britain, 125
Brown, Jacky, 58
Brubaker, Rogers, 14–15

Calhoun, Craig, 15
Camilleri, Carmel, 150, 152

Caribbean countries, 117
categorization and classification, 6–9, 48,
    49–51, 97–100. *See also* identity
Catholicism, 100, 149, 178
census data, 30
Cheb Mami (artist), 66
Chevènement, Jean-Pierre, 180
Chicago, Illinois, 60
Chirac, Jacques, 51, 62
Choppin, Alain, 112
la cité des Courtillières: and crime, 72; de-
    scribed, 59–67, 73–89; living condi-
    tions, *75–81;* police violence in,
    70–71; "rabbit cages," 43; and racial
    barriers, 194; renovations, 75
citizenship, 13, 55–57, 86–87, 90, 92, 112
Clarke, Kenneth B., 67
class divisions, 96, 113, 128, 132
classification. *See* categorization and classi-
    fication; identity
Clinton, William Jefferson, 28
co-education, 153
colonialism and colonization: and the Al-
    gerian War, 123; and immigration
    policy, 47; and language, 119–121;
    psychology of, 89; and racism, 7, 101;
    and school curricula, 109–110; and
    slavery, 190; and symbolic struggles,
    10, 191; textbook treatments of, 117
Le comité contre l'esclavage moderne,
    167
Committee against Modern Slavery, 167
common culture: Bourdieu on, 97–100;
    and education, 126; and franco-con-
    formity, 4, 100–110, 146; and French
    literature, 112–116; and language,
    104; in national education, 91–97;
    and school curriculum, 149, 154;
    and textbook selection, 110–112,
    112–116, 116–126
Communist Party, 59
Comtian positivism, 101
conformity, 4, 91, 146–156. *See also* assim-
    ilation
conscription, 125–126
contraception, 148–150
conversion, 173
Cooper, Frederick, 14–15
Coq, Guy, 179
Côte d'Ivoire, 44, 167, 190
Courtillières. *See la cité des Courtillières*
courts, 80, 182
crime, 68–69, 71–72, 84, 137, 158–166.
    See also violence and abuse

cross-sectional analysis, 25
cultural issues: adaptation, 35; and assimi-
    lation, 146; cultural literacy, 18,
    102–103; cultural supremacy, 57;
    "deculturation," 103–104; diversity,
    2, 66–67, 116, 135; and domestic vi-
    olence, 158–166, 167–169; and edu-
    cation, 10, 36, 98–100, 106;
    gatekeepers, 182; and language,
    106–108, 119; and public housing,
    74; versus religious observance,
    184–185; and textbooks, 111–113,
    117. *See also* assimilation; common
    culture; popular culture
curriculum: and common culture, 105,
    109; and family tensions, 150–151;
    and history texts, 116–126; and liter-
    ature textbooks, 112–116; and reli-
    gious observance, 147–156; and
    testing schedules, 143. *See also* edu-
    cation
customs, 74, 186. *See also* cultural issues

Dandicat, Edwidge, 16–17
Dark Ghetto: Dilemmas of Social Power
    (Clarke), 67
data collection, 8, 26, 27, 127, 135–136
De ce côté du monde: 33 parc des Courtillières
    (documentary), 61
De la colonisation chez les peuples modernes
    (Leroy-Beaulieu), 101
Declaration of the Rights of Man and the
    Citizen, 177, 178
Decolonising the Mind (Ngugi), 119
decolonization, 109–110, 117, 121,
    124–125
deindustrialization, 61
delinquency, 68–69
demographics of schools, 131
demonstrations. *See* protests and demon-
    strations
Denton, Nancy, 67–68
deportation, 12, 20, 72
Diallo, Amadou, 70
Diallo, Katiatou, 70
Diawara, Manthia, 21–22
Dibango, Manu, 68
Diop, Moustapha, 63
Diouf, Babacar, 38, 172
discipline, 34, 39, 169, 170
discrimination: African Americans in
    Paris, 22–23; in education, 105–107;
    in internships, 140; in public hous-
    ing, 64–65, 70, 87–88; racialized,

48–49; in social structures, 8; in student sorting practices, 133–134; U.S. and France compared, 7–8; in the workforce, 127

diversity, 2, 116, 135. *See also* multiculturalism

divorce, 171, 175

doctrine, 186

documentaries, 61

Doillon, Jacques, 61–62

domestic labor, 167–168, 175–176

domestic violence, 158–166, 167–169

Dreyfus Affair, 118

drug trade, 84

Du Bois, W. E. B., 5

Durkheim, Emile, 97, 112

ebonics, 108

Echenberg, Myron, 125

écoles sensibles programs (EP), 130

economics: and deindustrialization, 61; and exams, 115–116; financial assistance for schools, 130–131; in immigrant neighborhoods, 18; informal economies, 72, 84; and living conditions, 65, 83–85; socioeconomic backgrounds, 92; and textbook selection, 110; and women in the workforce, 74; and workforce discrimination, 127; and xenophobia, 50

education: access to, 91; achievement levels, 41, 128, 136–137, *139*, 170; and affirmative action, 6; and citizenship, 90, 92; and common culture, 10; and employment, 69; and ethnicity, 86; and forced marriage, 53–54, 57; gatekeeper courses, 133–134; general studies, 138–140, *139*, 141, 143; Henri III high school, 134–145; higher education, 74; homework, 85, 150–151, 152, 167; inequality in, 103, 132, 141; and language, 108–109; and living conditions, 84–85; and national identity, 99–100, 102; and parenting, 26, 43; physical education, 142, 147, 152–153; and politics, 128–134; private schools, 99; and religious symbols, 1–4, 12, 16, 20, 31, 47, 52, 99, 147, 155, 179, 184–192; school renovations, 76; and social inclusion, 89; and social inequality, 132, 145; sorting practices, 133–134; student

protests, 28, *75*, 91, *93*, *94*, 105, 111; and symbolic struggles, 13; teaching styles, 141; textbook selection, 110–112, 112–116, 116–126; tracking students, 17, 128, 140; tutoring, 145; university studies, 115, 139; vocational studies, 37, 41, 43, 127, 136, 138–141, *139*. *See also* curriculum

Egypt, 45, 159, 162, 173

El Saadawi, Nawal, 74, 162, 166

elections, 10, 51, 181, 195

employment, 12, 115–116, 140–141

L'enfant noir (Laye), 113

England, 7, 54

English language, 154–155

Enlightenment, 100, 101

The Equality of the Human Race (Firmin), 7

Essays on the Inequalities of the Human Race (Gobineau), 101

ethical issues, 29–30

ethnicity: and education, 86; ethnic cleansing, 29; ethnic neighborhoods, 73; methodological issues, 8; and race, 9; versus race, 9; of teachers, 114

Eurocentrism, 2, 9, 100, 114

exams, 107, 114, 115–116, *138*, 138–140, 141–142

excision, 44, 53, 159–162, 167

expatriates, 157–158

extended family, 171

"Eye of Fatima," 40

family structure, 38

Fanon, Frantz, 89

fashion/dress, 33–35, 69–70, 73–74, 135, 184–185

Fatima (subject): on gender issues, 174; home environment, 169, 170; interviewed, 39–40; on religious observance, 185, 189–190; school performance, 137; self-image, 1

Fatou (subject): background, 36–39; home environment, 169; introduced, 25; on *la laïcité*, 188; living conditions, 82, 85; on public housing, 77; on religious observance, 187; school performance, 106, 116, 128, 136, 141; on tutoring, 145

female circumcision, 44, 53, 159–162, 167

Les femmes médiatrices sociales et culturelles, 73

Ferry, Jules, 90–91, 100–102, 112, 116, 126, 178–179

Ferry Educational Laws, 108
Fifth Republic, 122
Fire Eyes (film), 161
Firmin, Anténor, 7
forced marriage, 5, 33, 37–38, 44, 52–53, 53–57, 161
Fourth Republic, 122
foyers, 63
France Telecom, 176
franco-conformity, 4, 100–110, 146
French Council of the Muslim Religion, 180–181
French Revolution, 100
French West Indies, 124
fundamentalism, 19, 85, 99, 180–181, 183

Gaulle, Charles de, 122
gender issues: constraints on Muslim girls, 194–195; and cultural traditions, 5, 172; and educational setting, 39; and female independence, 171–172; and generational change, 174–175; and home environment, 31, 158, 170–171; and independence, 172–173; and *la laïcité*, 185–186; and school curricula, 113
general studies, 138–140, *139*, 141, 143
generational change, 172, 174–175, 189
genital mutilation, 44, 53, 159–162, 167
German language, 154–155
ghettos, 67–73, 131
Gilroy, Paul, 4
Gobineau, Arthur de, 7, 101
Gramsci, Antonio, 132
Grellet, Isabelle, 112–113, 114
Gréou, Hawa, 5, 53, 162

Habiba (subject): on Algeria, 148; background, 43–44; on cultural difficulties, 166–167; on gender roles, 175; home environment, 170; on housewives, 176; introduced, 25; on *la laïcité*, 189; on Morocco, 155; on religious observance, 187; school performance, 136–137; on school renovations, 76
Haby Law, 105
Hall, Stuart, 4
Harkis, 191
headscarf bans: and assimilation, 99, 147; and cultural differences, 52; expulsions from school, 155; and *la laïcité*, 179, 184–192; and national identity,

47; protests against, 16; public perceptions of, 2–4; and racism, 20; resistance to, 31
Hebrew, 155
Henri III high school, 134–145, *138*, 153
higher education, 74, 127
history, 92, 116–126
Holocaust, 122
homeland security laws, 69
homeless population, 66
homework, 85, 150–151, 152, 167
honor codes, 164–165, 173–174
hooks, bell, 16
human rights issues, 5, 167. *See also* excision
Human Rights Watch, 57, 117
Human Subjects requirements, 30
humanitarian efforts, 28

identity, 46–53; defining, 13–16, 14; and language, 40; and media, 28; outside France, 41; politics of, 13–16, 195; and power of names, 48; and relative power, 47; and researcher's perspective, 24; self-image, 3, 5, 12, 14, 27, 32, 35, 38–40, 44–45, 46–53, 132–133. *See also* national identity
ideology, 104, 132
Imhotep (artist), 66
L'immigration (Sayad), 62–63
immigrants and immigration: African Americans in Paris, 22; anti-immigrant legislation, 11–12; and assimilation, 94; and categorization, 48; and colonialism, 47; and incarceration, 71–72; and labor exploitation, 62–63; legal status, 48–49; and national identity, 32; and symbolic struggles, 11. *See also specific groups*
incarceration rates, 71–72
independence, 172–73
The Inequality of the Human Races (Gobineau), 7
infibulation, 44, 53, 159–162, 167
informal economies, 72
Instituts universitaires de formation des maîtres (IUFM), 105
integration, 73, 94, 107, 147–148, 185, 190. *See also* assimilation; common culture
interdisciplinary perspective, 23–24
internships, 140
intolerance, 109
Iraq, 28

Islam, 42, 44–45, 68, 164, 186. *See also* Muslims

Israeli-Palestinian war, 49, 118

Jacobinism, 100

Jamila (fictional name), 158

journals, 26, 35, 89, 96, 149–150, 152–153, 187–188

Juppé, Alain, 180

juvenile delinquency, 68–69

Kant, Immanuel, 101

Karembeu, Christian, 51

KDD (Kartel Double Détente), 72

Keddie, Nikki, 164, 186

Kelkal, Khaled, 19

Kelman, Gaston, 7

Kepel, Gilles, 191

Khadija (subject), 44, 142, 185, 187

Khosrokhavar, Farhad, 185–186

Kingston, John, 54–55

K-Mel (artist), 66

Konte, Fatoumata, 53–54

Koran, 147, 164, 186

Kosovo, 29

Laamirie, Abdeljalil, 122

labor exploitation, 62–63

Lacoste-Dujardin, Camille, 47

la laïcité, 177–184, 184–192

Lake, Obiagele, 157

Lang, Jack, 121

language and linguistics: addressing handicaps, 142; African Americans in Paris, 22–23; Arabic, 45, 154; and assimilation, 92, 103–104; and common culture, 10, 104; and culture, 36, 119; curriculum, 154–155; and discrimination in education, 106; ebonics, 108; English, 154–155; and exams, 115; German, 154–155; in the home, 42–44; and identity, 40; in immigrant families, 35; and integration, 107; and multiculturalism, 104, 108–109, 142; and racism, 8; regional languages, 104; varieties, 108–109; written French, 143–144

laws: and abuse, 40; anti-immigrant legislation, 11–12, 71; enforcement, 70–71; and forced marriage, 54, 56–57; headscarf bans, 1–4, 16, 20, 31, 47, 52, 99, 147, 155, 179, 181–184, 184–192, 193; homeland security laws, 69; and human rights issues, 49; Islamic, 164; National Codes, 11; against polygamy, 38; and secularism, 178, 179–180, 189

lawsuits, 78, 79–80, 82, 132

Laye, Camara, 113

Le Dain, Jean-Michel, 122

legal status, 48–49

Leïla (subject), 45, 104, 170

Leroy-Beaulieu, Paul, 101

Lévi-Strauss, Claude, 14

Libération, 51

Lies My Teacher Told Me: Everything Your American History Textbook Got Wrong (Loewen), 117

literature textbooks, 112–116

living conditions, 65–66, 73–89, *75–81*

Loewen, James, 117

The Logic of Practice (Bourdieu), 1

Louisa (hip-hop artist), 157

Maghrebins, 3, 11, 47, 65, 70, 86, 113, 191

Malewska-Peyre, Hanna, 150, 152

Mali, 42

Manesse, Danièle, 112–113, 114

Mariama (subject), 1, 42, 52, 82

Marie-Ange (colleague), 21, 25

marriage, 38, 41, 45, 54–55, 174. *See also* forced marriage

Marx, Karl, 97

Mas, Sara Miangu, 73

Massey, Douglas, 67–68

Mémoires d'immigrés, 63

media: and American politics, 28; and Eurocentrism, 51; on forced marriage, 57; on gender violence, 166; on headscarf issues, 181; on living conditions, 61–62, 82; and stereotypes, 68; and urban violence, 2

Méhaignerie law, 11

Mehdi, 160, 162–164

menstruation, 154

Mernissi, Fatima, 186

methodological issues: census data, 30, 48–49; consent, 29–30; cross-sectional analysis, 25; data collection, 8, 26, 27, 50, 127, 135–136; data shortcomings, 30, 127; definitions, 14; and ethnic origins, 8; interdisciplinary perspective, 23–24; limitations of the study, 27–30; measuring racism, 50; selection bias, 17; and social reproduction theory, 17

Michalak, Laurence, 63

migrant labor, 62–63, 167–168
Ministry of Education, 102–103, 105, 111, 116–117, 135–136, 181
Ministry of Foreign Affairs (Norway), 55–56
Mire, Soraya, 161
Miss France Pageant, 52
Miss Italy Pageant, 52
Mitterand, François, 117
modesty, 5–6, 149, 151–153, 164
Le monde, 181, 193
Le monde diplomatique, 117
Morin, Edgar, 102–103
Mormons, 54–55
morning-after pill, 148–149
Morocco, 44, 45, 155
Mucchielli, Laurent, 69
multiculturalism: in French schools, 18; hostility toward, 92; and language, 108–109, 142; versus national unity, 33; in public housing, 66, 83. *See also* diversity
murder, 5, 164
Muslims: anti-Muslim violence, 118; and assimilation, 99; conscripts, 125; Diaspora, 173, 189–190; and domestic violence, 158–166; and franco-conformity, 146; in Kosovo, 29; population estimates, 86; religious observance, 44–45; and school curricula, 147–156. *See also* Islam
Myrdal, Gunnar, 7–8

Naïma (subject): background, 45; home environment, 169; on honor codes, 173; on *la laïcité,* 188; school performance, 127, 143
Les nanas beurs, 164
National Codes, 11
National Company for the Construction of Housing for Guest Workers, 63
National Consultative Commission on Human Rights (CNCDH), 49–50, 96, 114
national education. *See* education
national identity: and education, 92, 99–100, 102; and popular myths, 18; and racial classification, 6–9; and racism, 18–19; and secularism, 5; and self-image, 46–53; and stereotypes, 2–3; and "suitable enemies," 193; and symbolic struggles, 9–13; and textbook selection, 124. *See also* assimilation; common culture; identity

nationalism, 89
natural sciences, 142, 147–152
naturalization, 11–12, 48, 71, 86–87
Nazmiyé (subject), 5, 164
Negritude, 113
neighborhoods, 59
Neither Whores nor Submissive (Ni putes ni soumises), 164
neoliberalism, 64
New York Times, 179
Ngugi Wa Thiong'o, 119
Noguera, Pedro, 128
Noiriel, Gérard, 47, 92–94
Norway, 55–56
nudity, 5–6, 151, 152

Obadina, Lionel, 70
Ohio, 60

Pantin: background, 59; described, 25; diversity in, 135; public housing management, 65, 82, 84, 86; school district, 129; test performance, 138, *138,* 139, *139*
parallel economy, 84
parenting, 29–30, 34, 151–152
Paris, France, 18–24, 60, 130, 157, 194
"Parisiens du Nord" (song), 66
Pasqua, Charles, 20
Pasqua law, 11
Passeron, Jean Claude, 96, 98, 145
patriotism, 102, 117, 124
Petits frères (film), 61–62
physical education, 142, 147, 152–153
Pialoux, Michel, 69–70
Poiret, Christian, 38
police brutality, 70–71
policy analysis, 49
politics: of education policy, 128–134; and headscarf ban, 181–183; and identity, 13–16; and *la laïcité,* 180–181; political organization, 180–181, 191–192, 195; and textbook selection, 110–112; and urban violence, 2
polygamy, 38, 54–55
popular culture, 28, 47, 66, 69, 72, 166, 171
Portes, Alejandro, 35
Poupeau, Franck, 128
poverty, 60–61, 82–85, 129
priority education zones (ZEP), 129, 130, 136
prison system, 71–73

private schools, 99
projects. *See* public housing
le projet d'établissement, 143–144
Prost, Antoine, 96
Protestantism, 101
protests and demonstrations: against gender violence, 165; student protests, 28, *75*, 91, *93*, *94*, 105, 111; transportation strikes, 20
public housing: described, 59–67, 67–73, 73–89; France and the U.S. compared, 24; impact on residents, 58–59; and racism, 22; as research site, 25; subjects residing in, 42–44. See also *la cité des Courtillières*
public opinion, 50, 68–69, 109, 181
public policy, 85
public services, 73
public transportation, 65

Quiminal, Catherine, 38, 53, 172
Quran, 147, 164, 186

race and racism: anti-racism groups, 117; biological race, 101; black/white paradigm, 8–9; and classification, 6–9, 48; CNCDH report on, 96; and colonialism, 101; and color consciousness, 3; data on, 8–9, 50; defining race, 98; and discrimination, 127, 180; and ethnicity, 9; and headscarf ban, 183–184; in history textbooks, 119–120; and living conditions, 84; and national identity, 18–19; and nationalism, 89; and police violence, 70–71; and public housing, 22, 64–65; racial antagonisms, 194; reports on, 49–51; scientific racism, 7; and self-image, 35; student sorting practices, 133–134; and textbook selection, 114; and violence, 49; in the workplace, 140–141; and world events, 20; xenophobia, 49–51, 71, 96
Raissiguier, Catherine, 140–141
Ramadan, 147, 152, 191
le regard des autres, 173–174
religion and religious observance: and assimilation, 99, 146–148; church influence on education, 178; contradictions in, 189; conversion, 42, 173; versus fashion, 184–185; fundamentalism, 85; and headscarf ban, 181–183; observance in public

housing, 86; and polygamy, 55; and school curriculum, 147–156; and self-image, 35, 38–40; and veils, 186–187
rents, 66
réseaux prioritaires (REP), 129–130
resistance, 13, 18, 31, 128, 146–156
resource allocation, 130
reunification programs, 62
"reverse anthropology," 21
Rhein, Catherine, 61
Rima (subject): background, 42; on housewives, 175; introduced, 25; living conditions of, 60; on religious observance, 189; on school curriculum, 152; school performance of, 137
Rosette, Bennetta Jules, 21
Rumbaut, Rubén, 35

Samori-Touré, 120
Saracens, 190
Sarkozy, Nicolas, 180
Sartre, Jean-Paul, 89, *163*
Sayad, Abdelmalek, 62–63
scapegoating, 18–19, 71–72, 88, 193. *See also* "suitable enemies"
Scholl, Hans, 122
Scholl, Sophie, 122
Sciences Politiques, 132
secularism: and access to education, 189–190; and assimilation, 146; and education, 90–91, 99–100, 174; and *la laïcité,* 177–184; and public housing, 85; resistance to, 31
segregation, 17, 63, 67, 125, 133–134, 194
Seguin, Boris, 107
Seine-Saint-Denis, 59, 128, 130–131, 135, *138*, 138–139
selection bias, 17
self-image, 3, 5, 12, 14, 27, 38–40, 46–53, 132–133
Senegal, 32, 53, 113, 191
Senghor, Léopold, 113
September 11 attacks, 2
Serpentin, 78–81, *79*
Sétif massacre, 121–122, 124
sexuality: and cultural custom, 52, 158–166; and genital mutilation, 44, 53, 159–162, 167; and parenting, 34; and Parisian society, 5–6; and school curricula, 147; sex education, 148–149, 150–151; sexism, 175; sexual violence, 164; virginity, 39–40, 148. *See also* forced marriage

Sikhs, 182
Simon, Patrick, 65
slavery, 7, 117, 167–168, 190
Small, Stephen, 7
social engineering, 64
social exclusion, 4, 17, 91, 95–99,
    103–104, 127, 129, 183
social services, 73–75
socialization, 11, 59, 96
socioeconomic backgrounds, 92, 136
SOS Racisme, 70, 117, 121, 180
Spain, 2
sports, 39. *See also* physical education
stereotypes, 2, 62, 68
Stern, Nicholas, 61, 87
"The Stranger" (poem), 21
strikes, 20, 28, 91, *93, 94,* 111. *See also*
    protests and demonstrations
student protests, 28, *75,* 91, *93, 94,* 105,
    111
Su'ad (subject), 25, 43–44, 76, 88, 136,
    170, 189–190
Suárez-Orozco, Marcelo, 52
sub-Saharan Africa, 9, 65, 172
Sudan, 28
"suitable enemies," 7, 19, 23, 72, 174,
    191, 193–194
Sylvie (subject), 42, 173, 188
symbolic violence and struggles: Bour-
    dieu on, 97–100; and colonialism,
    191; described, 13; and exams,
    115–116; and franco-conformity,
    100–110; and headscarf bans,
    183–184; in national education,
    91–97; and textbook selection,
    110–112, 112–116, 116–126. *See also*
    violence and abuse

Talbott, John, 132
technology, 176
television, 61–62, 152
terrorism, 2, 19–20, 33, 68
testing, 17, 111, 114–116, 124, 130–131,
    137–142, *138*
textbooks, 110–112, 112–116, 116–126
Thatcher, Margaret, 121
Third Republic, 178
Thuram, Lilian, 51
tirailleurs, 191
traditionalism, 171
Tunisia, 42, 185
Turkey, 65
tutoring, 145

Une esclave moderne (Lafon), 168
unemployment, 6, 69, 71, 83
United Nations (UN), 49, 57
United States: affirmative action in, 129;
    census data, 49; class divisions in ed-
    ucation, 132–133; color conscious-
    ness, 7; compared to France, 8–9, 24,
    195; cultural literacy, 18; education
    policy, 128; France compared to, 67;
    history curriculum, 117; inner cities,
    67; polygamy in, 54–55; prison sys-
    tem, 72; public housing in, 60;
    racism in, 1, 22; and school texts,
    126; terrorism in, 2
urban planning, 66–67
urban violence, 2, 19, 194
urbanization, 66–67

Vasconcellos, Maria, 140
veils, 174, 181, 186–187. *See also* head-
    scarf bans
Venel, Nancy, 185–186
Vichy regime, 8
Vietnam War, 117, 126
violence and abuse: abductions, 53; anti-
    Arab, 3; bombings, 19–20, 33; com-
    bating, 180; and cultural differences,
    5, 6; and delinquency, 69; and de-
    pendency, 175; domestic, 158–166,
    167–169; excision, 44, 53, 159–162,
    167; and forced marriage, 52, 53,
    55–56; against girls, 31; in history
    textbooks, 122; and living condi-
    tions, 59; murder, 5, 164; parental,
    40; police brutality, 70–71; and pris-
    ons, 72–73; in public housing,
    87–88; racial, 49, 84; and school se-
    curity, 134; and "suitable enemies,"
    23; textbook treatments of, 118;
    urban violence, 2, 19, 194; U.S. and
    France compared, 1. *See also* symbolic
    violence and struggles
virginity, 39–40, 148
vocational studies, 37, 41, 43, 127, 136,
    138–141, *139*
Voltaire, 101
voting, 51, 195

Wacquant, Loïc, 8, 71, 72
Wade, Abdoulaye, 54
Wadud, Amina, 186
Weber, Max, 97, 184
Weil, Patrick, 11–12, 87, 94

West Africa, 11
white flight, 61
Wikan, Unni, 55–57
women and women's issues: and excision, 44, 53, 159–162, 167; forced marriage, 5, 33, 37–38, 44, 52–53, 53–57, 161; in history textbooks, 121; and school curricula, 113; vulnerability, 74. *See also* gender issues
World Cup, 51
World War II, 59

The Wretched of the Earth (Fanon), 89

xenophobia, 49–51, 71, 96, 114

Yourcenar, Marguerite, 113
youth culture, 47, 61, 71, *95*

"zero tolerance" policies, 69
Zidane, Zinedine, 51
zones d'éducation prioritaires (ZEP), 129, 130, 136

 **Trica Danielle Keaton** is Assistant Professor of African American and African Diaspora Studies at Indiana University Bloomington.